THE $16 TACO

THE $16 TACO

CONTESTED GEOGRAPHIES OF FOOD, ETHNICITY, AND GENTRIFICATION

Pascale Joassart-Marcelli

UNIVERSITY OF WASHINGTON PRESS
Seattle

Design by Katrina Noble
Composed in Iowan Old Style, typeface designed by John Downer

25 24 23 22 21   5 4 3 2 1

Printed and bound in the United States of America

UNIVERSITY OF WASHINGTON PRESS
uwapress.uw.edu

LIBRARY OF CONGRESS CATALOGING-IN-PUBLICATION DATA

Names: Joassart, Pascale, author.
Title: The sixteen-dollar taco : contested geographies of food, ethnicity, and gentrification / Pascale Joassart-Marcelli.
Other titles: $16 dollar taco
Description: Seattle : University of Washington Press, 2021. | Includes bibliographical references and index.
Identifiers: LCCN 2021005235 (print) | LCCN 2021005236 (ebook) | ISBN 9780295749273 (hardcover) | ISBN 9780295749280 (paperback) | ISBN 9780295749297 (ebook)
Subjects: LCSH: Food preference—California—San Diego—Case studies. | Ethnic food—California—San Diego—Case studies. | Ethnic restaurants—California—San Diego—Case studies. | Gentrification—California—San Diego—Case studies.
Classification: LCC GT2853.U5 J63 2021 (print) | LCC GT2853.U5 (ebook) | DDC 782.1—dc23
LC record available at https://lccn.loc.gov/2021005235
LC ebook record available at https://lccn.loc.gov/2021005236

To all immigrant and refugee food workers in San Diego.
Often underpaid and mostly invisible, you are the backbone of our
food economy and the pillars of our cosmopolitan foodscape.

All food is ethnic food.

CONTENTS

ACKNOWLEDGMENTS

Writing a book is at once a lonesome experience and an accompanied project made of connections with others. I have enjoyed both aspects of the work and am infinitely thankful for all the people who have supported me in this not-so-lonely adventure.

Thank you to my colleagues in the Department of Geography at San Diego State University, where I have found a supportive and caring home to carry on the work I love. Stuart Aitken, Kate Swanson, Trent Biggs, Arielle Levine, Tom Herman, and many others have opened my mind to new ideas and helped me become a better geographer. Fernando Bosco has been my research companion since I arrived at San Diego State, and this book would have never been possible without the brainstorming, fieldwork, teaching, writing, and conferencing we did together. Giorgio Curti has pushed me to engage with different perspectives, broaden my understanding of geography, and sharpen my project. His sense of humor and friendship got me through difficult times.

Thank you to my students who not only read and discussed draft sections of this work but also participated in various parts of the research by collecting valuable data. I am inspired by their passion, outrage, and insight. I hope this book speaks to them. I am especially thankful to Blaire O'Neal, my first doctoral student, who wrote her dissertation as I was working on this book. She probably helped me as much as I helped her.

Thank you to the unnamed people who trusted me with their stories and let me into their lives, sharing their struggles and joys of working in the food industry and procuring food for their loved ones. They are mothers, restaurant workers, food entrepreneurs, and shoppers, mostly immigrants, living under a system of food apartheid. I hope that I represented their experiences and perspectives truthfully. I am also grateful for Dian Moss and the people at Project New Village who have taught me so much over the past ten years. I am excited to see the Good Food District growing as a model of food sovereignty that is led by and for people of color.

Thank you to my mentors, Michael Dear and Jennifer Wolch; long ago, when I was a recovering economist, they turned me into a geographer. Their support in my early career means everything.

I am also thankful for the financial support I have received from the National Science Foundation and San Diego State University. The former funded a four-year project called Food, Ethnicity, and Place (award 1155844), which I directed with Fernando Bosco and became the basis of this book. Through two small grants and a sabbatical, San Diego State University gave me resources for fieldwork and time to write.

Thank you to my editor, Andrew Berzanskis, for believing in this project when it was just an idea, and to anonymous reviewers for their insightful suggestions.

Thank you to my friends Kelly, Sarah, Dacely, Cindy, and Shahnaz, who provided companionship, distraction, and support when I needed it, even if it meant listening to me lecturing about food, immigration, or other political issues. I am lucky to have them in my life.

Most important, thank you to my family: my husband, Enrico, and my sons, Luca and Adrien. They have supported me in more ways than they know. They put up with me sitting far too many hours at my desk. Through lively dinner conversations, they helped me clarify and substantiate my arguments. They were my research partners when new restaurants needed to be "studied." Their love gave me the space and confidence I needed to put my thoughts on paper. I hope the result makes them proud.

Finally, I would like to acknowledge that I live and conduct research on stolen Kumeyaay land. Long before becoming "ethnic" or "cosmopolitan,"

San Diego's foodscape was Indigenous. Today's foodscape is layered on the food geographies of Indigenous people who have been expropriated, displaced, and erased by successive generations of settlers who have refashioned it to meet their needs, twining the past, present, and future.

THE $16 TACO

Introduction

I HAD JUST DELIVERED a presentation on ethnic food markets at a conference and was sitting on a homebound plane, eating pretzels and flipping through the airline magazine in search of distraction. Between advertisements for business centers, dating services, chain steakhouses, and wrinkle-free shirts, my eyes settled in great disbelief on a colorfully illustrated article praising the "second renaissance" of Barrio Logan.[1] The neighborhood, located just a few miles from my home and the focus of my ongoing research on "ethnic" food in San Diego, was described as "a thriving hub of Chicano culture emerging from the shadows." Readers were taken on a quick tour of Logan Avenue—"the coolest stretch of Mexican culture north of the border." Aside from a vintage store and a swimsuit designer shop, recommended stops were all about food and drink. They included a craft brewery with "flavors for the Latino crowd like the horchata golden stout," a "super legit" "street-meets-foodie" hot-dog stand that "pushes the envelope," a café that "serves drinks like watermelon lemonade in a sweet-and-spicy rimmed glass" and "throws all these events from craft fairs to latte-art competitions," and a taco shop that is "not just a taco shop." The illustrations featured a Frida Kahlo look-alike holding a steaming cup of coffee imprinted with a Virgin of Guadalupe design. They also included a group of people with monochromatically light skin tones eating tacos at a communal table. In the former image, formally educated upper- and middle-class readers likely recognized ubiquitous symbols of Mexican culture. In the latter, they might have also recognized themselves.

Most residents of San Diego have never visited Barrio Logan, having found no reason to venture in the "Mexican barrio" dissected by freeways and typically described as gang-infested, polluted, and poor. Yet United Airlines was suggesting to the broad national and international readership of *Hemispheres* to take a stroll along its main street. The potential appeal of Barrio Logan to these readers reflects a particular moment in our changing food culture: a moment characterized by a seemingly growing openness to cultural diversity often described as cosmopolitanism. The short article validated a trend that had begun several years ago and was unfolding in many urban neighborhoods around the United States.

In recent years I have observed a small but growing number of "educated" consumers and "trendsetters" taking notice of Barrio Logan. Often, they present themselves as "urban pioneers" willing to venture in unknown territory in search of otherness and authenticity, which they have found in a few iconic Mexican restaurants, the Chicano murals covering the pillars of the Coronado bridge, and the occasional lowrider gathering. They wrote about their adventures in blogs and lifestyle magazines, posted photographs and comments on social media, and discussed them at dinner parties, piquing the interest of like-minded people and unknowingly setting in motion an economic, social, and cultural transformation of the neighborhood. Not far from Barrio Logan, in North Park, City Heights, and Little Italy, food was also playing a transformative role, by refashioning neighborhoods and making them more attractive to outsiders, including tourists and suburbanites in search of "good food."

This phenomenon is not unique to San Diego; in cities across the United States and much of the world, cultural elites have been turning their backs to traditional fine dining in favor of seemingly more casual, democratic, authentic, and cosmopolitan food experiences. The condescension of haute cuisine and the affectedness of nouvelle cuisine, typically associated with France, have been replaced by the unpretentiousness and authenticity of comfort food from around the world as symbols of good taste. This fascination with exotic yet down-to-earth food extends to the places where such food can be found—be it the hills of Tuscany, the streets of Oaxaca, or the gritty neighborhoods of American cities. The current popularity of food trucks, taquerias, ramen bars, donut shops, and beer gardens attests to this desire for simplicity and authenticity.

Places like the Mission District in San Francisco, Boyle Heights in Los Angeles, Williamsburg in Brooklyn, Jamaica Plain in Boston, Pilsen in Chicago, Brixton in London, Kreuzberg in Berlin, and Little Portugal in Toronto—to name a few—have been "discovered" by outsiders who are attracted by their historical character, presumed authenticity, and cultural diversity, which is almost invariably tied to their "vibrant" food cultures and history as immigrant destinations and ethnic enclaves. In fact, food is central in establishing the authentic and multicultural identity of these neighborhoods. Street vendors, "hole-in-the-wall" restaurants, food trucks, ethnic grocers, corner stores, and community gardens contribute to creating a seemingly cosmopolitan foodscape that is particularly appealing to young, college-educated, and affluent individuals. Yet very little is known about how this trend is transforming these neighborhoods and affecting the everyday life of residents, most of whom are first-, second-, or third-generation immigrants and people of color.

Several months before the *Hemispheres* article was published, fears about the negative effects of the so-called "second renaissance" of Barrio Logan were brought to the surface by a potential new addition to the local foodscape that upset many local residents. Going by the name Barefoot Bohemian, a young woman whose whiteness, wealth, and privilege are evident in her blogs and social media posts was attempting to open a "modern frutería" in the neighborhood. Her goal, as she explained in a Kickstarter video online, was to "bring healthy food to the barrio." Dismissing—or perhaps appropriating—the licuados, jugos, chamangos, frutilocos, aguas frescas, and other fruit specialties found in local Mexican eateries, she proposed a menu of smoothies, lattes, and fruit bowls at inflated prices. This infuriated many community members who interpreted it as a symbol of gentrification, an expression of cultural appropriation, and another manifestation of colonialism. The community response was so fierce that the Barefoot Bohemian abandoned her project, temporarily leaving an empty space on Logan Avenue.

Tensions have risen elsewhere too, as new visitors and residents come to enjoy the "burgeoning" food scene of ethnic neighborhoods while longtime residents increasingly feel like outsiders in a place whose cultural identity and physical landscape is changing quickly. Boyle Heights, a mostly Latino neighborhood of East Los Angeles, has become a battleground between developers and antigentrification advocates, who often target new restaurants, cafés, and craft breweries as both symbols of and actors in the transformation of their neighborhoods. In Pilsen, a Chicago neighborhood with a strong Mexican identity, the opening of a new coffee shop was disrupted by such signs as "Sugar with your gentrification?," "Fascism roasted daily," "Wake up and smell the gentrification," "Racism and classism smell like your coffee," and a more controversial "White people out of Pilsen." In these communities, as in Barrio Logan, these acts of resistance signal the emergence of grassroots collective action to oppose the changing food environment in which longtime residents no longer feel at home and struggle culturally, socially, economically, and emotionally to retain a sense of ownership and belonging.

These examples point to a need to critically examine cosmopolitanism—particularly as it relates to food—and go beyond celebratory accounts to consider the social tensions it may hide. Cosmopolitanism is the notion that "all people, regardless of cultural, national or other affiliations, do or can belong to a single, universal community of human beings that should be cultivated."[2] Although the transformation of Barrio Logan and other immigrant and ethnic neighborhoods across the country may signal a form of multiculturalism worth celebrating, it also raises important questions regarding the potential of food to bridge racial divides and create a more inclusive society. Does the popularity of ethnic foods and the "cosmopolitanization" of ethnic neighborhoods lift up the communities and places associated with them? What are the economic and social impacts of this new cultural appreciation on concerned communities, including the many immigrants who own and work in ethnic food businesses? Who benefits from food-based cross-cultural encounters, and who defines their terms? What kind of social relationships emerge from "eating together"? Why and how are public officials, developers, and nonprofit leaders encouraging food gentrification? In other words, how does the growing interest in cosmopolitan food transform ethnic neighborhoods and the immigrant communities who have long inhabited them? These are the questions I seek to answer in this book.

I approach these questions through the lens of foodscape—the social, political, economic, and cultural setting in which food acquires meaning and value—to explore the dynamic relationships between food, ethnicity, and place, which are inextricably bound to one another. Specifically, the book contextualizes the growing popularity of ethnic food within the immigrant neighborhoods where such food originates and investigates the effects on its inhabitants and their communities. The book centers on the process of transforming foodscapes from ethnic to cosmopolitan, paying attention to both discursive and material changes as well as the way they reinforce each other. It is not a book about ethnic food in an abstract— timeless and placeless—sense. Instead, it is about the evolution of places where ethnic food is produced, lived, and consumed by different urban actors. Focusing on foodscapes offers a unique perspective that acknowledges the symbolic and material as indivisible and helps conceptualize ethnic food dynamically as a geographic encounter that is full of tensions and contradictions. Using in-depth case studies from several immigrant neighborhoods of San Diego, and drawing parallels with examples from other places, this book examines the multiple ways in which immigrants contribute to the production of vibrant urban foodscapes while simultaneously being marginalized and excluded from them. It illustrates how food can both *emplace* and *displace* immigrants, shedding light on the larger process of food gentrification and the emotional, cultural, economic, and physical displacement it produces. The sixteen-dollar taco— an actual overpriced aberration of lobster and filet mignon offered at a new local restaurant—is a product and representation of these contested geographies.

GOALS AND CONTRIBUTIONS

The distinction between ethnic and cosmopolitan foodscapes provides a useful starting point and conceptual framework to consider how food geographies are socially produced in ways that reflect and influence race relations and the everyday lives of immigrants and people of color. Distinguishing between these foodscapes is partly a question of perspective: what angle is adopted to frame the landscape, what is made visible and invisible, what is blurred or out of focus, and what colors, lights, or tones are emphasized. While ethnic foodscapes foreground the experience of immigrants and racialized ethnic inhabitants who live and work there, cosmopolitan foodscapes are designed by and for multicultural elites who consume those spaces. The term *ethnic* is problematic and this distinction is obviously an oversimplification, which I hope to refine and elaborate upon in this book. My intention is not to set cosmopolitan and ethnic foodscapes as binaries but instead to focus on how urban foodscapes are produced and transformed to *become* ethnic or cosmopolitan and what this transformation means for immigrants and people of color who live there. In that sense, the distinction between ethnic or cosmopolitan foodscapes is more than a matter of perspective: it involves real lives that unfold and refold within them.

The "cosmopolitanization" of ethnic foodscapes is not merely a reflection of evolving attitudes and emerging cosmopolitan sensitivities prompted by global mobility and hyperdiversity. Rather, it is caused by economic investments, politically motivated interventions, and changing consumption habits. These changes are facilitated by and contribute to the growing invisibility and displacement of immigrants and people of color from cosmopolitan foodscapes. This symbolic and material exclusion has important yet poorly understood effects on well-being to the extent that visibility shapes abilities to define ownership and control over food. The stigmatization, reification, commodification, colonization, and appropriation of ethnic food that occur in the process of cosmopolitanization usurp economic opportunities, health benefits, memories, social connections, and sense of belonging that food may bring to immigrants and racialized ethnic people. This process is entangled into a larger process of gentrification that begins with the historical devaluation of ethnic neighborhoods and their foodways and ends with the displacement of longtime residents for the benefit of newcomers in ways that have yet to be explored.

This book goes beyond deconstructing cosmopolitan narratives that erase immigrant and nonwhite lives and contributions; my aim is to shed light on how immigrants and people of color participate in, navigate, and are resilient in the face of the cosmopolitanization of their foodscapes. As most students of landscape do, I acknowledge the importance of perspective and angle, but I also wish to emphasize materiality and lived experience as central to the construction and meanings of landscape as foodscape. By drawing attention to the invisibility, exclusion, and displacement of immigrants and ethnic others from cosmopolitan foodscapes, my work builds upon several interdisciplinary literatures and supports an antiracist agenda. In particular, it contributes to critical research in urban studies, food studies, and race and ethnic studies.

Within urban studies, I help generate a better understanding of gentrification by focusing on the role of food—an element that until recently has been ignored or interpreted as a by-product or mere symbol of urban change. By considering food as an agent in the transformation of neighborhoods, I shed light on contemporary forms of gentrification and bring together consumption and production aspects, bridging an ongoing divide within this broad body of work. In the extensive literature on gentrification, many scholars have adopted a political-economy approach and attributed gentrification to the logic of neoliberal capitalism in which investors are encouraged to take advantage of rent-gaps, altering the housing stock and triggering social displacement.[3] Following the cultural turn in much of the social sciences, however, researchers began to draw attention to the role of culture in shaping cities and social exclusion. From this perspective, gentrification is driven by changes in consumer preferences, including new politics of identity formation increasingly linked to consumption and lifestyles.[4]

Yet consumption and production need not be separated; they operate in tandem and reinforce each other. Similarly, the narratives and discourses surrounding cosmopolitan landscapes need not be divorced from their materialization as lived and felt embodied experiences. As Fran Tonkiss has put it: "Within the process of gentrification, the material and the symbolic production of space come together, as shifts in cultural meanings help to secure the ground for social and spatial restructuring."[5] Motivated by this recognition, I revisit the concept of landscape, including its symbolic and material relationships to race and ethnicity, and I illustrate its relevance for understanding the role of food in the process of gentrification. My research is engaged in and influenced by emerging dialogues on the complex relationships between food, race, and gentrification, including the recently edited volume by Alison Alkon, Yuki Kato, and Joshua Sbicca to which I contributed.[6]

This book also reaffirms the centrality of displacement in gentrification, challenging claims that gentrification is good for everyone. By paying attention to everyday embodied practices, including those related to feeding and eating, I broaden understandings of displacement as more than the physical loss of housing to include the disruption of everyday life and threats to sense of place and belonging. I am inspired by the work of Leslie Kern, who focuses on embodied (and gendered) practices of gentrification.[7] She documents the new tempos and rhythms of everyday life in a gentrifying Toronto neighborhood, showing how older residents and their needs are marginalized and rendered invisible—a process Kern describes as the "slow violence" of gentrification.[8] Food practices are an important element of daily rhythms that are transformed in the process of gentrification. In addition, I draw upon extensive work on the "right to the city" and the "right/fight to stay put" to explore practices of everyday resistance and survivability within broader political and economic structures, including the role that food may play in disrupting those structures.[9]

Within food studies I contribute to research on ethnic and cosmopolitan food as well as food security. I provide an important corrective to approaches that view ethnic food either "from below" (as a romanticized form of self-identification imbued in nostalgia) or "from above" (as an elitist discourse and a consumer-driven cosmopolitan commodity). My focus on foodscapes, particularly the distinction I make between *ethnic* and *cosmopolitan* foodscapes, helps advance understandings of how food, ethnicity, and place are coproduced. This provides opportunities to acknowledge interaction between the symbolic and the material and highlight the agency of ethnic entrepreneurs, workers, and consumers within structural constraints like economic inequality and racial discrimination. It broadens the field of food studies, where the theorization and investigation of place and landscape, particularly as it relates to ethnicity and race, remain in their infancy. It also strengthens the emerging field of geography of food by revisiting the concept of landscape and reconnecting foodscape to its theoretical origins in geography. Doing so provides a framework to think about the relationship between food security and race/ethnicity in geographic terms. In particular, the idea of "food apartheid" (to which I devote attention in chapter 2 and return throughout the book), draws attention to the fact that food insecurity is socially and politically produced by spatial processes that partition, segregate, label, and expropriate urban landscapes along color lines.[10]

This brings me to a third interdisciplinary area of research: critical racial and ethnic studies. My emphasis on immigrants and ethnic "others" answers calls for more research on the racialization of immigrants, including Latinx and Asian people, in the United States.[11] Like Patricia Price, I wonder "what is racialization if not a powerful social construction that renders a person or group impervious to belonging, mobility, and rights, due to a presumably immutable condition?"[12] Answering in the affirmative places most immigrants alongside other racialized groups and opens up possibilities to expand and intersect thinking about race, ethnicity, and immigration. Doing so broadens scholarship on immigration and ethnicity, which has historically shied away from critical race studies. A focus on race helps conceptualize ethnicity as a socially produced category that structures social relations, as articulated in Michael Omi and Howard Winant's racial formation theory.[13]

In this context, ethnicity is more than a cultural phenomenon based on seemingly voluntarily chosen attributes such as beliefs, language, religion, and lifestyle. "Ethnics" are not just European immigrants— "whites of a different color"—who presumably join the melting pot and assimilate into an increasingly color-blind, multicultural, and hyperdiverse society, shedding their cultural peculiarities with each generation. They are Black, Asian, and Latinx people who face deeply entrenched, often covert, systems of racial injustice demonstrated by the persistence of racial inequality in education, health, housing, employment, and the justice system. Thus, instead of reducing race to ethnicity as conservative and liberal thinkers have done in the post–Civil Rights era, Omi and Winant conceptualize ethnicity as race. To reflect this orientation, I often use the term *ethnoracial* and employ ethnicity, race, and immigration in the same spirit and interchangeably.

By focusing on food, foodscapes, and embodied practices of everyday life, I contribute to studies that explore the materialization of race and ethnicity as an ongoing spatial process resulting from interactions between bodies, objects, and places. As noted, I am more interested in understanding how ethnicity (or race) is lived and experienced in particular places than in the ways it is represented, although I acknowledge the relationship between the representational and nonrepresentational. I challenge myths surrounding notions of cosmopolitanism and multiculturalism, including the idea that geographic encounters through ethnic food supports social inclusion, economic integration, and cultural appreciation by drawing attention to the racialized foodscapes in which these encounters take place, including the materialities of food apartheid and uneven access to food. Doing so, I build upon a rich body of work in geography on the complex spatialities of race and recent efforts to reontologize race as a spatial assemblage of materials, discourses, and practices that make race "stick" in particular contexts.[14] The work of Ashanté Reese, which examines how race structures uneven access to food and shapes the way people navigate these constraints through place-based practices of refusal and self-reliance in a Black community of Washington, DC, provides wonderful inspiration for centering race in food studies and examining the food geographies of other racialized communities.[15]

Ultimately, *The $16 Taco* is about food sovereignty and contributes to this area of research and activism.[16] It challenges us to see the lives of different ethnoracial groups and recognize the tensions, contradictions, and injustices in a food system that adopts cosmopolitan aesthetics. Despite the fact that people of color, especially immigrants, are a major source of labor throughout the food industry—from orchards to slaughterhouse to canning factories to restaurant kitchens—they are often invisible to those of us who depend on their labor. Paradoxically, this invisibility remains true in cosmopolitan foodscapes and within the so-called alternative food movement, where the immigrant and ethnic experience is flattened by the erasure of racial oppression, dispossession, and exclusion.

By making immigration and race visible and disclosing the working of racialization in the cosmopolitan foodscape, my project aligns with a larger antiracist project of denaturalizing and decentering whiteness. It fits within research that points to the limitations of a contemporary food movement that is dominated by ethical consumerism and normalizes white food habits at farmers' markets and community gardens as the standard for good food practices.[17] Similarly, it outlines the hypocrisy of celebrating a cosmopolitan food culture without immigrants and people of color. By foregrounding ethnoracial perspectives, this book asserts the possibilities of a food justice movement premised on meaningful and transformative encounters with and through food—encounters that make visible the contributions and struggles of immigrants and challenge participants to manifest necessary change.

CRITICAL ETHNOGRAPHY AND MIXED METHODS

The $16 Taco focuses on several urban neighborhoods of San Diego, including Barrio Logan, City Heights, Golden Hill, Little Italy, North Park, and Southeastern San Diego, which I describe more thoroughly in chapter 2. These neighborhoods are located within close proximity to downtown and are home to ethnically diverse populations, although the size of these populations has evolved over time. Indeed, these neighborhoods are all undergoing demographic and socioeconomic transformations and experiencing gentrification pressures with varying intensity.

Compared with New York, San Francisco, or Los Angeles, San Diego's food landscape may appear provincial and less cosmopolitan. No local restaurant has earned any Michelin star, and fewer than a handful have caught the attention of food critics compiling "best of" lists of restaurants and chefs in America. Indeed, San Diegans often pride themselves in the laid-back atmospheres of their restaurants and the casualness of local food. Known for the California burrito and craft beers, San Diego rarely sets culinary trends. Yet this characteristic makes it an ideal setting to study the process of "cosmopolitanization" that is unfolding not just in "global cities" but also in small and midsize cities that are becoming increasingly diverse.

Framing my work through the lens of foodscapes encourages an ethnographic approach to understanding the relationship between food, place, and identity. The bulk of the evidence has been gathered through interviews and participant observations in San Diego. Since the early 2010s, I have been doing fieldwork and collaborating with community-based organizations on food security and food justice issues in the neighborhoods that are the focus of this book. I conducted hundreds of food store and restaurant audits in Southeastern San Diego (n = 167), City Heights (n = 221), and Barrio Logan (n = 63), beginning in 2014 and updating them in 2020. I also surveyed customers who shopped at ethnic food stores in City Heights (n = 42) in the summer of 2016 and conducted interviews of food store and restaurant owners and managers (n = 34), employees (n = 6), and consumers (n = 33) in all three neighborhoods between 2016 and 2018. In earlier projects I gathered data from farmers' markets and community gardens. Finally, I led a photo-voice project with high school students in City Heights (n = 38). These various data-collection efforts generated a wealth of mostly qualitative information about immigrants and subsequent generations' relationship to food as consumers, business owners, and workers.

During this period, I got to know City Heights, Barrio Logan, and Southeastern San Diego in a more familiar and intimate way than traditional research would allow. I walked everywhere, shopped at local stores, ate in restaurants and homes, went to farmers' markets, pulled weeds in community gardens, and attended numerous community meetings and events. In addition to informal conversations and formal interviews, I took pictures and wrote field notes in an effort to record nonverbal data, including the elusive but important smells, sounds, and rhythms of foodscapes. I collected a large amount of news clips, magazine articles, restaurant reviews, and social media data, which I have used extensively in this analysis. The US Census is another important source of data. I have used Summary Files data at the Census tract level to describe and analyze neighborhood change and gentrification over time, and I have relied on the Public Use Microdata Sample to supplement my analysis of workers in San Diego's food service economy. By combining these various data sources, this book exemplifies a mixed-method approach.

Much of the fieldwork was undertaken with Fernando Bosco, my colleague in the Department of Geography at San Diego State University, to whom I am intellectually indebted. Together, with funding from the National Science Foundation, we conducted research and gathered data on the food practices of children and families in three ethnically diverse central neighborhoods of San Diego. We cotaught several versions of a community-based geographic research course, allowing us to work with both undergraduate and graduate students on service-learning projects related to our research. These classes were built around collaborative projects with community partners to document various elements of local foodscapes at the neighborhood scale, including small stores, ethnic businesses, farmers' markets, and community gardens.[18] We worked closely with young people in a participatory project to explore their "food journeys"—the ways they navigate local foodscapes (often painted as food deserts) through everyday food practices.[19] This work led to a coedited volume titled *Food and Place*, where we laid out the foundations for studying food from a place perspective.[20] In short, my research, teaching, and activism over the past decade, especially the collaborative work with Fernando Bosco and students at San Diego State University, have given me a rich and intimate understanding of San Diego's foodscape.

In recent years I have become increasingly concerned by gentrification, noticing how changes in the food environment of immigrant neighborhoods were having unanticipated consequences. Community gardens, farmers' markets, new grocery stores, and food-based community development programs seem to be attracting new residents to such neighborhoods as Barrio Logan, changing the demographic composition of these neighborhoods and rebranding them as cosmopolitan. I worry about displacement, including the displacement of renters who can no longer afford escalating rents, but also the displacement of ethnic businesses that have a hard time competing with newcomers, and ultimately the displacement of longtime residents' cultures and ways of being. This book emerged from these concerns and explores the role of food in the transformation of urban neighborhoods, with a particular focus on the experiences of immigrants who live there, running businesses, feeding families, building communities, and creating homes.

Although this project is primarily an ethnographic undertaking, it also engages with other methods and types of data, including media content and public data analysis, photography, and mapping. Using mixed methods permits me to oscillate between the material and the symbolic, merging qualitative and quantitative data about immigrants' relationship to food and place, as told by participants in my study, visualized through photography, portrayed in the media, documented in Census data, and experienced in the field. It also allows me to go back in time and consider how places became constructed as ethnic or cosmopolitan foodscapes through a combination of demographic and housing shifts evidenced by Census data, new business activities recorded in city registries, changing embodied practices documented through interviews and participant observations, evolving built environments revealed by photography, and emerging narratives embedded in various media sources.

Some might view this undertaking of raising the visibility of immigrant lives in cosmopolitan foodscapes as naïve or, worse, hypocritical. What right do I have to tell immigrants' stories? How could I possibly do justice to these struggles? Will this not, after all, reproduce the sort of cosmopolitanism that I criticize for reflecting the perspective of affluent and primarily white consumers? As an immigrant who has spent approximately half of her life in the United States, I have experienced firsthand the capacity of food to bring people together and generate a sense of place and belonging. It would not be an exaggeration to say that my family and closest friendships have been formed at my dinner table—around food inspired by my country of origin and shaped by my new home. Cooking for others has been one of my greatest pleasures; it has made strangers into friends, given me confidence, and helped me keep my children in touch with their transnational roots. However, unlike many of the immigrants portrayed in this book, I do not cook for a living. I also come from a county—Belgium—that has not been the object of strict immigration restrictions and does not figure into the popular imagination as a problematic source of immigrants. I have had no difficulty obtaining the required authorizations to study, live, and work in the United States and eventually becoming a citizen. As many food scholars, I must acknowledge the privileged position from which I engage with food as a white, highly formally educated, internationally mobile, and relatively affluent woman.

Although these attributes certainly influence my work and will generate a less-than-perfect ethnography, acknowledging and reflecting on my positionality will hopefully produce meaningful work and shed light on the complex and multidirectional power relations underlying the relationship between food, immigration, and place. Following anthropologist Wendy Luttrell's advice, I aim for a "good enough" method—one in which the nitty-gritty research decisions regarding site selection, subject involvement, case studies, data recorded, comparisons, and so forth are assessed "in terms of what is lost and what is gained rather than what might be ideal."[21] She makes a useful analogy when she argues that, like the "perfect mother," the "perfect researcher" does not exist. However, "it is possible to be a 'good enough researcher'—that is a person who is aware that she or he has personal stakes and investments in research relationships; who does not shy away from frustrations, anxieties, and disappointments that are part of any relationship; and who seeks to understand (and is able to appreciate) the difference between one's self and another."[22] This is the kind of person I try to be in my research, including the work that led to this book.

A MAP OF THE BOOK

I begin with an overview of foodscapes as the primary theoretical frame for my research (chapter 1). The remainder of the book traces the cosmopolitanization of foodscapes in several immigrant neighborhoods of San Diego, beginning with the production of ethnic foodscapes as deprived of good food—a process I describe as "food apartheid" (chapter 2)—and their significance in the everyday life of immigrants and people of color both as workers toiling in various sectors of the food and restaurant industry (chapter 3) and as consumers struggling with food insecurity (chapter 4). I then turn my attention to the "urban food machine" that is reshaping ethnic foodscapes into cosmopolitan destinations through "gastrodevelopment" (chapter 5) and explore how the emerging "taste of gentrification" favors white, middle-class, and young consumers while displacing older residents economically, culturally, and affectively (chapter 6). The book concludes with hopeful but cautionary suggestions on how we may fight food gentrification so that food can become a medium to create meaningful cultural encounters, disrupt racism, provide economic opportunities, and sustain immigrant and working-class communities of color.

1

Foodscapes

From Ethnic to Cosmopolitan

URING THE PAST decade, the term *foodscape* has been adopted by a growing number of scholars as a useful way to situate food within particular cultural, economic, political, and social landscapes. I, too, am inspired by this idea as a promising framework to situate the study of ethnic food within the places where it is materially and discursively produced. A foodscape approach shifts the analytical gaze from food itself to the larger geographic context in which it is prepared, advertised, imagined, sold, and ingested, drawing attention to everyday food practices and the social relations and hierarchies of power in which they are embedded.

Going back to the example of the frutería mentioned in the introduction, from a foodscape perspective the fruit bowl that the Barefoot Bohemian had hoped to sell in Barrio Logan would be more than a combination of healthy ingredients. It would have to be interpreted relationally, within the material and discursive context in which residents carry out a multiplicity of everyday food-related activities that help them earn an income, feed their families, and remake their home. Acknowledging that this landscape has been shaped over time and through space by immigration, environmental racism, political neglect, and capital withdrawal would generate a better understanding of the significance of this fruit bowl well beyond its nutritional value—as a symbol of gentrification and a geographic encounter between longtime residents of Barrio Logan and white, middle-class consumers and entrepreneurs who "battled" over it.

In this theoretical chapter, I trace the origins and evolution of foodscape as the primary concept I use to frame my analysis of ethnic food throughout the rest of the book. I engage with work in geography, food studies, and racial and ethnic studies to articulate a dynamic, geographic, and power-laden notion of foodscape in which ethnic food is produced, negotiated, and contested. I then distinguish between ethnic and cosmopolitan foodscapes. While the former foregrounds the experiences of immigrants and ethnic others in procuring food, the latter privileges the consumption practices of more affluent and primarily white consumers. This distinction underlies the main argument I make herein regarding the changing nature of ethnic food and the impacts of its growing popularity on the people and places that have historically produced and consumed such food.

CULTURAL LANDSCAPES

The idea of *landscape* has a long tradition in cultural geography, where it carries different meanings and is closely associated with notions of place and space. Many in the discipline, beginning with the influential work of Carl Sauer in the 1920s, view landscapes as records of human activity.[1] As such, they are representation of cultures that can be interpreted and analyzed, like a text or a painting. Landscapes are both the "scenery" and the "frame" through which it is viewed. They reflect unique *ways of seeing*—a view of spatial arrangements or place from a specific perspective.[2]

A more recent body of work emphasizes the materiality of landscapes as lived places that are socially constructed and imbued with power—the ongoing production of interactions between humans, objects, and environments. Instead of uncovering fixed cultural traits in the landscape, contemporary geographers have turned their attention to the social dimensions of landscapes and their relationship to culture. Inspired by Marxism, many scholars have turned to capitalism, including the profit motive driving inflows and outflows of capital, as an explanation for contemporary landscapes. For Don Mitchell, landscapes are dialectic; they are both the outcome of social processes and the driving force shaping and reshaping these processes.[3] By dividing and segregating landscapes along the lines of class and race, capitalism reproduces the differences on which it thrives. In that view, landscapes are dynamic and always in flux. Other scholars, influenced by cultural and feminist geography, draw attention to the everyday experiences and practices that concretize landscapes.[4] They view landscapes as the raced, classed, gendered, and sexed microcosms of daily activity that arise from and simultaneously condition everyday practices. It is within these landscapes that cultural notions of whiteness, patriarchy, and heteronormativity are reproduced but also negotiated, contested, and resisted with material consequences for those who inhabit them.

Bridging these two broad perspectives—landscape as representation and landscape as process—and ignoring for now the long-standing debates within and between them, I think of landscapes as symbolic and material; experienced, produced, and imagined; processual and relational. Stephen Daniels has summarized this characteristic as the "duplicity of landscape" that "can neither be completely reified as an authentic object in the world nor thoroughly dissolved as an ideological mirage."[5] This duplicity makes landscapes particularly useful to approach the study of food and its relationship to race and ethnicity, which is at once symbolic and material. It is equally helpful in thinking about gentrification that produces its own landscape characterized by shifting demographics, changing rhythms of everyday life, and new ways of seeing old places.

FOODSCAPE: EMERGENCE OF A NEW CONCEPT

Following Arjun Appadurai's lead, scholars began attaching the suffix *-scape* to a variety of terms (e.g., mediascape, ethnoscape, technoscape) to emphasize the perspectival aspect of cultural and economic phenomenon that are "inflected by the historical, linguistic and political situatedness of different sorts of actors."[6] Combined with *food*—as in *foodscape*—the term refers to spatial contexts of food production and consumption as they may appear to particular viewers, close to what may be described in popular parlance as the "food scene." Foodscapes are much more than the physical spaces where people obtain food, however; they also include symbolic, imaginative, and emotional components. Echoing this idea, Josée Johnston and Shyon Baumann think of the foodscape as "a dynamic social construction that relates food to places, people, meanings, and material processes."[7] As physical and discursive spaces, foodscapes are shaped by power and influence how people relate to food. In short, foodscapes incorporate the social, cultural, political, and economic factors that influence the way people interact with food and with each other through food in particular places.

One of the very first references to the term *foodscape* is found in Gisèle Yasmeen's study of small shops selling prepared food in Bangkok.[8] Emphasizing the experiences of women in a city undergoing rapid urbanization and economic restructuring, she situated local food habits within the broader context of Thai gender relations and global urban change. Her geographic research helped define foodscapes as dynamic spatial assemblages of food practices and ideologies that are experienced differently by people based on their gender, class, or other social categories. Since then, the term has gained popularity among scholars who are interested in understanding the multifaceted relationships between food and place from a variety of disciplinary angles, including public health, sociology, geography, and the broader field of food studies. However, as *foodscape* became more frequently used, its theoretical underpinnings were gradually ignored, leading to confusion as to what the term actually represents.

Public health researchers have been keen to adopt the idea of foodscape as a way to conceptualize the effects of the food environment on health behaviors and outcomes, such as diet and obesity. Over time, however, the concept lost its multivalence and became synonymous with the food environment, specifically the built environment. For instance, for Thomas Burgoine, "the foodscape, or the food environment, incorporates all opportunities to obtain food within a given region."[9] As health researchers prioritized the measurement and quantification of food deficits and obesogenic characteristics of particular places, they often lost sight of the perspectival, dynamic, and social aspects of foodscapes that are crucial to understanding the well-being of communities. Foodscapes simply became physical containers of corner shops, fast food restaurants, and supermarkets, offering a very narrow perspective of the relationship between food and place. Urban planners have adopted a similarly restricted perspective by focusing on design or built elements of the foodscape that may be conducive to sustainability and conviviality.[10]

Sociologists, in contrast, have been inspired by the notion of foodscape as a way to frame analyses of the social relations in which food practices are embedded. For instance, Johnston and Baumann's work on "foodies" describes a gourmet foodscape that is both increasingly democratic and simultaneously exclusive.[11] They focus mostly on the discursive aspect of foodscapes—the representation of food in magazines, cookbooks, blogs, and television shows—and demonstrate how these narratives are framed by class relations. Relying primarily on media content analysis, they argue that "foodies"—people with passionate interests in food—exhibit an ambivalent or conflicting class position in their attitude toward food. While seemingly embracing democratic, cosmopolitan, and ethical values in their food choices, the criteria they set to define "good food" (e.g., organic, fairly traded, local, authentic) remain unattainable to most because of cultural and economic restrictions and geographic obstacles. Johnston and Baumann's research has been very influential in refining the concept of foodscape and shaping critical food scholarship, including my own work. Yet their focus on the discursive foodscape is centered on the experiences of foodies as cultural elites and does not address the effects of these narratives on the people they render invisible.

THE PLACES, SPACES, AND SCALES OF FOODSCAPES

Without it being acknowledged, the concept of foodscape that has come to dominate public health, sociology, and much of food studies, privileges space over place—two important geographic ideas related to landscape. Although there is much debate on the meaning of *space* within geography, it is typically understood as the surface on which natural and social phenomenon occur, giving these events some structure or pattern. However, as nodes in increasingly global flows of ideas, people, and objects, *space* is not necessarily attached to territory.[12] In their research on foodies, Johnston and Baumann equate foodscapes to discursive spaces; they emphasize the media as the space where knowledge about food is being formulated and legitimized. Scholars interested in access to healthy food, use foodscapes to represent retail and consumption spaces, aligning themselves with a more Cartesian definition of space as a physical surface on which we can objectively measure location and distance.

In contrast to space, *place* is more concrete; it is generally defined as space that has been transformed by human activity and is imbued with cultural values, social meanings, and personal experiences.[13] Steve Harrison and Paul Dourish distinguish *space* from *place* in the following way: "Space is the opportunity; place is the understood reality. . . . We are located in space, but we act in place."[14] Many geographers emphasize landscape's connections to place. For instance, Edward Relph claims that "landscape is both the context for places and an attribute of places."[15] Doreen Massey, building on her notion of place as fluid, provisional, unstable, and contested, argues that landscapes are events—"provisionally intertwined simultaneities of ongoing, unfinished, stories."[16] I argue that it may be time to revisit the concept of foodscape and reconnect with the idea of landscapes as a set of lived and imagined places in which inhabitants—not just cultural elites, corporate leaders, or financiers—relate to each other through food in material and sensory ways. Doing so would draw attention to the inseparability of the symbolic/discursive/representational and the material/everyday/lived. It would also provide a framework to better consider how race and ethnicity are signified, experienced, and constituted geographically through food.

In trying to relocate foodscapes in particular places, geographers have focused on a variety of *scales* from the global to the body. Several scholars have emphasized the *global* political and economic relations that underlie our everyday food practices, using *foodscape* to describe the global neoliberal capitalist food system. For instance, Lewis Holloway and Moya Kneafsey have written about a "placeless foodscape" to describe a global and industrial food system where we no longer know where our food comes from.[17] They contrast this to the "local foodscape" of farmers' markets, where consumers are economically, socially, and culturally connected to the places where food is produced. Attending to the perspectival aspect, Michael K. Goodman, Damian Maye, and Lewis Holloway focus on "ethical foodscapes"—a sort of geographical imaginary in which organic, local, fairly traded, and alternative foods are viewed as morally superior.[18] They conceptualize these landscapes as products of neoliberal capitalism that promotes market-based solutions and espouses the idea of consumer responsibility. Along those lines, several observers have pointed out that the "corporate-organic foodscape" hides enduring labor exploitation and ecological destruction.[19] Furthermore, it reproduces social inequality by labeling those unable to partake as consumers in the market-based "alternative foodscape" as uneducated, irresponsible, and amoral, with severe consequences for their economic, physical, and emotional well-being.[20] Ironically, this includes most of the people who work in the vastly underpaid and highly exploitative agrifood industry as fruit pickers, meat cutters, waiters, cooks, and dishwashers, many of whom are immigrants and people of color who live in places abandoned by supermarkets and mainstream food retailers.

Others have located foodscapes at the *urban* scale, focusing on changing cities and their relationships to food. With my colleague Fernando Bosco, I have written about the rise of the cultural economy as a critical influence on contemporary urban foodscapes.[21] Inspired by Sharon Zukin, whose research in New York City stresses cities as consumption sites of commoditized urban experiences, we argued that eating out and shopping for food has become a quintessential and highly marketable aspect of urban life.[22] In a context where the worth of cities is increasingly measured by their cultural life, food has become more important than ever in defining places and is an essential aspect of the cultural economy of cities. Food is both a marker and a maker of cultural identities understood in a neoliberal context as fluid expressions of individuality through lifestyle and consumption choices that shun rigid categories such as class, race, or gender.[23] The social capital that food provides is enhanced by the desirability of the places where it is consumed. As Ian Cook and Philip Crang have put it, "foods do not simply come from places . . . but also make places as symbolic constructs, being deployed in the constructions of various imaginative geographies."[24] In other words, food, place, and identity are coproduced. Yet much of the research on the cultural economy of food focuses on urban elites who presumably have greater purchasing power and tends to ignore the role of other actors such as food workers and lower-income consumers.

The recognition of the symbolic value of food has justified a new approach to urban governance and planning in which local government agencies focus their energy and resources on building so-called "creative cities" by transforming their foodscape. In cities across the United States and around the world, we have seen an expansion of food halls, public markets, farmers' markets, food truck gatherings, and food festivals meant to revitalize urban neighborhoods by attracting relatively affluent and educated consumers and tourists. Real estate advertising increasingly relies on foodscapes as selling points, banking on proximity to cafés, local eateries, world-class restaurants, and weekly farmers' markets to raise property values. Lists of "best places for foodies" abound in lifestyle and tourism magazines. Cities and neighborhoods compete with each other in terms of food, with the most diverse, authentic, communal, sustainable, festive, and/or ludic foodscape winning the contest in attracting desirable businesses, consumers, and residents.

Yet it is becoming clear that many groups, including people of color, immigrants, and the poor, are often socially and spatially excluded from these new urban food spaces. It is well documented that access to healthy, fresh, affordable, and culturally appropriate food is highly uneven within cities. The notion of food apartheid specifically ties this uneven access to racism, which involves policies, practices, and ideologies that produce and normalize racial inequalities resulting in food insecurity for Black, Brown, and Indigenous people and food abundance for white people.[25] These inequalities have explicit territorial dimensions that are expressed and constituted in the landscape. As race relations continue to evolve and cities become increasingly multicultural, new racial projects emerge to maintain the exclusion of nonwhites from the material and symbolic rewards of power and reproduce white supremacy. A burgeoning area of research to which I have contributed links food to the gentrification of urban neighborhoods, showing how newly discovered restaurants, community gardens, food halls, specialized boutiques, or high-end supermarkets transform neighborhoods by attracting more affluent residents and displacing previous ones.[26] The consequences of food gentrification for urban dwellers, including the complexities of displacement, remain poorly understood and are a key topic of this book.

This brings us to a third significant scale—the human *body*—which has animated some of the most creative and critical work on foodscapes. Conceptualizing the body as a foodscape calls attention to the ingestion of food and how eating connects us viscerally—through the gut—to what is around us.[27] Social difference is metabolized and can be "read" and "inscribed" on the body. Food has a transformative effect on bodies, but this effect goes well beyond the relationship between caloric intake and weight. In the act of eating, we ingest place—its biophysical elements as well as the social relations and cultural norms that underlie it. There is a metabolic and affective interchange between the body and the envionment that subverts dichotomies between human bodies, landscapes, and self. The physical environment—whether healthy or polluted—becomes part of foodstuff and therefore part of the body. The same could be said about the built environment, which influences access to food and diets. The social environment, including the labor that produces food, is also absorbed into the body; although this is rarely acknowledged, eating connects us to the many people who touch and handle our food. In addition, the body as an always emerging element of the foodscape also refers to the ways we, as a society, think about bodies and attach moral value to particular types of bodies and ways of eating—for instance, linking fatness with laziness or decadence. In other words, as feminist thinkers have long shown, the body is political.

In that sense, race can be thought of as embodied—produced through situated social interactions that result in othering and inequality. The embodiment of race—the production of whiteness and otherness through repeated practices—takes place in the foodscape, among other landscapes of daily life. Race structures the foodscapes in which it is materialized through food experiences that mark and differentiate bodies as white, black, ethnic, or other. Racism is experienced in the foodscape as material violence directed at racialized bodies in the form of hunger, malnutrition, exploitative physical labor, and health disparities as well as representational violence that erases, denigrates, and caricaturizes these same bodies. For instance, gentrified landscapes enable and promote particular embodied practices involving food such as shopping for artisanal products, snapping pictures of food, sitting at a café with a laptop, seeking out supposedly authentic dishes, purchasing locally grown produce, following food trucks on social media, or ordering salad dressing on the side. The raced and classed bodies that do not partake in these new habits are "out-of-place" and become disciplined, displaced, or erased.[28] Thinking about foodscape through the body shifts our entrance point from the constitutive elements of the landscape (e.g., the built environment) to the processes that relate elements to each other through events, including eating and feeding. In an embodied perspective, what becomes important is the different ways in which people enter, move through, dwell in, and occupy the foodscape. It emphasizes doing, feeling, sensing, and experiencing food as processes through which bodies and place become immanently entangled.[29]

This book engages with these geographically inspired and critical visions of foodscapes at multiple scales including the urban and the body. For me, thinking about foodscapes in urban settings makes tangible the idea that they are produced both physically through the labor of those toiling in the many sectors of the food industry and the capital that is directed at restaurants, food stores, and other food-related spaces and events, as well as culturally through the various ways we use these spaces in our everyday activities and imagine, describe, and package them for consumption. My approach uniquely seeks to unpack the mutual complication of the economic/material and cultural/symbolic. I do so by focusing on the urban places where ethnic food is a significant part of the landscape, as a material and symbolic commodity that is produced, exchanged, and consumed by actors with different attachments to ethnicity. This urban lens calls attention to the spatial unevenness and variegated nature of urban foodscapes, including the coexistence and evolution of what I describe as "ethnic" and "cosmopolitan" foodscapes that are foregrounded in different understanding of race, ethnicity, and immigration.

RACE, ETHNICITY, AND IMMIGRATION

This book focuses on the experiences of people who in dominant American society would most commonly be considered "ethnic" for lack of a better term. This includes immigrants from the Global South, subsequent generations, and people of color who do not fit into neat racial categories but do not view themselves and are not viewed by others as white. I have struggled coming up with a term to describe them without flattening or homogenizing their experiences. Finding it both impossible yet necessary to name the people at the center of this book, I have settled on the notion of *ethnicity*, which I view as a fluid and situational category related to immigration, race, and class.

Ethnicity is typically understood as an adopted or perceived identity based on shared characteristics such as language, religion, ancestral origins, and cultural traditions. The idea that everybody has an ethnicity underlies the popular notion of multiculturalism and assimilationism that tend to erase the significance of race and ignore the existence of structural racism. It assumes that ethnicity is voluntary rather than ascribed. As Stuart Hall and other race scholars have argued, however, ethnicity is not simply a form of self or collective identification; it is also a way to classify racialized "ethnic others" whose language, skin color, and/or food habits differ from what is understood as the norm.[30] Therefore *ethnicity*, like race, is socially produced as difference from a dominant group whose ethnicity has become naturalized and invisible and, like race, it has real-world material affects and effects. *Race* is as much about whiteness as it is about Blackness or otherness. In their theory of racial formation, Michael Omi and Howard Winant have argued that racial categories—including ethnicity—are "created, inhabited, transformed and destroyed" in sociohistorical processes involving both social structure, cultural representation, and everyday practices.[31] For them, "race operates at the crossroads between social structure and experience. It is both historically determined and continuously being made and remade in everyday life."[32] Geographers would add that race is also spatially produced: *materially* through racial segregation and uneven development and *symbolically* through coding of space as white or nonwhite, both of which deprive people of political, social, and economic power and shape everyday corporeal experiences of race.[33] As noted earlier, race can be thought of as embodied—inscribed materially and symbolically on the body through situated experiences.

Ethnicity, race, and immigration often overlap and are similar in their relationship to whiteness—the socially constructed normalcy and presumed superiority of white ways of being. I use these three terms interchangeably despite the fact that *race* often relates to skin color, *ethnicity* is typically about a common culture linked to ancestry and religion, and *immigration* generally refers to foreign national origins. In an attempt to be more specific, I also use the term *ethnoracial*, which emphasizes the connections between race and ethnicity—the fact that "race and ethnicity play hide-and-seek with each other."[34] To be clear, I am not suggesting lumping the experiences of all racialized groups together under an all-encompassing notion such as ethnorace, which would erase or dissolve ethnic and racial difference and differentiation. Rather, I posit that the experiences of nonwhite immigrants and subsequent generations are structured by racism, even if they do not fit neatly in a grand narrative or a Black/white binary. What is important here is that race, ethnicity, and immigration are not based on innate, immutable, natural, or objective characteristics but are socially produced categories that define people as different based on visible biological characteristics with real consequences for their present and future well-being.

As such, the meaning of these terms evolves over time and varies across space: they are situational, contingent, indeterminate, multiplicitous, and subjective. For instance, at the turn of the nineteenth century, Irish, Italians, and Jews were considered *ethnic*, but today, with a few exceptions, they are perceived as white and enjoy many of the privileges that come along with this association. The French and the Japanese, whose cuisine is regarded as highly sophisticated, are often perceived as distinctly foreign but rarely described as *ethnic*. In contrast, Latinos, including those who have been citizens of the United States for many generations and may define themselves as white, are viewed as ethnic, immigrant, and nonwhite. Finally, Black people rarely have the luxury of defining themselves or their food as *ethnic*, even if they come from places as diverse as the Caribbean, Africa, and Latin America. Arabs and Native Americans also occupy ambivalent ethnic categories that reflect a process of racialization rather than self-identification based on culture.

ETHNIC FOODSCAPE

Informed by the definition of *ethnicity* as socially produced and materially experienced, I use the term *ethnic foodscape* to describe the environments (e.g., kitchens, restaurants, streets, gardens, shops), bodies (e.g., cooks, chefs, immigrants, tourists, foodies, ethnics), objects (e.g., ingredients, carts, cookware, recipes, dishes) as well as ideologies, feelings, and imaginaries (e.g., domesticity, taste, smells, nostalgia, authenticity, exoticism) that work together to link food, place, and people to one or more ethnicities. The ethnic foodscape is therefore relational; it includes tangible elements that can be observed and counted as well as less tangible aspects of how people engage with these food-related elements in their daily activities. It foregrounds the everyday lives of "ethnic" people as they navigate the structural constraints of racism in and beyond their neighborhoods by engaging in unique food procurement practices.

Considering the breadth of writing on food and ethnicity, particularly as it relates to immigrants, it is surprising that the idea of ethnic foodscape has not gained more traction in critical food studies. Perhaps this is due to a lack of spatial thinking as well as the persistent divide within the interdisciplinary academic literature between those who focus on immigrant and diasporic foodways and those who study the racialized narratives surrounding ethnic food and its consumption. To date, few researchers have focused on the geographic encounters between the producers and consumers of ethnic food and how the symbolic nature of ethnic food and its everyday material reality are interwoven.

The first broad group of scholars includes anthropologists, historians, sociologists, and geographers who conceptualize food practices as symbolic and reflective of identity. Ethnicity is seen as a given and fixed identity to be discovered in cooking techniques, flavors and seasoning, table manners, and other socially condoned food behaviors. These researchers emphasize how immigrants use food to maintain cultural heritage, preserve memories, hold on to a threatened identity, and recreate a sense of community.[35] Immigrants perform a cultural identity that they brought with them through their migration journeys. Such identity may even become exacerbated over time through an idealization of the food left behind.[36] Food, especially when prepared and consumed at home, is thought to bring comfort and respite in a hostile context where immigrants are unable or hesitant to reveal their "true" identity publicly. Over time, however, it is assumed that immigrants assimilate and take on new identities reflected in the gradual adoption of Americanized diets. Then, only a few select nostalgic foods are preserved, more as a sign of distinction than as a necessity.

In that literature little attention is given to how identity is shaped and reshaped through situated interactions with others. Yet ethnic food is more than symbolism and self-identification in a few iconic traditional dishes. While ethnicity is performed by members of specific ethnic groups, it is also consumed and appropriated by others. It is also lived. In fact, people rarely call their own food ethnic; such labels usually come from interactions with others. As Pierre van den Bergh has put it: "Like ethnicity itself, ethnic cuisine only becomes a self-conscious, subjective reality when ethnic boundaries are crossed."[37]

From this recognition, a different perspective is put forward by scholars who study food through the lens of race and emphasize how racialized "ethnic others" are (re)produced—not just revealed or expressed—through food.[38] The work of bell hooks, especially her essay "Eating the Other," has been influential in promoting thinking about exotic food from the perspective of white consumers who seek it as a source of pleasure and distinction without any real appreciation for the people who create and produce it. She associates this to a commodity culture within which "ethnicity becomes spice, seasoning that can liven up the dull dish that is mainstream white culture."[39] For these scholars racialized discourses become embodied, thereby materializing race. For instance, the food of immigrants and ethnoracial groups has been disparaged historically as greasy, spicy, pungent, smelly, and/or unhealthy. These judgments have in turn translated into disgust toward the Brown and Black bodies that prepare and ingest such nasty food—a form of racism with very tangible consequences.

Although today's consumers appear to be much more open to a diversity of ethnic foods, several authors have argued that this openness is equally problematic in the way that it essentializes race/ethnicity and denies its significance through a process of decontextualization. Ghassan Hage has summarized this aptly as "multiculturalism without migrants," suggesting that consumers are interested in exotic and multicultural foods but overlook the immigrant communities from which such food is appropriated, often reducing them to "diversity."[40] Similarly, in his study of the food consumption practices of white middle-class consumers in a gentrifying neighborhood of London, Jon May has identified a process by which consumers pride themselves on an interest in other cultures while revealing racists stereotypes, including homogenizing descriptions of ethnic food businesses and their owners as uncivilized, slightly unsafe, and unsanitized yet cheerful, colorful, spiritual, and quaint.[41] Lisa Heldke in

Exotic Appetites has described her own experiences as a form of culinary colonialism characterized by "the quest for exoticism, the desire for authenticity, and the view that the Other is a resource for my own enrichment."[42] Jennie Germann Molz has made a similar point regarding culinary tourism, which she argues is not motivated by a desire to know or experience another culture but instead is "about performing a sense of adventure, adaptability, and openness to any culture" that grants travelers cultural capital and reinforces their sense of superiority.[43]

These two opposite perspectives on ethnic and immigrant food are useful but problematic for two somewhat similar reasons. First, they privilege the representational at the expense of the material, ignoring the structural realities of everyday experiences. Second, they tend to view race and ethnicity as fixed, whether self-selected or externally imposed, rather than negotiated, contested, and created through repeated interactions. In both perspectives, interactions between producers and consumers are rarely acknowledged as a possible source of identity or ethnoracial formation. In the first, immigrant and ethnic producers seek to preserve their identities by using food according to their own rules and circumstances— often in the privacy of their homes and kitchens. In the second perspective, white consumers seek to increase their cultural capital while ignoring or erasing the ethnic other. The focus is primarily on what ethnic food symbolizes or represents, less on what it actually does to places and bodies. By focusing on foodscapes, I seek to move beyond this representational and dichotomous framework and attend to the material, fluid, contingent, situated, and embodied nature of ethnicity. Framing ethnic food practices within foodscapes draws attention to the interplay between oppression and agency, between the structural forces of racism that shape food experiences and the everyday practices that challenge, transform, or reproduce these structures, and between the macrogeographies and microgeographies of ethnic food. Doing so shifts the focus away from identity as a rigid category to difference as a lived experience.

Indeed, foodscapes are continually formed through practices such as cooking dinner at home, eating a quick breakfast, shopping for ingredients at the corner shop, renovating a restaurant, upgrading a menu, opening a new food store, sharing meals with family and friends, chopping vegetables, discussing recipes, watching food shows on television, serving picky customers, washing dirty dishes, growing produce, counting calories, exchanging cash, and posting online reviews. These activities are structured by capitalism, racism, and neoliberalism, which underlie food apartheid and create vastly different setting for these activities, making it much more difficult for some to obtain food, earn a living in the food economy, and partake in the pleasures that food could provide. At the same time, these mundane food practices require social interactions between consumers and producers that shape conviviality—the act of living together. In that sense the ethnic foodscape is relational and dynamic; it involves a negotiation and exchange between numerous actors that shape its built environment, demographic characteristics, sense of place, and geographic imaginaries. Studying ethnic foodscapes opens up possibilities for examining the agentic capacities of ethnic food and the people engaged in its production, distribution, and consumption, while acknowledging structural constraints that exist but are not immovable or infinite.

The interplay between oppression and agency is at the core of the few studies that frame ethnic food in terms of foodscape. For instance, Sylvia Ferrero has argued that transnational consumerism has led to ethnic foods being "disembedded" from their original contexts and reembedded in new contexts where the identities of individuals and the peculiarities of food can be renegotiated and adapted.[44] She shows how Mexican restaurant owners in Los Angeles actively construct and sell new self-identities in their interactions with consumers, including an increasingly cosmopolitan clientele:

> Mexican food, as a foodscape, can become a forceful device to twist power relations in the ethnic food industry and corporate business. It shows how Mexican business people claim authority and cultural capital over the authenticity of Mexican food items and culinary practices. It also reveals how Mexican food becomes a means to break into the American economic and cultural system, a way of legitimizing social networks and establishing new ethnic roots.[45]

Ferrero does not ignore the social structures that constraint the agency of many immigrants and ethnic minorities, including poverty, racism, and discrimination. She points out that whether ethnic food is used as a symbol and expression of cultural identity or as an object of consumption and means of distinction, it "entails forms of power that disclose themselves according to circumstances and contexts."[46] This argument is in line with critical and geographic understandings of foodscape that seek to locate food within political, cultural, economic, and social contexts. For Ferrero, "ethnic food . . . must be regarded as a foodscape, . . . revealing how movements of ethnic food are intertwined with the different movements of ethnic groups, financial capital, and business, hence with different configurations of power." In the ethnic enclave, ethnic food may become "an economic source, a social collector, and a tool of cohesion."[47]

As Jean Duruz has noted, however, it is important not to overstate the capacities to enact agency of those who are both culturally and economically marginalized.[48] She is concerned that Ferrero's argument about the empowerment potential of ethnic food "might encourage us to romance the ghetto, as well as the marketplace, and to romance the plucky figure of the 'ethnic other' who challenges the forces of dominant society—whether through refusing to play the cyclamen game, or grinding corn 'authentically' for tourists, or reserving 'real' Mexican food for Mexicans (and sympathetic Anglo-Americans)."[49] Yet Duruz concedes that Ferrero avoids that trap by focusing on "intersecting regimes and sites of power" in which complicated "alliances, conflicts, and accommodations" emerge crossing gender, class, and ethnic lines. In short, the strength of her approach lies in anchoring the concept of foodscape in place.

Questions regarding the agency of "ethnic others" are echoed in Krishnendu Ray's work on ethnic restaurateurs, in which he portrays them as creative "taste-makers" meeting and challenging consumers' expectations and reworking their place in the city, "playing with power in spite of relative subordination."[50] Inspired by Ghassan Hage, Ray argues that ethnicity cannot be separated from the ethnic restaurateurs who have been left out of most studies, which typically focus on immigrant homemakers or white privileged consumers.[51] Providing a much-needed corrective to this bias, Ray shows ethnic restaurateurs as always involved in a process of negotiation with white folks and others through "inhabitation."[52] Although he does not use the term *foodscape*, his emphasis on the sites where "those feeding us might have power over us"[53] suggests attention to place-based interactions. To the binary between resistance and domination, Ray posits the "vast intermediate landscape of making do, of living, of making ends meet, of insinuating one's intentions between the expectations of others, of poaching, of mimicking, of mocking, of explaining to white folks, of dismissing them, of interpreting the rest of the world to them, of plain fabrication of one's self as the ponderous native informant, the gorgeous pleasures of subversion and subterfuge, which may not be available to righteous theorists, but is important to practical others, including migrant restaurateurs peddling food as much as notions of it."[54]

The recent work of Ashanté Reese examines how Black residents of Deanwood, a neighborhood of Washington, DC, navigate and resist unequal food access through self-reliance.[55] She shows that although anti-Blackness produces particular foodscapes where food access is limited and Black lives are threatened, these foodscapes can also become sites for healing, reclaiming, caring, remembering, seeing and being differently, and flourishing. Through gardening, entrepreneurship, food activism, and everyday food practices, residents "refuse to accept the boundedness of neighborhood spaces, . . . to give up hopes that another way is possible, . . . to allow the absence of supermarkets to completely define their foodways."[56] What she calls geographies of self-reliance emphasize "how spatial, historical, and racial dynamics intersect and insist that Black folks navigate inequities with creativity that reflects a reliance on self and the community . . . making way out of no way."[57]

Duruz, Ferrero, Hage, Ray, and Reese's research focus on foodscapes as public or semipublic spaces in which bodies engage with difference through food, paying less attention to the private spaces of homes favored by anthropologists. While the distinction between public and private may be a false dichotomy, encounters and negotiations between "ethnic" and "nonethnic" tend to take place in public, especially in the commercialized spaces of restaurants, food stores, festivals, and mass media. Building on this body of work, my research privileges urban neighborhoods: the streets, gardens, and commercial spaces where urban dwellers interact with one another and make space for themselves. I am interested in understanding how foodscapes function as sites of encounters with ethnic difference and how these capacities change over time and space. In contrast to the ethnic foodscape, which foregrounds the food practices of immigrants and subsequent generations in a racialized space, a new multicultural or cosmopolitan foodscape appears to be emerging where ethnic residents are taking secondary stage to consumers as ethnic food is being reinvented, stolen, misappropriated, or alienated as hip and trendy.

COSMOPOLITAN FOODSCAPE

In recent years, acknowledgments of the significance of place-based encounters with difference, including race and ethnicity, has generated much optimism among scholars, who have celebrated the emergence of cosmopolitan spaces as a sign of increased openness to diversity across national borders that may destabilize racism. For Paul Gilroy, the ordinariness of diversity and cross-cultural encounters in postcolonial cities, where the ethnic composition has been altered by increased migration from the Global South, is engendering a form of "cosmopolitan conviviality" characterized by cohabitation and pragmatic interaction between people of different national origins.[58] Conviviality, he argues, "makes a nonsense of closed, fixed, and reified identity" and opens the door for unpredictability and nonbinary ways of seeing and being.[59] Gilroy does not posit "the absence of racism or the triumph of tolerance," but the existence of new settings where different people can learn to live together.[60]

Other scholars have written about "everyday" or "ordinary" cosmopolitanism, challenging its elitism and drawing attention to the role of habitual engagement and interdependence in promoting meaningful cultural exchange.[61] According to Elijah Anderson, even in the most divided cities, there exist urban islands of civility or "cosmopolitan canopies" where a "kaleidoscope of urban dwellers" can be observed peacefully interacting with each other and demonstrating practices of civility.[62] These are spaces such as markets, parks, sidewalks, and other mostly public places where "racially, ethnically, and socially diverse peoples spend casual time together, coming to know one another."[63] Through various examples from Philadelphia, Anderson illustrates how cosmopolitan canopies allow people "to take leave of their particularism and show a certain civility and even openness towards strangers."[64] Food often features prominently in these hopeful cosmopolitan spaces, providing a means through which people connect with each other, breaking down stereotypes, and encouraging respect for differences. As many have argued, food has the potential to bring strangers together and highlight commonality across difference. Middle Eastern food is a classic example, with hummus and falafels being conceptualized as bridges to peace between Arabs and Jews.[65] In the United States some have interpreted the popularity of Mexican and Chinese cuisine as a sign of assimilation and changing attitudes toward these ethnic groups.

Recognizing that food and place are intimately connected, scholars of cosmopolitanism have begun paying attention to foodscapes too, noting that certain environments are more conducive to social interaction and cultural exchange. In particular, public markets, food festivals, community gardens, and farmers' markets appear to function as cosmopolitan canopies—places where people of different backgrounds come together with a common interest in "good food" and an openness to diversity. Without being fully fleshed out, the term *cosmopolitan foodscape* has emerged recently to describe urban settings where food diversity is part of the built environment, the everyday eating practices of residents, and the postcolonial imaginaries associated with those particular landscapes.

There is no doubt that food habits in the United States have changed dramatically over the past several decades, particularly in large cities. In an era of unprecedented global interconnectedness and mass migration, consumers are exposed to an increasingly broad and constantly changing array of commodities, including foods associated with many different countries and regions. Commercial streets, with their variety of ethnic eateries, have become key sites and symbols of cosmopolitanism. The main street of my neighborhood in San Diego is home to French, Italian, and Mexican restaurants as well as Afghan, Ethiopian, Greek, Indian, Indonesian, Japanese, Korean, Lebanese, Salvadoran, Thai, and Vietnamese. On any given night, I can choose to "have a little taste of something more exotic."[66] Such cosmopolitanism has become a defining characteristic of urban lifestyles in postcolonial and neoliberal contexts.

As debates within the literature suggest, however, it is unclear whether exposure to diversity in general, and ethnic food in particular, actually produces new ways of understanding, seeing, and being. While everyday interactions between strangers may forge new hybrid cultures and even nudge established patterns of power, it is important not to romanticize intercultural contact. In fact, evidence suggests that it often hardens prejudicial attitudes, breeds defensiveness, and results in the import of white habitus.[67] To identify meaningful encounters that actually produce the sort of cosmopolitan citizenship celebrated by many, Gill Valentine focuses on the geography of encounter because exposure to difference takes place in specific contexts—such as streets, public transportation, schools, restaurants, parks, and so forth—that are shared by many people; it "never takes place in a space free from history, material conditions, and power."[68] Her perspective takes us away from the shallowness of postracial celebrations and colorblind cosmopolitanisms and brings us back to the significance of place, space, and landscape and the power relations that are enacted and enforced through them.

The transformative potential of multicultural encounters unfolding in the cosmopolitan foodscape depends on to the nature of these encounters—the dynamics of who is included, participates, initiates, and controls the interaction as well as what is exchanged, learned, and taken away through it. Looking at these questions from a geographic perspective requires that we attend to how the cosmopolitan foodscape is socially produced and enacted in the everyday. One of the most important criticisms leveled at cosmopolitanism is its elitism. As a disposition of openness and tolerance, cosmopolitanism is typically associated with urban elites who have the economic, social, and cultural capital needed to navigate hyperdiversity and use it to strengthen their position in a rapidly changing world. For Valentine, "tolerance is a dangerous concept . . . it conceals an implicit set of power relations. It is a courtesy that a dominant or privileged group has the power to extend to, or withhold from, others."[69]

Indeed, much of the work on cosmopolitanism, including a growing body of work within food studies, has been focused on cultural elites, attempting to make sense of the attitudes and dispositions of white and affluent people toward "others." This focus presumes that the cosmopolitan foodscape is controlled—used and defined—by cosmopolitan elites, including white, affluent, and internationally mobile foodies. Although the cosmopolitan character of urban neighborhoods may be attributed to the ethnic entrepreneurs who have settled in these places and opened grocery stores, bakeries, restaurants, and cafés, it is the presence and visibility of cultural elites that make them cosmopolitan. It seems paradoxical that a concept so closely linked to ethnic diversity would be primarily defined by white elites, as if only white people must contend with diversity.

Another concern with cosmopolitanism is the notion that all ethnicities are commensurable, even if temporarily at different positions on the path to assimilation. Like in colorblind multiculturalism, cosmopolitanism often reduces race and ethnicity to culture without acknowledging the dynamic social, economic, and political processes that underlie the production of racial and ethnic difference. Recognizing the diversity and hybridity of subjective positions and cultural identities should not imply that ethnicity is purely symbolic, discursive, and ideological. Doing so erases the very different material circumstances, experiences, and opportunities of racialized groups living in a hyperdiverse environment. Indeed, immigrants and ethnic others are often made invisible in cosmopolitan foodscapes—an important difference with ethnic foodscapes. Caroline Knowles explains that the presence of "ethnic-migrants" in cities can be registered in multiple ways though bodies, food, clothing, performances, commerce, artifacts, and buildings.[70] Their presence, however, is only partially registered, providing a distorted and racialized understanding of diversity. What or who is seen in the cosmopolitan landscape matters in terms of how it is valued, both symbolically and materially. Invisibility has serious political, economic, and social consequences. John Berger and Jean Mohr hint at questions of invisibility when they write: "Landscapes can be deceptive. Sometimes a landscape seems to be less a setting for the life of its inhabitants than a curtain behind which struggles, achievements, and accidents take place. For those who are behind the curtain, landmarks are no longer only geographic but also biographical and personal."[71]

Likewise, liberal depictions of cosmopolitan foodscapes ignore or make invisible the socioeconomic obstacles that underlie the everyday life of those producing cosmopolitan food. Although some ethnic restaurants, as depicted in magazines, may be seen as fashionable gathering places for the cosmopolitan creative class, what happens in the kitchen is out of sight. The back of restaurants where food is prepared almost exclusively by underpaid immigrant workers from the Global South gives a very different perspective on ethnicity as a lived experience. Don Mitchell makes a similar point in his work on the agricultural landscape of California when he points out the invisibility of Mexican labor.[72]

Although the struggles of immigrants working in the food economy, procuring food, and running food businesses are significant parts of the ethnic foodscapes, they are absent from cosmopolitan foodscapes, except perhaps in reified forms. This distinction is a key theme that I examine as I explore the "cosmopolitanization" and gentrification of San Diego's ethnic neighborhoods through the symbolic lens and material entrance point of food. Cosmopolitan foodscapes differ from ethnic foodscapes in several ways: politically, economically, socially, and culturally. Although both are characterized by ethnic diversity and might look similar on the surface, they embody different political histories, economic trajectories, social dynamics, and cultural sensitivities. My goal is to challenge the racial biases of cosmopolitanism by making more visible the struggles and daily experiences of immigrants and ethnoracial people.

2

Food Apartheid

The Production of Tasteless Landscapes

THE FOOD DESERT metaphor has come to dominate much of
the public discourse on food and health. In just a few years, it has
become a ubiquitous phrase to describe foodscapes characterized by
limited access to healthy and affordable food. The term has quickly made
its way into popular discourse, including news media, public forums, and
everyday conversations, influencing the way we think about particular
places. Yet it tells a very partial story.

In San Diego, local news reporters have been keen to label specific
neighborhoods, including many of the urban core areas on which this
book focuses, as food deserts where "it may be easier to find a bag of
potato chips than a head of broccoli" and "you don't have Whole Foods
or even an Albertson's; you have corner stores that sell Twix bars and
Mountain Dew."[1] Residents themselves use the term to draw attention to
food deficits where they live, as when someone in Southeastern San Diego
described his neighborhood as "a total food desert—the shittiest examples
of fast-food chains and poor grocery stores devoid of quality produce."[2]
Not surprisingly, elected officials are increasingly throwing this term
around as a policy priority they promise to address. For example, in a
recent interview, then county supervisor candidate Nathan Fletcher

claimed that "it is time to address the disproportionately concentrated low-income communities and communities of color who face higher rates of food insecurity, reside in food deserts and have very little access to fresh fruits and vegetables."[3]

The popularity and wide use of the term is no doubt linked to its capacity to capture a complex phenomenon through simple indicators. For instance, the most common measure of urban food desert is defined by the United States Department of Agriculture (USDA) based on whether residents of low-income neighborhoods have a supermarket, supercenter, or large grocery store within a half-mile distance of their home.[4] Although technically difficult to compute, the concept is fairly easy to grasp, especially when displayed on colorful maps that highlight deficient areas. Yet the idea of food desert is problematic for a number of reasons. In addition to methodological issues related to measuring access to food, there are deeper questions associated with what access means and how it matters in the everyday lives of urban residents. There is also a concern that the common narrative of food desert masks the historical dynamics that caused such places to become devoid of large food retailers.[5] Although it has not been widely used, food activists and critical scholars have recently suggested that *food apartheid* might be a better term to describe the segregation processes underlying urban foodscapes.[6] The term draws attention to the political and economic factors that produce food deprivation and have been mostly ignored in the mainstream literature. This lacuna may encourage policy interventions that fail to address the inequities that have contributed to the marginalization of urban neighborhoods and the desertification of their foodscape.

This chapter critiques the concept of food desert by documenting how such areas have been socially produced in San Diego through racially biased policy, planning, and business decisions. Narratives of food desert hide these dynamics and serve as a discursive device that stigmatizes low-income communities of color, devalues their food practices, and fails to acknowledge existing resources in order to justify outside interventions and pave the way for food-based gentrification. Instead, I adopt the concept of food apartheid, drawing attention to the material and discursive dynamics that divide the city and produce "tasteless landscapes," where food is either absent or insipid, cheap, and lacking in "taste" according to naturalized white notions of good food. In particular, I demonstrate that the historical devaluation of ethnic foodscapes, illustrated in their labeling as food deserts, has severe consequences for the well-being of residents who struggle with food apartheid.

FOOD DESERT: PRIVILEGING ACCESS AND STIGMATIZING PLACE

In San Diego County more than seven hundred thousand people lived in food deserts in 2010—that is about 23 percent of the population. The majority of census tracts identified by the USDA as food deserts (i.e., low-income areas lacking access to a supermarket) are located in highly urbanized and densely populated areas near and around downtown San Diego, including the three primary study neighborhoods of Barrio Logan, City Heights, and Southeastern San Diego. Additional food desert tracts are clustered in more distant locations such as the South Bay (National City, Chula Vista, and San Ysidro), North County (Oceanside, Escondido, Vista, and San Marcos), and the eastern cities of El Cajon and Santee.

How do residents of these areas differ from those of neighborhoods where food is allegedly more available? According to 2010 data from the US Census, residents of food deserts in San Diego have a much lower median household income than those in the rest of the county: $47,206 compared with $85,046. The average poverty rate in food deserts was significantly higher than in areas with access to supermarkets: 23 percent compared with 12 percent. Nonwhite people were also much more likely to live in food deserts. About a third of San Diego County's Latinx and Black residents lived in areas identified as food deserts, while fewer than a fifth of whites and Asians did. San Diego's food deserts are also concentrated in neighborhoods with large proportions of immigrants, with 28 percent of foreign-born residents and more than a third on non-naturalized immigrants living in a food desert.

The notion of a food desert emphasizes the absence of (healthy) food in such areas as Barrio Logan, City Heights, and Southeastern San Diego that can easily be identified on a map. In recent years it has come to be viewed as one of the primary explanations for poor health, particularly as it relates to obesity. A huge body of work has been built on the premise that health disparities could be explained by neighborhood differences in "access" to food, defined as physical proximity. Much of this research has focused on developing increasingly sophisticated measurements and mapping techniques of what boils down to a neighborhood food "deficit" that ultimately came to be known as "food desert." As the concept grew in popularity, so did its criticism. In addition to questioning it on methodological grounds, some have challenged the assumption that supermarkets are the only suppliers of healthy and affordable food.[7] They argue that small grocery stores, including much disparaged ethnic markets and convenience stores, play an important role in low-income neighborhoods.[8]

Similarly, several studies have documented the contribution of so-called alternative food provisioning sources like community gardens, farmers' markets, and mobile retailers. Along those lines, a number of researchers have questioned the bias underlying the assumption that people shop for food at the most proximate supermarket. Some suggest that we need to consider the negative influence of fast-food restaurants and have proposed new metrics that take into account both healthy and unhealthy food availability.[9] Many of these criticisms point to the need to gain a better understanding of food provisioning practices and urban mobility, particularly among those most likely to suffer from food insecurity—the poor, people of color, immigrants, and single mothers. They also hint at the diversity of circumstances and experiences within neighborhoods identified as food deserts. Simply walking along the commercial streets of places like Barrio Logan, City Heights, and Southeastern San Diego reveals very different foodscapes, suggesting that a quantitative indicator may not be appropriate to describe local food environments.

Despite these suggestions to rethink access to food, the notion of food deserts endures and researchers continue to use it to test a host of hypotheses regarding factors explaining the lack of access to healthy food and its effects on residents' health behaviors and outcomes. Numerous studies have documented lower densities of supermarkets and higher densities of fast food outlets in nonwhite and low-income neighborhoods, compared with white and affluent areas.[10] The patterns uncovered in San Diego are similar to those observed in cities across the United States and lend support to this vast literature suggesting that low-income communities of color are more likely to suffer from limited access to healthy food, as estimated by distance to supermarkets.

A less conclusive area of research has focused on the impact of food deserts on food-related health behaviors (e.g., fruit and vegetable consumption) and outcomes (e.g., obesity, chronic disease). Despite being poorly substantiated, the idea that living in a food desert encourages bad health behavior has gained significant political currency and has come to be taken for granted, informing a wide range of policy interventions to transform urban neighborhoods. For instance, the term *food desert* has appeared in several recent pieces of legislation, including the 2008 Food, Conservation, and Energy Act; the 2010 Healthy Food Financing Initiative; and more recently the Food Desert Act and the Healthy Food Access for All Americans Act, which are currently being reviewed and would support the establishment of grocery stores in underserved communities through state grants and tax credits. National policy research and advocacy organizations have made attracting supermarkets in deficient areas one of their policy priorities.

What is missing from food desert snapshots and the extensive literature on food environments, however, is a critical perspective that goes beyond documenting patterns and associations between race, income, and food access at a given point in time. These are symptoms of food apartheid that tell us little about how such a system is enacted. The very notion of apartheid, which is often associated with South Africa's brutal state-sanctioned system of racial segregation and discrimination against non-whites, underscore the socially constructed, politically imposed, and spatially enforced nature of ethnoracial food disparities. There is an urgent need for researchers to deal with the social and political dimensions of uneven food access and explore why these disparities in the food environment exist, how they came about, and the specific ways in which they shape everyday food experiences and race itself. Instead of asking whether limited access to healthy and affordable food in City Heights, Barrio Logan, or Southeastern San Diego has a negative impact on diet and health, it may be more useful to ask how social processes leading to the absence of food retailers in the neighborhood overlap with those threatening the ability of residents to lead healthy lives. Focusing on processes rather than conditions, opens up new lines of inquiry into the complex relationships between food, place, and well-being. It also requires that we pay more attention to place and landscapes as dynamic and look beyond the boundaries of food deserts to explore relationships across historical and geographic scales.

Without attending to the processes that produce uneven food access and underlie food apartheid, current narratives of food deserts rest on snapshots of food environments at a given point in time. This reinforces place-based stereotypes that Black, Brown, and poor people have dysfunctional relationships to food. While such discourse is no longer centered solely on individual responsibility, it continues to locate problems such as poor diets and illnesses within bounded neighborhoods. It blames individuals through place narratives that simplistically equate low-income neighborhoods and communities of color with problematic food practices, assuming that those places reflect residents' taste—or lack thereof. In these accounts, food deserts become stigmatized places where classed and raced bodies engage in destructive and irrational behavior. Little attention is given to the historical reasons why food deserts have emerged in particular neighborhoods, including the process of "retail redlining" by which supermarkets and chain stores stayed away or withdrew from neighborhoods of color.[11] Next, I offer a corrective to the reductionist concept of food desert by documenting the production of food apartheid in San Diego, revealing stories of abandonment, erasure, and displacement alongside resourcefulness, care, and survival.

BEFORE FOOD DESERTS: LOCAL FOOD OASES

To paint a more nuanced picture of food environments, one needs to go beyond an inventory of food desert and investigate the process by which such areas were created and the ways in which local residents have responded to these changes. I focus on three neighborhoods that illustrate food apartheid and its spatial dynamics. Labeled as food deserts, City Heights, Southeastern San Diego, and Barrio Logan seem to embody the presumed connection between nonwhite people and unhealthy foodscapes. Yet, prior to the massive divestment caused by rapid suburbanization in the 1950s and 1960s, each of the three neighborhoods was characterized by a distinct population and culture in which immigrants and subsequent generations played varying roles. Their retail landscape at the time reflected that ethnoracial diversity and included numerous food shops and restaurants meeting the needs of local residents, including people of Asian, Latin American, African, and European origins born in and out of the United States. In today's popular imagination, that rich history has been erased and replaced by a common narrative of poverty, crime, immigration, and urban decline in which food deserts flourish. Snapshots capturing today's limited access to healthy food say nothing about the unique histories of each neighborhoods and how they became known as food deserts. Similarly, they mask the social, political, and economic forces that shaped their fate and that of many inner-ring suburbs across the nation.

The current downtown area began to develop in the late 1870s as political functions and business activities relocated there from Old Town in anticipation of the extension of the transcontinental railroad. Speculators purchased land surrounding the so-called New Town of San Diego and created subdivisions to be developed. Logan Heights—the area in which Barrio Logan is located—was one of the first to gain population in the late 1800s, owing to its proximity to downtown, the rise in waterfront activities, and the arrival of the railroad. Prominent San Diego families hired architects to build mansions and settled in the hills looking over the bay. Most did not stay for long though. As industrial activity on the bay front expanded, multifamily dwellings and workers' housing came to dominate the landscape, making it less desirable to the affluent class. Japanese immigrants attracted by jobs in the fishing industry and Mexican immigrants escaping the revolutionary war in Mexico were among those settling in the new apartment buildings and bungalow courts. At the same time, the 1915 Panama-California exhibition prompted significant infrastructure development throughout the city, including the San Diego Streetcar, and encouraged rapid growth of other inner-ring suburbs around Balboa Park, where the international exhibition took place. Most affluent families relocated to Mission Hills, Kensington, and East San Diego. By the mid-1920s, Logan Heights had become San Diego's "residential section of the negroes, Mexicans, and Orientals."[12]

At that time a significant commercial district had developed along Logan and National Avenue, and the neighborhood was home to several grocery stores, bakeries, restaurants, and taverns, with many, such as the Tamale Factory, serving the needs of increasingly Mexican clientele. Archival evidence from City Directories reveals the existence of an active business district, including at least thirty-eight grocery stores, ten meat shops, and seven restaurants in 1926, for a population of fewer than two thousand.[13] The height of commercial activity appeared to have occurred in the early 1930s, with as many as fifty-five grocery stores, sixteen meat shops, and seventeen restaurants in operation in 1931. The vast majority of these food businesses were independently operated, with the owner's residence often listed in the directory at an adjacent address—above, behind, or next to the business. Although in 1925 most owners had Anglo-Saxon names (e.g., Wellington and Sorenson Grocery, Enright Bakery, Powell Meats, and Lewis Fruits), by 1931 a growing number of businesses were associated with Spanish names such as Ruiz Bakery, Santos Tamales, Duarte Restaurant, Guadalupe, and Amador Market (figure 2.1). The number of businesses began to decline during and after World War II, but the share of Spanish names among owners would continue to increase until 1957—the last year for which City Directories are available. Other businesses in the neighborhood reflected its increasingly industrial character, with a large number of junk yards, mechanics, and canning factories.

City Heights emerged in the early 1900s as East San Diego—an independent and conservative city with strict regulations against "liquor sales, gambling, dance halls, carrying guns, and driving faster than fifteen miles an hour" and the "golden rule" of treating others as one would like to be treated enshrined in its incorporation documents.[14] It was annexed by San Diego in 1923 and became the site of significant residential and commercial development. City Heights remained a predominantly white middle-class community well into the 1970s. The 1921 City Directory lists a wide range of food suppliers along its two main commercial corridors—University and El Cajon Avenues. There were at least thirty-eight grocery stores, ten meat or poultry shops, two bakeries, and seven restaurants, serving an area of approximately four thousand residents. Most of these businesses were owned by people with Northern European names. Commercial areas included a large number of gas stations, real estate offices, automobile dealers, furniture stores, dentists, and so forth, reflecting the demands of a growing middle-class population.

Southeastern San Diego was a semirural area for much of the late 1800s and early 1900s. Extending to the east of Logan Heights, it was advertised by developers as ideal for small suburban farms. Although the

FIGURE 2.1 View of M. C. Amador Jr. Market on National Boulevard and Beardsley Street in Barrio Logan, 1949. Photograph by Norman Baynard. Courtesy of San Diego History Center.

east side of the neighborhood, including Encanto, remained fairly rural for decades, the west side saw an increase in residential development and population density beginning in the 1920s. As the City of San Diego attracted large numbers of newcomers in the 1920s and 1930s, housing covenants became increasingly restrictive, particularly for the growing African American population migrating from the US South. Southeastern San Diego was one of the few areas where Black people were allowed to purchase and rent properties. Elsewhere, in Mission Hills, City Heights, and North Park, property titles included such clauses as "No part of said property, or any buildings thereon, shall be used or occupied by any person not belonging to the Caucasian race, either as owner, lessee, licensee, tenant, or in any other capacity than that of servant or employee."[15]

Thus the neighborhood became the heart of the Black community in San Diego. At first, Black folks concentrated in the few blocks east of 30th

Street between Ocean View Boulevard and National Avenue in what is known as Memorial Park and is still considered part of Logan Heights.[16] Over time, the Black community moved further east and settled in Mountain View, Mount Hope, Lincoln Park, and eventually Valencia Park—all distinct pockets of so-called Southeastern. By 1940 all of the city's Black churches were located within that neighborhood, and more than forty-five hundred Black people called it home.[17] The establishment of the 32nd Street Naval Station in the early 1920s and its subsequent expansion during World War II brought new residents to the neighborhood, including more Blacks, Latinos, and Filipino immigrants, who worked on the base and navy shipyard. Landowners and developers in Southeastern were eager to capitalize on this influx of middle-class families and would soon build some of the first suburban tract homes in places like Emerald Hills. The focus being mostly on residential expansion, the development of schools, amenities, and commercial facilities in the neighborhood lagged behind, with the majority concentrated in a few spots along Market Street and Imperial Avenue. According to City Directories, throughout the 1920s, 1930s, and 1940s, there were only five grocery stores in the area. No bakeries, butcher shops, or restaurants were listed.[18] By 1957 there were fifteen grocery stores, one bakery, two meat shops, and eight restaurants— significantly fewer businesses than in the other two neighborhoods of interest to this research. By then, the population had reached over sixty-five thousand, but the neighborhood lacked cohesion. It was a series of villages housing different population groups whose primary source of income was downtown or the waterfront.

Although their foodscapes differ, the three neighborhoods shared a reliance on small independent stores and restaurants that were typically owned and operated by local residents. Each community contained "oases" of food retailing filled with vibrant grocery and specialty food stores—a far cry from today's food deserts. In the densely populated neighborhoods of Barrio Logan and City Heights, grocery stores could be found on almost every block of commercial arteries, blending comfortably with residential buildings. They were often surrounded by butcher shops, bakeries, and restaurants. In the 1920s, however, supermarkets such as Waite's and Heller's emerged in San Diego. They were described by their owners as revolutionary to the extent that they allowed consumers to gather their own individually priced and packaged goods in the store, thereby saving labor costs and lowering prices. In the early years the "self-service" stores were relatively small and owned by a variety of local chains, but over time consolidation occurred and companies like Safeway—itself the result of various mergers and acquisitions—came to dominate the market.

By the 1930s, City Heights had the highest concentration of supermarkets, including three Humpty Dumptys, three Piggly Wigglys, three Safeways, and three MacMarrs along University Avenue. Barrio Logan also had two MacMarrs and two Safeway supermarkets on Logan and National Avenues. Southeastern San Diego only had one Safeway at the western edge and one MacMarr at the eastern edge. Based on historical photographs and parcel maps, the size of these stores was relatively small and comparable to many other grocery stores, temporarily maintaining diversity and balance in the retail environment.

In the following decades, Barrio Logan, City Heights, and Southeastern San Diego became absorbed into the urbanized core of San Diego, surrounded by a mass of ever-expanding suburbs where white and affluent residents relocated, along with such businesses as supermarkets, superstores, and shopping malls. Despite the unique character of the three study neighborhoods, they are often described in similar terms, which typically include references to poverty, crime, unemployment, race, and immigration. Food and health scholars have not escaped this tendency to confound low-income urban areas into an undistinguishable deficient and dysfunctional space. According to common indicators of food access, all three neighborhoods are equally problematic for the health and well-being of their residents: they are all food deserts.

Yet their unique and rich histories of food retailing suggest that the contemporary lack of supermarkets is the result of neighborhood transformation that led to the gradual disappearance of food stores and restaurants. As in many older inner-ring suburbs across the United States, post–World War II urban politics and race played a key role in transforming the foodscape of Barrio Logan, City Heights, and Southeastern San Diego. Federal housing and transportation policy, redevelopment efforts, local real estate practices, and municipal changes in zoning regulations, often motivated by race, brought about the devaluation and racialization of urban core communities, dramatically changing the regional foodscape.

Between 1930 and 1950, San Diego's population more than doubled. As the military and defense industry grew, particularly during World War II, thousands of workers and soldiers moved to the area in search of opportunities. This led to a housing crisis that was partly solved through the expansion of suburbs. Rapid suburbanization, however, led to a massive exodus of the middle-class from Barrio Logan, City Heights, and Southeastern San Diego, forever changing the urban geography of the city. As the more affluent residents left, so did businesses. The ensuing decline of central city neighborhoods is a well-documented phenomenon that transformed cities across the United States. Many urban scholars view neighborhood decline as a natural process; as housing stock ages, demographic composition changes and those who can afford it move elsewhere. Theories of "neighborhood succession," "life cycle," and "filtering" first developed by the Chicago School of urban ecology in the 1920s suggest that such changes are the inevitable and natural results of cultural assimilation, economic integration, and changing consumer preferences.[19] However, scholars increasingly recognize that this post–World War II urban transformation was far from inevitable, but instead was fostered by policy decisions that have encouraged the suburban exodus of white middle-class households and contributed to the devaluation of neighborhoods like Barrio Logan, City Heights, and Southeastern San Diego.[20]

Housing and transportation policies played a key role in the production of San Diego's highly segregated landscape, what Larry Ford and Ernst Griffin call "the ghettoization of paradise" that took place between the late 1940s and 1960s.[21] A survey of urban scholars regarding key influences shaping the past and future of American cities ranks the 1956 Interstate Highway Act and the mortgage policies of the Federal Housing Administration (FHA) as the two most important.[22] Beginning in the mid-1950s, federal expenditure funded the development of forty-one thousand miles of interstate highways that allowed people to travel more easily outside of the central city and turned rural lands into accessible suburban housing tracts, shopping malls, and office parks. In 1934, to fight the Great Depression, the FHA created a program to insure mortgages with low down payments, fixed interest rates, and long repayment periods, effectively making mortgage loans and home ownership more affordable to the middle-class.

Other housing initiatives, such as the mortgage interest tax deduction and the postwar Veterans Administration (VA) loan program, also promoted home ownership. Because the FHA *Underwriting Manual* was very specific about what types of projects the government would support, almost all FHA loans were made for new suburban constructions. Loans in central city locations were considered risky and were almost never guaranteed by the FHA and the VA. This is because, according to the FHA, "interior locations . . . have a tendency to exhibit a gradual decline in quality."[23] Together, these federal policies made suburban housing more desirable and affordable to middle-class families, raising the homeownership rate from about 40 percent after the war to 65 percent by the end of the 1960s. In other words, the federal government subsidized suburbanization at the expense of central city neighborhoods that saw their population and property values decrease rapidly. It encouraged the flow of capital outside of older urban neighborhoods and contributed to their decline.

The racist nature of these policies cannot be understated. Indeed, the suburban exodus is often described as "white flight" because those leaving the city were overwhelmingly white, while those left behind were primarily people of color. This too is not accidental. The guidelines provided in the FHA *Underwriting Manual* specifically discriminated against lending in communities with an "infiltration of a lower grade population" or "disharmonious racial groups."[24] These guidelines were translated into so-called redlining maps produced under federal supervision by the Home Owners' Loan Corporation for more than two hundred US cities. There is extensive literature suggesting that these maps, and the associated lending practices that lasted well into the 1960s, even after racist language was removed from the FHA manual, had a devastating effect on urban Black communities, denying them the opportunity to own homes and build equity, triggering a vicious cycle of divestment.[25]

Most of Southeastern San Diego and a large section of City Heights were identified as "red" or "hazardous," with many remaining parts of my study area described as "definitely declining." To this day, nonwhite residents remain concentrated in these neighborhoods, reflecting the lasting impact of racial policies (map 2.1). The rankings were determined by real estate agents, bankers, and assessors who lent their "expertise" to this initiative and provided neighborhood descriptions that highlighted housing characteristics as well as racial and class composition. For example, one part of Southeastern was described as having "a great many Mexicans with a definite trend of infiltration of this element." Another was "occupied by mixed races, colored, Mexican, lower salaried white race, laborers, etc." Although City Heights had "no concentration of any foreign element, . . . Mexicans [were] scattered throughout the area" making it less desirable. This sort of "infiltration" or "concentration of colored fraternity," which was explicitly linked to a "lack of restrictions and ordinances" was interpreted as a warning sign of neighborhood decline. Observers also commented on the quality of housing, noting that "homes show only slight degree of pride of ownership and are on the average negligently maintained."[26]

In other words, investment in these neighborhoods was discouraged—if not prohibited—by these rankings. In contrast, developers received numerous incentives to mass-produce suburban homes that would meet FHA preferences for single-family homes, separation of land use, low density, controlled and homogenous design, and "prohibition of the occupancy of properties except by the race for which they are intended."[27] In the subsequent decades the suburban expansion of San Diego would become one of the most extensive in the United States, hollowing out urban neighborhoods and spreading all the way to Orange and Riverside counties. Barrio Logan did not receive any residential rating but instead was classified as industrial and not worthy of housing investment. About a decade before the Home Owners Loan Corporation map was produced, the City of San Diego put together its first comprehensive city plan, known as the 1926 Nolen Plan, in which it established Logan Heights as the industrial zone of the city due to its proximity to the bay, downtown, and transportation facilities.[28] This was one of the first steps that would lead to the decline of Logan Heights, as the influx of industries and junkyards prompted the outflow of wealthier residents and businesses.

Local ordinances and zoning regulations in San Diego, along with real estate practices, have historically served to reinforce racial segregation. Affluent communities protected their property values by ensuring that only white people could move in. As noted, racist housing covenants that prohibited property owners from selling or renting to nonwhites were

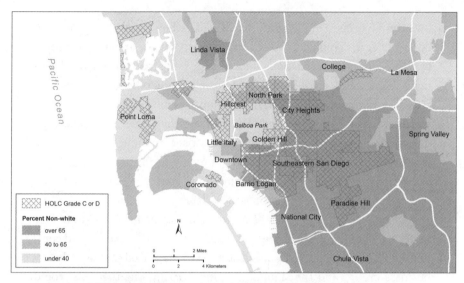

MAP 2.1 The legacy of *redlining*: Relationship between low Home Owner Loan Corporation (HOLC) ratings (i.e., C "definitely declining" or D "hazardous") in 1934 and percentage of nonwhite residents by US Census tract in 2012–17. Most of City Heights and Southeastern San Diego and parts of Barrio Logan were identified as "hazardous," which in the original HOLC map was highlighted in red (hence the term *redlining*). Map created by author with data from the US Census, "American Community Survey Five-Year Estimates, 2013–2017. Summary File Data" (2019); and shape files from Nelson and Ayers, "Mapping Inequality."

common and supported by local ordinances. Real estate agents steered people into neighborhoods based on their race. Regardless of income, Black people were shown properties in Southeastern San Diego, while white people were directed to various neighborhoods such as Mission Hills, Coronado, or La Jolla depending on their budget. Some agents engaged in the lucrative practice of blockbusting, spreading fear among white residents that their neighborhood was being "invaded" by people of color and prompting massive exodus, which would turn into lucrative sales to nonwhite households and rapid neighborhood change. There is some evidence that this practice contributed to the demographic transformation of City Heights in the late 1960s. Police harassment of Black people in "good neighborhoods"—a phenomenon that still occurs today—was another way to encourage isolation.[29]

Even after the Civil Rights Act of 1964, when racial discrimination became illegal, zoning ordinances continued to exclude low-income people by imposing costly restrictions under the guise of maintaining neighborhood character. Meanwhile, low-income neighborhoods were increasingly zoned for commercial, industrial, and multiple-unit residential land uses, which are typically considered less desirable than open space and low-density single-unit residential categories. Challenging these designations is an extremely difficult and politicized process, as illustrated by the tensions surrounding Barrio Logan's Community Plan. The plan has not been updated in forty years and proposed updates were recently repealed by San Diego voters in the midst of controversy. Residents' desire to reduce industrial land use in their neighborhood as outlined in the revised community plan they approved was silenced by an organized campaign led by business groups and the shipbuilding industry arguing that this would cause a major loss of jobs for the region.[30]

Freeway construction solidified the isolation of minorities and further divided San Diego along color lines. The 1936 FHA *Underwriting Manual* had suggested that in addition to deed restrictions and zoning ordinances, "natural or artificially established barriers will prove effective in protecting a neighborhood and the locations within it from adverse influences, . . . [including] prevention of the infiltration of business and industrial uses, lower-class occupancy, and inharmonious racial groups."[31] All three study neighborhoods suffered tremendous losses through the construction of highways that served overwhelmingly white suburban residents who owned cars and commuted between suburbs and central city areas.

Barrio Logan, as a name and a place, emerged from the 1963 construction of Interstate 5, which separated the "barrio" from other parts of Logan Heights. Five years later, the construction of the San Diego–Coronado Bay bridge began, leading to further displacement. Over the following decade, the population of Barrio Logan dropped from twenty thousand to five thousand. These changes were met by resistance from local residents, influenced by the growing Chicano movement that was encouraging Latinos to create change in their own communities. In 1971 residents, artists, and activists occupied the area at the foot of the bridge and claimed the space with murals depicting Mexican American lives and struggles. This social movement galvanized the community and continues to influence the identity and politics of Barrio Logan today. However, as in other urban neighbor-hoods, civil unrest in Barrio Logan also contributed to its stigmatization as a highly segregated, dangerous, and dysfunctional place. Southeastern San Diego and City Heights were equally devastated by highway construc-tion. In the late 1950s, State Route 94 created a barrier that artificially kept Black people from moving north. The subsequent extensions of Interstate 15 and 805 created additional rifts through both areas, leading to the demo-lition of hundreds of houses and the displacement of thousands. Schools and stores that had once been within easy walking distance were now inaccessible.

By the 1970s, Barrio Logan, City Heights, and Southeastern had been thoroughly transformed: many businesses, except for a few liquor and convenience stores, had been closed; single-family homes had been turned into apartments for low-income tenants; poverty, unemployment, and crime were seemingly on the rise; and the proportion of white residents had dropped significantly. It is around that time that redevelopment initiatives were adopted, following the 1974 Housing and Community Development Act. Several areas, including downtown and all three study neighborhoods, were considered "blighted" and designated as Enterprise Zones by federal, state, and/or local governments. These designations provided unique tax credits and incentives designed to stimulate business investment and spur job creation. Yet redevelopment efforts focused almost entirely on downtown as illustrated by the creation in 1975 of the Centre City Development Corporation (CCDC)—a public-private partnership with limited public oversight to promote the redevelopment of downtown.[32]

Meanwhile, in this new entrepreneurial model of urbanism, sur-rounding neighborhoods were ignored and left on their own to address mounting problems, including battling outdated and discriminatory zon-ing designation. As downtown reinvented itself by appealing to tourists and conventioneers, many of its neighboring communities, particularly those most severely damaged by early policy rounds, continued to struggle with a lack of job opportunities and basic amenities such as parks, schools, and food stores. They also had to contend with stereotypes asso-ciated with immigrant-filled, crime-ridden, and culturally dysfunctional neighborhoods—perceptions that extended beyond place to vilify resi-dents themselves.

Today's limited access to healthy food is the result of historical structural processes that have led to the creation of food apartheid—"a *human-created* system of segregation that relegates certain groups to food opulence and prevents others from accessing life-giving nourishment."[33] Contemporary food deserts coincide closely with areas that had been redlined in the late 1930s, unprotected by racial covenants, targeted for subsidized housing, isolated by freeways, labeled as blighted, and ignored by investors and policymakers. The history of retail business in San Diego and other cities reflects decades of discriminatory urban politics that have produced food apartheid and imposed grave long-term material consequences on the everyday life and health of the urban poor. In the first half of the twentieth century, food had been primarily supplied by small independent retailers who lived near their business. Densely populated urban areas like City Heights and Barrio Logan had grocery stores on almost every block of their main commercial streets. In the 1920s and 1930s small self-service markets began to appear, prompting smaller stores to adapt. A similar trend occurred with fast food restaurants that progressively replaced family-run businesses. However, it is not until the 1940s, when suburbanization and white flight accelerated, that the local retail sector began to struggle. The same forces that caused the devaluation and racialization of urban spaces also led to the demise of small businesses.

Transportation policy made the development of large supermarkets and shopping centers profitable by facilitating automobile access. Those with a car could afford to shop outside of their neighborhood, in stores with wide aisles, well-lit displays, refrigerated sections, and large selections of competitively priced items. According to Elizabeth Eisenhauer, during the 1950s the average size of supermarkets in the United States doubled to more than twenty thousand square feet.[34] The availability and lower cost of land in the suburbs prompted the construction of increasingly larger stores, including superstores with sprawling parking lots to accommodate car-dependent shoppers. Small markets could not compete with these new stores and, by the end of the 1960s family-owned and operated supermarkets had virtually disappeared. The closure of small urban markets and the growth of suburban supermarkets created a new geography of retail.

At the turn of the century, the three study neighborhoods increasingly resembled food deserts. Barrio Logan had no supermarket and City Heights and Southeastern only had one, leaving thousands of residents dependent on remaining small stores, including gas stations, ethnic markets, and convenience stores, to get food. As I discuss in chapter 3, these stores are often struggling to stay in business and cannot offer the same selection, prices, service, and shopping experience as larger chain stores. Yet there are millions of dollars of purchasing power in City Heights, Barrio Logan, and Southeastern San Diego that grocery chains have chosen to ignore and mostly flow out of these communities. The USDA "thrifty food plan" for a family of four is $645 per month—an amount estimating the food budget of people in the bottom income quartile based on current dietary recommendation data and food prices.[35] This low estimate suggests that residents of the three study areas have a combined annual food demand of at least $1.4 billion, which at this time is mostly diverted to stores in other neighborhoods. This persistent retail gap cannot be explained by neoclassical economic theory that would have predicted that supply would meet demand. Against this economic logic, structural forces, including racism, continue to stir capital away from low-income neighborhoods.

The mortgage policies that negatively impacted home ownership and housing investment in low-income communities of color had a similar impact on small businesses. Redlining and FHA guidelines influenced private lending practices and constrained small retailers who found it difficult to obtain loans to set up shop or support an existing business in low-income communities. As the food retail sector became increasingly concentrated, supermarket chains relied on this type of information to determine the location of new stores and progressively withdrew from central city areas—a phenomenon that Eisenhauer has called "supermarket redlining."[36]

To this day, lending to small businesses in marginalized areas remains limited. A recent study indicates that in San Diego County, businesses in low-income areas are far less likely to receive a small bank loan of less than $100,000, compared with those in high-income areas.[37] Based on lending activity data that financial institutions are required to share through the Community Reinvestment Act, only 24 percent of the former received such loans between 2012 and 2016, compared with 80 percent of the latter. A similar pattern is observed when comparing businesses in high

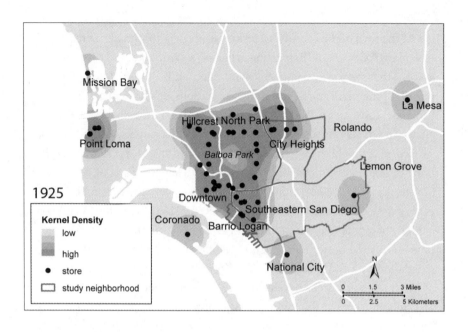

1925

Kernel Density
low
high
• store
▭ study neighborhood

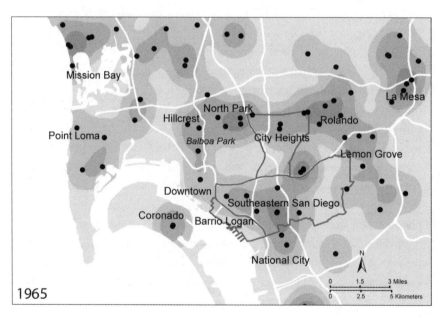

1965

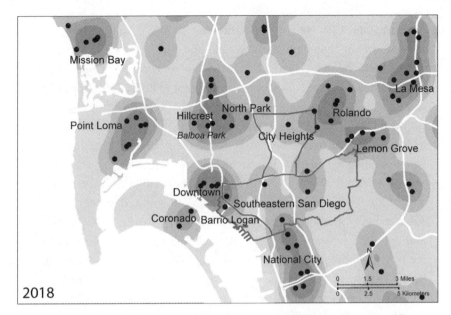

2018

MAP 2.2 Supermarket location and density in central San Diego, 1925, 1965, and 2018. Supermarkets were first concentrated in densely populated urban neighborhoods in the 1920s. They began spreading to suburban areas after World War II, which resulted in a more even distribution within the region in the 1960s. Eventually they withdrew from low-income neighborhoods of color, creating a more uneven pattern by 2018, with higher supermarket density in white and affluent neighborhoods and relatively lower density in Barrio Logan, City Heights, and Southeastern San Diego. Maps created by author with data compiled from historical business directories at the City Clerk Archives (2017) and ESRI's Community Analyst (2018).

minority areas against those in other places. Many small food businesses operating in low-income communities of color do not have any formal access to credit and rely entirely on cash for any business-related purchases. This restricts their ability to cope with temporary financial needs or expand their activities, having lasting consequences on local foodscapes and reproducing urban geographies of inequality.

Map 2.2 illustrates the evolving geography of food retail in San Diego, by tracking the density of supermarkets over time. In 1925 most supermarkets were located in the downtown area and around Balboa Park, with density declining in concentric patterns with distance from the urban core.

Barrio Logan, City Heights, and the western tip of Southeastern were located within that high-density zone and had several supermarkets. Throughout the 1930s, 1940s, and 1950s, however, density began to shift away from downtown, splitting north and east of Balboa Park toward the first suburbs. As City Heights gained supermarkets, downtown and Barrio Logan lost a few. By the 1960s, downtown and Barrio Logan had hollowed out and the overall density began shifting outward, with many new stores opening in suburban locations. This trend continued in the 1980s—an era in which all three neighborhoods lost a significant number of supermarkets. Today, density is higher in affluent and primarily white suburban neighborhoods. Following decades of gentrification, downtown and uptown have gained several new supermarkets. However, the three study neighborhoods have a lower supermarket density than most places in the region. In light of the demographic characteristics of residents, which underlie lower mobility, the lower density of supermarkets has a negative impact of food security, as I discuss in chapter 4.

To some, the absence of supermarkets is a reflection of the limited purchasing power of residents, whose median income was significantly lower than elsewhere in the city and county. To others, this is related to the dysfunctional food habits of immigrants, people of color, and the poor, who presumably have limited cooking skills and nutritional knowledge and favor "junk" food. The common narrative is that supermarkets left because there was not enough demand for healthy food in these neighborhoods. Therefore residents are to blame—not supermarket chains, developers, or policymakers. Research, including my own interviews, indicates that store managers often have negative perceptions of the customer base in low-income areas. They describe shoppers as "uneducated," "unwilling to try different foods," and "lazy."

In contrast, those in more affluent neighborhoods, consisting primarily of white consumers with more disposable income, are described as having healthy habits and being motivated by a desire to improve their diets. This bias is reflected in the media, where low-income neighborhoods are often described as dangerous wastelands saturated with fast food restaurants and liquor stores serving a population that does not know any better. Even among those working with nonprofit and grassroots organizations to improve community food security, the perception that people of color do not care about health endures.[38] In short, food apartheid in City Heights, Barrio Logan, and Southeastern San Diego is as much discursive as it is material. The devaluation of physical property and the disappearance of food stores have been accompanied by a racialization and stigmatization of the resulting foodscape that shifts the responsibility for this decline onto residents.

MAKING SPACE FOR GENTRIFICATION

Since about 2008, a number of initiatives have been put in place by various actors, ranging from federal government agencies to grassroots community organizations, in an effort to eliminate what has been called food deserts in San Diego. Because of the emphasis on the absence of supermarkets, interventions tend to focus on what is allegedly missing from the land-scape—grocery stores—rather than on the structural inequities that have led to the systematic devaluation of places and caused food apartheid.

Numerous scholars of gentrification have argued that devaluation is a precondition for gentrification. As Neil Smith noted more than three decades ago, "the steady devaluation of capital creates longer term pos-sibilities for a new phase of valorization" because it leads to a "rent gap" where "the ground rent capitalized under current land uses is substantially lower than the ground rent that could be capitalized if the land use were changed."[39] What is important here is that the process of devaluation is not accidental or driven purely by market forces; rather, it occurs *"precisely because* an effective *barrier* to new investment had previously operated there."[40] In the case of Barrio Logan, City Heights, and Southeastern San Diego, as in other inner-city neighborhoods across the United States, these barriers were the result of racist policy decisions that prevented investment and maintenance of capital in those areas for decades, underly-ing food apartheid.

There is another important aspect of devaluation: the territorial stig-matization and symbolic defamation of urban neighborhoods inhabited by low-income households, immigrants, and people of color. Not only is the negative image associated with certain neighborhoods—or "ghettos"— profoundly inscribed in the geographic imagination of policymakers and outsiders who may have never visited those places, they are also absorbed by residents who then tend to distance themselves from or denigrate their own communities. For Tom Slater, this stigma is politically activated and leads to "corrective political reactions driven by fright, revulsion, and condemnation, which in turn . . . penalize urban marginality."[41] In such a context, prescribed policies focus on restoring order, demolishing shameful elements such as public housing projects, and rebuilding with external capital. In Slater's words, "symbolic defamation can provide the groundwork and ideological justification for a thorough class transformation of urban space, usually involving housing demolition, dispersal of residents, land clearance, and then the construction of housing and services aimed at a more affluent class of resident."[42]

In the case of the retail environment, both physical and symbolic devaluation occur in tandem and reinforce each other. Physical devaluation can be observed in capital outflows linked to the closing of some stores or the lack of maintenance and repairs in remaining ones. Symbolic defamation is produced through overlapping narratives that paint these neighborhoods as dysfunctional. The food desert metaphor is one of such narratives. Viewed as empty, unkempt, and tasteless foodscapes, food deserts are now prime for reinvestment and justify drastic outside intervention. Indeed, in recent years a few supermarket chains have begun to realize the potential economic return of operating in areas where rents are low and purchasing power is higher than traditionally assumed. This realization has been buttressed by public policy programs designed to create incentives for supermarkets to locate in food deserts. Barrio Logan and City Heights each gained a new supermarket in 2016 as the result of community organizing and fiscal incentives.

Meanwhile, residents of Barrio Logan, City Heights, and Southeastern continue to seek alternative ways to address the lack of food options in their neighborhoods. Immigrants have been particularly entrepreneurial and have played an important role in maintaining small food businesses. Still, these efforts are constrained by the larger processes described throughout this chapter. Not only do they face limited resources in the form of capital, but they must also contend with stigmatization through narratives portraying them as "tasteless"—too poor or uneducated to care about good food. Today, older stores—many of which are ethnic businesses—must also face growing competition from newer businesses taking advantage of the so-called rent gap and bringing about change in the foodscape. In the next two chapters, I turn to the food provisioning practices of families and the experiences of ethnic food retailers to gain a better understanding of how living in a changing foodscape impacts the well-being of residents and reproduces existing inequalities.

3

Work in the Urban
Food Economy

Ethnicity, Invisibility, and Precarity

IN JANUARY OF 2020, Con Pane—a gourmet bakery that supplied several of San Diego's high-end restaurants—closed after a federal immigration audit discovered a large number of immigrant workers unauthorized to work. Customers were shocked by the sudden closing and bemoaned the fact that they would miss the raisin hazelnut bread, cinnamon rolls, and cheese sandwiches on oven-toasted rosemary olive oil bread.[1] Some "felt sorry for the owners," but less was said about the plight of the workers who were likely deported.[2] While inspections by the US Immigration and Custom Enforcement agency, known as ICE, are relatively rare occurrences, they shape the food economy by instilling a climate of fear and contributing to the marginalization of workers in an industry where immigrants fill many jobs. It is one of the many policies, ideologies, and practices that racialize and devalue food service work, ensuring a continuous supply of cheap labor to support the cultural economy and sustain gentrifying foodscapes.

The food service industry in San Diego—including restaurants, catering businesses, food stores, and delivery services—is one of the largest and fastest segments of the labor market, employing approximately 140,000 people. The industry is among the worst in terms of earnings, benefits, job security, and working conditions. Not coincidentally, it is one of the industries with the greatest proportion of immigrant and ethnic workers. Indeed, food provides a significant source of employment to the many residents of Barrio Logan, City Heights, and Southeastern San Diego who run or work in restaurants, catering businesses, and food stores both in their own neighborhoods and throughout the region. Ethnic and cosmopolitan foodscapes depend on this labor, which is often poorly paid and hidden from consumers, especially as the foodscape becomes increasingly oriented toward the consumption desires of outsiders.

Immigrants and people of color provide much of the labor needed in the contemporary food regime—from farming the fields to slaughtering meat, packaging food, and cooking in restaurants. Yet this labor is mostly invisible and therefore vulnerable and exploitable. Physically out of sight or symbolically irrelevant, invisible labor is "overlooked, ignored and/or devalued by employers, consumers, workers, and ultimately the legal system itself."[3] It is well documented that in California farm workers are principally immigrants, most from Mexico and many undocumented, who work in harsh conditions to earn very low wages.[4] Almost a quarter of farmworkers live in poverty, the majority do not have health insurance, and perhaps ironically many suffer from food insecurity.[5] Abuse and exploitation in agricultural fields have been the object of numerous studies, films, popular books, and classic literature. They have also motivated one of the most important labor movements by people of color in the twentieth century, including marches and boycotts organized by César Chávez, Dolores Huerta, and Larry Itliong in California. What has received less attention is the exploitation and hardship occurring in other segments of the food system, particularly the retail and restaurant sectors that are much more proximate to consumers than fields and factories.

Much hard and physical labor is performed by workers of color behind the kitchen doors and in the back of the food store. However, the commodification of food hides the labor process from consumers. This is true of the authentic and exotic foods that people crave; the hands that feed us are either invisible or reified into exotic commodities to enhance product desirability. Even workers who are in plain sight remain socially invisible to consumers who push their cart past the shelf stockers and look away from servers and bussers in restaurants. This invisibility is somewhat surprising given that cosmopolitan consumers are often enticed by the multicultural aspects of ethnic food and the possibility of cultural exchanges through food. Food service workers are closer to consumers on the food supply chain than farm workers, often working in the very spaces where consumption occurs and directly contributing to the consumption experience itself through their social interactions with consumers. Yet it appears that foodies may value what Ghassan Hage has called "multiculturalism without migrants," as their interest in "diversity" applies to exotic foods but does not necessarily extend to the immigrants who bring those foods to them.[6] As Alison Alkon and Julie Guthman have suggested, the emphasis we put on consumption choices in contemporary food politics lifts up ethical eaters but remains blind to the workers who struggle throughout the food system.[7]

The invisibility of labor, which facilitates and hides its exploitation, is tied to race/ethnicity and the need for capitalism to both divide labor and segregate space in order to expand. Merging theories of racial capitalism and labor geographies suggests that the production of racially divided landscapes is instrumental to the process of labor exploitation and capital accumulation.[8] Rendering certain ethnoracial groups invisible and restricting their mobility to specific spaces—such as the plantation, the farm labor camp, the factory, the ghetto, the ethnic enclave, the prison, the warehouse, the back of the store, and the restaurant kitchen—ensures a supply of cheap and subservient labor that is essential to the reproduction of capitalism. These not-so-new ideas are inspiring exciting new work on race in geography.[9] However, to date, little attention has been given to ethnic workers, including immigrants, whose position in the labor market is spatially and racially constituted.

The ethnoracial segmentation of the labor market in which workers are assigned to particular spaces and occupations based on their race and ethnicity is a component of food apartheid: it is part of a system that undermines food security among people of color by dismantling their food provisioning mechanisms including devaluing food work and livelihoods. This chapter sheds light on the working realities of those who labor in the food economy, the Black and Brown bodies that remain invisible in the cosmopolitan foodscape and have been equally absent from most research on food. Krishnendu Ray's work on ethnic restaurateurs stands out as a notable exception, but like other research of food service work, it focuses on restaurant workers and leaves out store clerks, produce stackers, street vendors, delivery assistants, and the many others who bring urbanites their food.[10] This chapter relies on a combination of US Census data, qualitative interviews, and secondary sources, to document the diversity of work in the food economy and examine the role of ethnicity in structuring food work and occupational segregation. We begin by unpacking the popular ethnic entrepreneurship narrative.

BEYOND ETHNIC ENTREPRENEURSHIP

When thinking about ethnic food, most people think about ethnic entrepreneurship. They envision small Italian delis, Mexican taco shops, Indian buffets, Korean food trucks, Peruvian rotisseries, Greek cafés, and Chinese dim sum restaurants in neighborhoods where people and businesses with similar ethnic identities coexist. Places like City Heights, Barrio Logan, and Southeastern San Diego are full of small ethnic businesses that match these geographic imaginaries. There is an enduring and romanticized perception that ethnic food economies consist primarily of entrepreneurial immigrants whose economic mobility is driven by hard work, business savviness, social connections, and unique knowledge. Historically, immigrants have been highly entrepreneurial in both serving their own ethnic communities and marketing food to others in their new place of residence.[11] In the United States, in 2013, 53 percent of grocery stores, 43 percent of liquor stores, 38 percent of restaurants, and 35 percent of specialty food stores were owned by immigrants—well above their 16 percent share of the labor force.[12] Although the trope of entrepreneurship dominates research on ethnic and immigrant food economies, in reality the role of ethnicity in the food economy is much more complex.

The privileging of entrepreneurship in the popular imagination and in research on ethnic food economies is both misleading and revealing. Ethnic food entrepreneurship is often interpreted as the result of a cultural affinity toward this type of work, an entrepreneurial spirit embodied in the decision to migrate, and a desire to create a sense of place and express one's identity through food. For example, in the United States the prevalence of Italian, Korean, Cuban, Jewish, Greek, Middle Eastern, and Indian immigrants in restaurant businesses, and their replacement by other groups over time, has been explained by cultural characteristics and the process of assimilation.[13] Ethnic niches are seen as building the cultural and social capital of immigrants and ethnic minorities and providing a form of apprenticeship to workers who eventually branch out into other occupations as they assimilate.[14] Social connections within ethnic enclaves enhance this entrepreneurial disposition and strengthen the ethnic economy, suggesting that residential segregation is an opportunity rather than a curse.

Other scholars, however, are more skeptical of these cultural explanations that, they argue, fail to consider the larger context in which various immigrant groups seek to make a living, including the role of economic conditions, employment alternatives, immigration policies, race relations, and access to capital—what some call the opportunity structure.[15] Specifically, anti-immigrant and xenophobic attitudes, restrictive immigration policy, economic downturns, racial discrimination, limited access to financial capital, heavy regulations, and competition from the corporate sector may create significant barriers of entry in the labor market for immigrants and people of color, forcing them to start their own business as a survival strategy. These structural constraints, which are often premised on racial assumptions regarding skills, work ethics, creditworthiness, and so on, vary across time and space and influence the ability of immigrants and people of color to find remunerative employment. Work arrangements in the ethnic food economy, including the relative role of self-employed, waged, informal, and unpaid labor, need to be examined within the institutional and social contexts of global, neoliberal, and postindustrial urban economies.

Saskia Sassen's work on global cities has had a tremendous impact on the way we understand ethnoracial divisions of labor.[16] She has argued that globalization has led to a restructuring of the global economy that manifests itself most clearly in the new urban occupational structure of large cities that is polarized into two parallel sectors dependent on each other: a high-end stratum consisting of well-paying high-skill jobs involved in controlling the global economy (e.g., finance, design, engineering) and a low-end stratum made up of low-wage producer and consumer service jobs filled primarily by immigrants, women, and people of color. Most ethnic entrepreneurs, especially those involved in the food industry, are found in this lower segment of the labor market, where they struggle to earn a decent income and often work informally. Although the increase in immigration from the Global South beginning in the 1970s has fueled this low-wage and informal economy, for Sassen it is the insatiable demand for low-cost services and cheap labor by the higher segment of the economy that sustains these jobs. In service-oriented and postindustrial urban economies, food and entertainment have become important economic drivers that stimulate consumption and attract the so-called creative class.[17]

Yet these sectors rely on a large low-wage labor force that includes janitors, cooks, waiters, retail clerks, and drivers, many of whom are immigrants and people of color who often work informally or under precarious conditions. Sassen connects this new labor demand with gentrification, pointing out the continuing need "for low-wage jobs required by high-income gentrification in both its residential and commercial settings—the increase in numbers of expensive restaurants, luxury housing, luxury hotels, gourmet shops, boutiques, French hand laundries, and special cleaners that ornament the new urban landscape."[18] Sassen's contribution is to shift our analytical lens away from proximate influences, such as entrepreneurs' individual characteristics, immigrant shared culture, or ethnic enclaves' social networks, onto the global structural factors shaping the growth of a low-income service sector, including the ethnic food economy that caters to the needs of the globally connected urban elite in the postindustrial economy. In her framework, ethnic entrepreneurs, street vendors, and low-wage food workers are all operating in the same segment of urban space produced by globalization.

In *Servant Class City*, David Karjanen has built a convincing case that San Diego's efforts to become a global city have resulted in the creation of a large class of service workers.[19] Revitalization, including downtown development projects such as the Horton Plaza mall in the 1970s, the convention center in the 1980s, the ballpark in the 1990s, and more recently the waterfront, has mostly created jobs in low-wage service occupations. By subsidizing amenities and commercial real estate downtown, the city has sought to promote tourism, attract investors, and draw highly educated and creative workers to the region. This neoliberal approach to urban development, which has been adopted by countless cities around the world, has resulted in a spatially and socially divided local economy.[20] With the bulk of public and private resources directed to downtown, surrounding neighborhoods such as Barrio Logan, City Heights, and Southeastern San Diego have suffered from chronic neglect. Affordable housing has become increasingly scarce, schools are underfunded, and infrastructure is crumbling. Instead of bringing about shared prosperity by creating middle-class jobs, neoliberal policies have produced a large number of low-wage jobs that support capital accumulation at the top by providing a host of necessary producer and consumer services at low cost—just as Sassen predicted. This includes jobs in the food economy that guarantee a variety of attractive dining options for tourists and creatives alike.

While globalization and neoliberalism have changed the supply and demand for low-wage labor, racist ideologies, policies, and practices have ensured that Black and Brown bodies are available to fill these jobs at low cost. Using immigration laws to control workers, ignoring existing labor laws, allowing informal labor arrangements to flourish, and maintaining barriers of entry into better-paying jobs have kept wages low and built the food industry on the back of ethnic workers. Although shaped by structural forces operating at larger scales, these processes unfold locally. Thus this chapter sheds light on labor arrangements in San Diego's food service economy, paying attention to the role of race, ethnicity, and immigration in shaping occupational segregation and making food service jobs "ethnic." My focus is on the urban landscapes where globalization, economic restructuring, neoliberalism, and racism coalesce and interact with the intimate and the mundane. I place ethnic entrepreneurship alongside other labor arrangements within the context of food apartheid and engage with notions of precarity and informality.

ENTREPRENEURSHIP AND ETHNIC LABOR IN SAN DIEGO'S FOOD ECONOMY

According to recent US Census data, San Diego's food service industry amounts to 138,648 jobs, or 8.6 percent of the county's workforce. These food retail and restaurant jobs represent the most public interface of the cosmopolitan foodscape, where cashiers, cooks, servers, hosts, and vendors interact with consumers, even if many people also work behind the scenes stacking shelves, washing dishes, and cooking food.[21] What I call the food service industry, for lack of a better term, excludes farming and manufacturing—not because immigrants and ethnic minorities are less important in these industries but because these jobs are further removed from the everyday social interactions that characterize the changing foodscape I seek to better understand. If those were taken into account, food-related employment would reach more than two hundred thousand jobs. Food services, especially the restaurant industry, is one of the fastest growing sectors of the local economy, doubling its number of jobs since 1990 and growing twice as fast as the overall economy.[22] These jobs include self-employed and hired workers from many different ethnicities laboring in a variety of occupations with widely different skill requirements. To examine this diversity, this section relies heavily on US Census data, especially the Public Use Microdata Sample (PUMS) of the 2013–17 American Community Survey five-year estimates, which provides individual-level data that allow for detailed computations and cross-tabulations.[23]

In San Diego County the majority of self-employed workers in the food service industry are immigrants: 50 percent of restaurateurs and 57 percent of food retailers. This confirms the finding in a previous study that almost 50 percent of so-called "main street" businesses (e.g., stores, repair shops, hair salons, restaurants) are owned by immigrants.[24] Indeed, among those working in the food service industry, immigrants are much more likely than nonimmigrants to be self-employed: about 2.5 times in food retail (11.4 percent versus 4.2 percent) and almost twice in restaurants (2.7 percent versus 1.5 percent). These findings seem to support the notion of restaurants and food retail businesses as quintessential immigrant enterprises—a way to integrate in the economy by capitalizing on authenticity without incurring huge exorbitant starting costs. This perspective, however, is problematic for two reasons. First, many food workers are not self-employed but instead enter into a wage relation with an employer. There are just 4,316 self-employed workers in San Diego's food service industry, compared with 134,332 employees. Thus 97 percent of food service jobs are filled by workers who sell their labor for a wage.

Second, the vast majority of food service workers are not immigrants but people who were born in the United States and belong to a variety of ethnic groups perceived as nonwhite. As described in chapter 1, *ethnic* is a fluid category that is associated with race, immigration, and ancestry. In popular parlance, the term is used more often to describe things like food or restaurants that are different from normalized white things than it is to describe people. In this context, however, *ethnic* or *ethnoracial* refers to all nonwhite workers, including Latinx, Asian, Black, Native American, Pacific Islander, and mixed-race people as defined by the Census. Almost three-quarters of workers in the food service industry are ethnic or nonwhite. No other large industry, except for agriculture, has such a high proportion of ethnic workers. Of the 35,946 food retail jobs in San Diego, 71 percent are filled by nonwhite workers, 32 percent by immigrants, and just 4 percent by self-employed ethnic immigrant entrepreneurs. Similarly, of the 102,702 restaurant jobs, 73 percent are filled by nonwhite workers, 36 percent by immigrants, and just 1 percent by self-employed ethnic immigrant entrepreneurs. Thus the ethnic food economy is much more about wage labor than it is about entrepreneurship. Nevertheless, like immigrants, ethnic food workers are more likely to be self-employed than whites. Although US-born white people are engaged in self-employment in other industries, very few do so in food services, perhaps because these activities are less remunerative and perceived as entry-level occupations reserved for immigrants and minorities—a side effect of the enduring myth of the immigrant ethnic entrepreneur.

Aggregating all ethnic groups, however, is not particularly useful to identify how ethnicity might work to produce different work experiences and create ethnic niches. Here I turn to country of origin or ancestry as an indicator of ethnicity. I include people with ancestry in southern and eastern Europe (e.g., Italians, Greeks, Russians, Hungarians) because historically they have played an important role in the American ethnic foodscape and, although they primarily identify as white today, they were not always viewed as such. Just above half of ethnic workers employed in San Diego's food sector claim a Mexican origin or ancestry (table 3.1). The next largest groups identify the Philippines, Italy, Iraq, Vietnam, Japan, and China as their country of origin or ancestry. Black people born in the United States are included in the analysis and constitute an important "ethnic" group in San Diego's food service sector. People with Polish, Guatemalan, Korean, Indian, Russian, Native American, Puerto Rican,

Iranian, Brazilian, Guamanian, and Thai identity also play a significant role in the food economy, although their numbers are smaller than other groups. The representation of various ethnic groups in the food service industry partly reflects the overall distribution of immigrants in San Diego, which is dominated by Mexicans, followed by Filipinos, Vietnamese, and Chinese as well as a host of much smaller populations, including many refugees from Southeast Asia, eastern Europe, East Africa, and the Middle East, making San Diego a relatively diverse region.

These absolute numbers hide concentration patterns that are revealed by looking at the share of people from a given ethnic group who hold jobs in the food industry. In total, 8 percent of the workforce is employed in food services. Thus, if the proportion of workers from a particular ethnicity is higher than 8 percent, this ethnic group could be considered overrepresented. Interestingly, the largest groups are not necessarily those who are overrepresented. For example, despite their relatively large numbers, a small proportion of Filipinos, Italians, African Americans, and Vietnamese work in the food service industry. In contrast, Bosnians, Burmese, Iraqis, Thais, and Haitians are overrepresented in food jobs, with large shares in these relatively small groups finding work in food services. This overrepresentation suggests the presence of ethnic niches that are shaped by the unique histories and opportunity structures of each groups. It is interesting to note that, although a large proportion of Mexicans are employed in the food sector, their strong presence owes more to their sheer numbers than to processes of ethnic clustering—at least at this point in time.

Self-employment in the food service industry also varies by ethnicity, with some of the largest ethnic groups in San Diego (i.e., Mexican, Filipino, African American, and Vietnamese) less likely to work in their own business than smaller groups like Haitian, Lebanese, and Indian do. Among the midsize groups, Italians and Iraqis are more likely to be self-employed. Indeed, many restaurants in San Diego—not just in Little Italy—are owned by Italian Americans. Similarly, a large number of food stores are operated by Iraqis, who own numerous convenience and grocery stores. These differences in rates of self-employment suggest that labor market opportunities and dynamics vary between ethnic groups. Given the popularity of Mexican food and the large number of Mexican restaurants in San Diego, it is surprising that not more people of Mexican

TABLE 3.1. Indicators of ethnic representation in the food industry, by country of origin or ancestry, ranked

LARGEST ETHNIC GROUPS	Total number employed in food industry	OVERREPRESENTED GROUPS	Percentage employed in food industry (%)	MOST ENTREPRENEURIAL GROUPS	Percentage in food industry who are self-employed (%)	GROUPS WITH LARGEST PROPORTION OF IMMIGRANTS	Percentage in food industry who are immigrant (%)	GROUPS WITH LARGEST PROPORTION OF IMMIGRANT ENTREPRENEURS	Percentage self-employed in food industry who are immigrant (%)
Mexican	52,458	Bosnian	42.6	Haitian	73.1	Burmese	100.0	Guatemalan	100.0
Filipino	7,119	Burmese	35.6	Lebanese	31.8	Bosnian	100.0	Korean	100.0
Italian	4,406	Iraqi	26.6	Indian	31.4	Thai	92.4	Russian	100.0
African American	4,050	Thai	22.0	Iraqi	17.7	Colombian	92.0	Iranian	100.0
Iraqi	3,098	Haitian	20.2	Burmese	17.6	Haitian	86.5	Burmese	100.0
Vietnamese	2,082	Guatemalan	15.3	Iranian	17.5	Iraqi	85.5	Lebanese	100.0
Japanese	1,764	Japanese	12.8	Japanese	11.2	Chinese	83.3	Haitian	100.0
Chinese	1,627	Mexican	12.6	Italian	10.7	Vietnamese	78.8	Iraqi	95.1
Polish	1,206	Brazilian	12.3	Korean	9.6	Guatemalan	76.1	Indian	87.3
Guatemalan	857	Guamanian	11.5	Chinese	4.90	Indian	75.5	Chinese	72.5

Korean	726	Samoan	11.0	Laotian	71.7	Filipino	69.0
Indian	650	Hungarian	9.9	Lebanese	70.8	Mexican	68.2
Russian	603	Lebanese	9.6	Korean	67.8		
Native American	581			Iranian	65.3		
Puerto Rican	520			Filipino	63.0		
Iranian	487			Mexican	55.9		
Brazilian	480			Ukrainian	54.7		
Guamanian	438			Japanese	53.9		
Thai	435						

Source: Computations by author using US Census, "American Community Survey Five-Year Estimates, 2013–2017. Public Use Microdata Sample," US Census Bureau, 2019.

ancestry are self-employed in food services, suggesting the presence of barriers of entry tied to ethnicity, immigration status, and access to resources. For instance, the majority of Iraqis came to San Diego with refugee visas, giving them the opportunity to access social services, work, and eventually become citizens. In contrast, a significant share of immigrants from Mexico came without authorization to work—a restriction that has repercussions for their economic integration and the well-being of subsequent generations.

As I have argued, the ethnic food economy is much larger than the immigrant food economy. Yet for a few groups the majority of those involved in food services are immigrants. This is the case for Burmese, Bosnian, Thai, Colombian, Haitians, Iraqi, Chinese, Vietnamese, Guatemalan, and Indian food workers. For these ethnic groups food services may provide economic opportunities to those who recently arrived in the United States. However, subsequent generations are unlikely to stay in this line of work, branching off into more remunerative industries. In contrast, many US-born Mexicans, Brazilians, Salvadorans, Russians, Polish, Hungarians, and Ukrainians work in food services, suggesting that these occupations are more than a stepping-stone to other jobs. It is worth noting that for a number of ethnicities, self-employment is very much related to immigration. All self-employed workers from Haiti, Lebanon, Burma, Iran, Korea, Russia, and Guatemala are immigrants. The vast majority of entrepreneurs from Iraq, India, China, the Philippines, and Mexico are also immigrants. These groups may reflect the sort of entrepreneurial immigrant enclaves favored in much of the ethnic entrepreneurship research.

Countries listed in all five panels of table 3.1 represent ethnic food economies as traditionally understood given their large numbers, over-representation in the food industry, high rate of self-employment, and significant presence of immigrants. In San Diego the only country/ethnicity meeting this criterion is Iraq. No Latin American or Asian countries were listed in all five panels, although Mexico, Japan, China, the Philippines, Thailand, Korea, and India appeared multiple times. The circumstances of Iraqis in San Diego are worth expanding. Consisting primarily of refugees who arrived in the 1990s after the first US war in Iraq, they faced significant hurdles. At the same time, being recognized by immigration authorities as refugees and thus eligible for assistance and citizenship, belonging to the Chaldean Christian community, and being highly educated gave them some advantages that other groups, including, for example, undocumented immigrants from Central America or low-income Black people, do not have. Today there are about 550 self-employed Iraqis in San Diego who primarily run small grocery and convenience stores, hire friends and family members, and work together with the Neighborhood Market Association, originally called the Chaldean Grocers Association, to expand their activities and protect their interests. As a tight and organized community, they have been more successful than other larger ethnic groups in establishing businesses and creating jobs, reflecting differences in opportunity structures.

PRECARITY AND INFORMALITY

Does working in the food service industry provide immigrants and ethnic minorities with decent income and upward mobility, as the ethnic entrepreneurship literature would have us believe? Answering this question requires data on earning, working conditions, employment security, and long-term trajectories. Some of these are available in the US Census, which I use to generate an overall picture of work in the food economy. However, to better understand the experiences of working in the ethnic food economy, including questions of job security, informality, and relationships between owners, managers, and workers, I turn to interviews I conducted in 2016 and 2017 with twenty-four owners and managers of ethnic stores in City Heights, seventeen restaurant operators in City Heights and Barrio Logan, and eighteen restaurant workers in Little Italy, North Park, City Heights, and Barrio Logan. These interviews help shift our attention back onto the ethnic foodscape and the everyday experiences of work.

According to my analysis of US Census data covering the 2013–17 period, the median individual earnings in food services were $18,500 per year, about half of the median for all industries combined. Median earnings in food sales are significantly higher than in the restaurant industry ($25,000 versus $17,000), although this remains well below the regional median of $36,000. More than 90 percent of workers earned less than $50,000 per year. Only a couple of thousand workers in the top 1 percent earned incomes above $100,000, suggesting that very few become wealthy by working in the food industry. These numbers are slightly worse, but not drastically different, if we look at ethnic workers separately. Translating these figures in hourly wages indicates that food service workers earn a median of $11.76 per hour, close to the $11 minimum wage and significantly lower than the $19.78 median for all other employed workers in San Diego. Estimates of living wages necessary to live in specific metropolitan areas indicate that in San Diego an hourly wage of $37.01 would be required for a full-time worker to support a household of one adult and two children.[25] This living-wage figure assumes full-time employment, yet in the food service industry full-time employment is much less common than in other sectors (55 percent compared with 77 percent).

Poverty is about twice as high among food workers (12 percent) as it is for the entire workforce (6 percent). Given the very high cost of living in San Diego, economic hardship might be more accurately measured by raising the poverty threshold to 200 percent of official cutoffs—an approach commonly used by researchers and government agencies. With this adjustment, poverty among food workers rises to 39 percent, compared with 19 percent for the rest of the workforce. Precarity among food workers is reflected in several other indicators of economic hardship. For instance, according to US Census data, more than one in five workers in food services does not have health insurance coverage, about twice as many as in the total workforce. Poverty is so prevalent that 11.5 percent of food service workers use Food Stamps (CalFresh) to purchase basic food, almost twice the 6.7 percent rate for all workers. Given the high number of immigrants in the food industry and the fact that noncitizen and recent immigrants are not eligible for CalFresh, this figure likely underestimates food insecurity, with many hungry households going without public assistance. That people feeding others for a living are unable to feed themselves is a sad irony, which I revisit in chapter 4.

In San Diego, where the housing market is one of the least affordable in the nation, food workers disproportionately struggle to put a roof over their head. On average their households spend 36 percent of their income on housing, and very few are able to own their home. The rate of homeownership for food workers' households is 37 percent, compared with 52 percent for all working households. The majority of food service laborers live in urban neighborhoods like City Heights, Southeastern San Diego, and Barrio Logan, where rent was historically lower. Indeed, there are several census tracts in these neighborhoods where up to a third of employed adults work in the food service industry. While some run or work in ethnic businesses in these neighborhoods, the majority are employed outside of the community and commute to work, creating additional hardship for those who must contend with an underfunded public transportation system that is not designed to meet the needs of workers with unusual work schedules. Today these neighborhoods are experiencing gentrification as more affluent and primarily white people move in and put pressure on rents. Although this is likely to displace longtime renters who cannot afford higher rents, it might also support local ethnic businesses through increased consumption—a complex phenomenon I explore in depth in chapter 6.

Job security, which is more difficult to measure with Census data, also appears to be less tenable for those working in food services. As noted, a significant share of food workers is employed part-time. The median number of hours worked in the week preceding the Census was thirty-five for food workers and forty for all. People employed in the food service industry are also more likely to work unusual hours, starting work before 6 a.m. and/or ending after 6 p.m. In fact, a recent survey of restaurant workers in San Diego found that many worked unstable schedules, with irregular hours and frequent last-minute changes—often in violation of labor laws.[26] Although these practices afford employers some flexibility, they create challenges for employees, especially for parents of young children, who struggle finding affordable childcare, and those who do not have a car and rely on public transportation.

Although most of the food workers I interviewed were hesitant to talk about income, they confirmed what the Census makes clear: they struggle financially and live on a month-to-month, if not week-by-week, basis. Many mentioned their desire to work more hours and get better job security. They often described having to combine jobs to pay their bills, especially in the restaurant industry. Low wages and poor working conditions in the food service industry are linked to economic informality—the fact that many employers are willing and able to avoid existing labor laws, leaving workers unprotected. This is especially true when work is performed out of consumers' sight in the back of stores and restaurants. Indeed, research on the informal economy suggests that the food industry is one where informal or casual labor arrangements are widespread. *Informal labor* is defined as labor that is unprotected in a context where regulations and safety nets have been put in place to ensure safety and minimize abuse.[27] This typically occurs because employers fail to observe existing rules, state agencies do not enforce them properly, and workers are poorly organized or represented. Informal work is also prevalent among the self-employed who may work without proper permits or fail to report all of their activities.

I have been studying the informal economy in Southern California for more than twenty years, beginning with my doctoral dissertation, and to date there remains no definite count of its size, mostly because it is extremely difficult to measure and must be estimated indirectly.[28] In a study I conducted with colleagues at the Los Angeles Economic Roundtable, we estimated that on a typical day in 2004 there were 679,000 informal workers in Los Angeles County—about 15 percent of the workforce.[29] We showed connections between informal work and immigration status and found this relationship to be particularly strong in restaurants where the number of undocumented immigrants was larger than in any industry. We estimated that 18 percent of restaurant workers were immigrants who did not have the authorization to work in the United States, making them especially vulnerable to labor abuse. A report about San Diego County estimated that more than one hundred thousand undocumented immigrants were employed in the region, with food and recreational services and retail among the top five industries.[30] Zooming in on City Heights, they estimated that hundreds of undocumented immigrants worked in food services. This estimate is not surprising at all considering the presence of small and informal ethnic food businesses in the neighborhood, including many street vendors selling fruits, tamales, hot dogs, *tostilocos*, *paletas*, and various other foods. Indeed, immigration status turns out to be a very good indicator of employers' willingness to avoid existing regulations in low-wage industries like food services, construction, manufacturing, and agriculture.

In the only published study of the informal economy in San Diego, James Bliesner and Mirle Rabinowitz Bussell have shown that in City Heights food was one of the most common items that surveyed residents obtained in the informal economy, primarily through street vendors.[31] They found that 87 percent of respondents purchased produce from the informal economy and 65 percent bought food from street vendors. The informal economy provides an important community resource and contributes to food security in immigrant neighborhoods where formal sources of food are lacking (discussed further in chapter 4). However, for workers who make and sell food informally, the risks are high and the payoffs limited. Jill Esbenshade's report on the restaurant industry in San Diego confirms the informality of labor arrangements in the food economy by providing staggering evidence of various types of labor abuse and lack of protection in the restaurant industry.[32] For instance, wage theft was extremely common, with more than three-quarters of the 337 surveyed restaurant employees having lost earnings or tips stolen in the previous year. A vast majority also reported that their employers ignored labor laws pertaining to break requirements, overtime pay, scheduling, and other matters. Very few workers reported receiving benefits such as paid sick days and health insurance. Violations were more common among women, Latinx, and back-of-the-house workers. A multicity survey of the low-wage labor market also found overwhelming evidence of violations of labor laws, including minimum wage and overtime laws, in industries such as restaurants and grocery stores, especially among Latinx workers and women.[33]

The restaurant and store employees I interviewed confirm this high level of informality and poor working conditions. Many complained about scheduling uncertainty, lack of breaks during long shifts, and the limited benefits they received. This was especially true in small stores where one or two employees were expected to fulfill many tasks such as receiving deliveries, stocking shelves, cutting meat, making sandwiches, and working the cash register. For instance, Berta, a Latina worker in a small convenience store in City Heights, told me: "I am here all day. I don't really get a break. Sometimes, if it's busy and the owner is not here, I work all day without a break. I don't eat lunch. I can't even stop to use the restroom. If someone would steal something when I am not looking, I'd be responsible. I'd have to pay for it. So, it's hard." Restaurant workers—mostly cooks and waiters—also told me about harsh and abusive working conditions. Rodrigo, a young Mexican American man who cooks for a restaurant in Little Italy, claims that "substance abuse is so common in the restaurant industry. Most of the guys in the kitchen are on some sort of drugs. That's the only way you get through the night. Working in restaurant kitchens is so stressful and physically demanding, you know. I don't think people understand, it's really rough. They want to work in restaurants, but they have no idea. . . . It's not just where I work, it's everywhere. I worked in many restaurants and everywhere is the same." When I asked him how women fared in this environment, he answered that the kitchen was not a place for women, echoing a common perception about professional cooking that may explain the relative low number of female chefs and restaurant managers.

The majority of the people I interviewed, especially those who worked in large restaurants catering to tourists in the downtown area, were clearly dissatisfied with their job. However, they indicated that finding work in other sectors would be difficult, suggesting that they had limited employment opportunities. José, a Salvadoran immigrant who works as a dishwasher in a Mexican restaurant downtown, told me:

> I have been working here for seven years and I never got a raise. . . . Waiters do not share their tips with us, so I basically make $9 an hour when they make $20 or more. Some are college students, white kids. . . . It's not a fair system. Of course, I am thankful to have a job! But it's not right. . . . Sometimes I am tired of this job and I look for other jobs, but it's really tough. I never find anything better. I could work in another restaurant, but it will be just the same. At least here they know me.

José's experience, like that of other workers I interviewed, suggests that many food service jobs are dead-end jobs that do not offer upward economic mobility either within the organization—for example, form a dishwasher to a waiter position—or outside of the organization into other industries with better paying jobs.

OCCUPATIONAL SEGREGATION: RACE AND SPACE

Why are there so many immigrants and people of color seemingly stuck in food service? How do workers end up working in this industry? Answering these questions require that we focus on occupational segregation not as an outcome but as a process in which certain jobs are simultaneously assigned to specific ethnoracial groups and devalued. Documenting the association between ethnicity and poor labor outcomes is not enough. We must interrogate how ethnicity is used to produce these differentiated outcomes. The notion of racial capitalism suggests that race, and by extension ethnicity, play an essential organizing role in the economy by institutionalizing the sort of inequality required by capitalism. One of the ways that race shapes the economy is through occupational segregation.

Within the food service industry itself, there are clear divisions along ethnic lines between jobs in terms of prestige, labor relations, earnings, and working conditions. The differentiation between formal/visible/living-wage and informal/invisible/poverty-wage jobs correlates strongly with race and ethnicity. Jobs where people of color and immigrants are overrepresented pay the lowest wages, are less likely to provide health benefits, and tend to be part-time. These are mostly invisible jobs like washing dishes, peeling vegetables, baking birthday cakes, wrapping sandwiches, unloading trucks, and sorting through produce boxes—jobs performed behind kitchen doors and in grocery stores' storage rooms, hidden from the public and thus more prone to labor law violations and exploitation.[34] In contrast, jobs requiring direct interaction with customers or suppliers—including managers, cashiers, bartenders, and waiters—tend to be less informal and pay slightly higher wages. These are also the very jobs where white workers are more likely to be found. Gender also shapes occupational segregation. Women, who represent 45 percent of food service workers, are concentrated in specific occupations such as waitresses and hosts—an unsurprising finding given the very gendered nature of this type of work, which consist of serving consumers.[35] In contrast, they are severely underrepresented as chefs, bussers, and dishwashers, which are perceived as physically demanding and masculine positions.

Restaurant labor can be seen as performative, with an important distinction between "frontstage" and "backstage." Frontstage workers such as waiters, hosts, and bartenders interact directly with consumers, performing emotional labor of serving and pleasing clients. Such body work requires attention to language, facial expression, dress, skills, and manners and tends to privilege bodies seen as clean and docile. These are often white workers or ethnic workers that embody reverence, tradition, and authenticity. For instance, in San Diego several restaurants hire Indigenous Mexican women who, dressed in traditional attire, make tortillas by hand on a large wood-fired comal placed prominently in front of the restaurant. In contrast, backstage performance emphasizes physicality, associated with strong, sweaty, and dirty bodies.[36] These embodied performances translate into a rigid division of labor within the food service sector that is related to race, ethnicity, and gender and affects earnings and working conditions. For instance, in San Diego this disparity is illustrated by the income gap between bartenders who are mostly white males and earn almost $14 an hour—a figure that probably does not include tips—and dishwashers, many of whom are undocumented immigrants of color, who earn $9.50 an hour, below the local minimum wage. Indeed, within the food service industry the earnings of white, male, and US-born workers are above the median, while those of women, immigrant, and ethnic workers are below. Among the latter, Black and Latinx workers are at the bottom of the pay scale.

These findings align with Restaurant Opportunities Center (ROC) United's claim that in the United States and in California "restaurant workers are effectively segregated by race and gender by a partition between livable-wage server and bartender positions and poverty-wage busser, runner, and kitchen positions."[37] Their research, including qualitative data from interviews of restaurant employers, employees, and customers, reveals the prevalence of racism in California's restaurant industry and the existence of strong racial biases that keep people of color in low-wage positions like busser, dishwasher, runner, or prep cook. For instance, restaurant owners and managers often hold explicit and implicit biases, relying on racist stereotypes and unexamined race-related assumptions when making hiring and promotion decisions. Biases also influence customers who judge the quality of restaurants—and the price they are willing to pay for food and service—by the race and appearance of chefs, bartenders, and waiters (explored further in chapter 6). Even workers show internalized bias when they sort themselves into specific positions based on their own race and gender. For example, Latinx workers in the ROC United survey rarely applied for front-of-the-house positions because they did not view themselves as qualified. Similarly, few women consider kitchen jobs in high-end restaurants because these environments are typically dominated by men and perceived as unfriendly to women.

I have observed similar processes taking place in San Diego's retail sector, where employers revealed strong racial biases in assigning people to jobs. For instance, most produce handlers in supermarkets and grocery stores are Latinx. So are workers who put together prepared meals such as sandwiches and salads. When asked about this, a white store owner explained that "Mexicans have a background in farming and know their produce. . . . I could not have them work at the cash register; they do not have the necessary computer skills. Appearances are also important, you know, the way people dress and interact with consumers." Yet racism is more than bigoted or biased attitudes by a few individuals. It is a set of policies, ideologies, and practices that lead to the persistence of inequality between ethnoracial groups. As geographers point out, racialization and racism are spatialized processes that have territorial dimensions. Combined with residential segregation, the spatial organization of local labor markets play a role in sustaining occupational segregation. Some describe this as spatial mismatch between good jobs and affordable housing.[38] Others draw attention to the raced and gendered social networks that connect workers from particular communities to employment opportunities and deepen the ties between ethnicity and work.[39]

As noted, the majority of food service workers live in low-income urban neighborhoods east and south of downtown San Diego. These include City Heights, Barrio Logan, and Southeastern San Diego, where there is an active ethnic food economy and where the proximity to downtown means that many restaurant jobs are relatively accessible. Thus there are important spatial and social connections between where people live and where they work. Access to job is both geographically and socially constrained. Employers often seek people of specific ethnicities to fill certain jobs. This is especially true of people with Mexican ancestry who they perceive as having unique skills and being willing to work for low wages. To find such workers, employers often turn to specific neighborhoods. A white grocery store owner told me:

> I went to Chula Vista [a city south of San Diego with a large Mexican immigrant population] to find my tortilla guy. . . . I wanted to have fresh tortillas in the store. Nobody else does this here. So, I found this Mexican guy who was working in a tortillería and I stole him. I paid him a few extra cents and he came to work for me. It's been a great success. If I need more bakers, I just go down to Chula Vista. Same thing with the taco shop out front. . . . It's not hard to find workers. You just have to look in the right places. There are plenty of people looking for work. You just have to be smart and pick the right guy. . . . Sometimes I have problems with people who come in late or call in sick, but I don't keep them. I tell them: "There are plenty of guys out there willing to take your job."

These sorts of associations between place, race, and labor are also reproduced by the social networks that immigrants and co-ethnics (i.e., people who share the same ethnicity) build in their communities. In my earlier research with Latina immigrants in Los Angeles, I found that social networks were central to the concentration of women in specific segments of the informal economy where wages tend to be lower, working conditions harsher, and abuse of labor regulations rampant. These networks often operate along ethnic lines, with Salvadoran, Guatemalan, and Mexican women employed in different niches. Indeed, several studies have shown that ethnic social networks may be exploitative or constraining, including in the restaurant industry.[40] This phenomenon needs to be understood in a context where there are important race-related barriers to employment and social connections are one of the primary ways to gain access to jobs. Under these circumstances, those able to obtain a job in the food service sector through friends and family often feel indebted to them as well as their employer or supervisor. This can create an imbalanced relationship and makes room for exploitation. In short, race and ethnicity are critical to understanding why people work in food service jobs and why these jobs fail to pay decent wages, offer benefits, and provide safety and dignity.

ETHNIC ENTREPRENEURSHIP: A WAY UP?

Could working in one's own business prevent this sort of exploitation and allow immigrants and people of color to flourish in their own communities? The popular narrative of the American dream would have us believe that hard work, and perhaps a little bit of luck, typically lifts ethnic entrepreneurs into the ranks of the middle class. Although hard work is indeed a defining characteristic of most ethnic enterprises, unfortunately it does not automatically translate into economic success. The data I presented earlier in this chapter indicate that ethnic entrepreneurship in the food industry is not as common as could be surmised from the large number of stories and studies on this topic. In San Diego, according to US Census data, there were 3,531 ethnic food entrepreneurs in 2017, of whom 2,312 were immigrants. These are very small numbers in comparison to the thousands of hired workers reported above. Yet they represent the vast majority of the 4,316 food entrepreneurs in the county.

How do these workers fare economically? Analysis of Census data reveals that self-employed workers in the food industry earn higher wages than those working for someone else, with median hourly earnings of $18.15 compared to $11.76. This earning gap between self-employed and hired workers holds true for ethnic ($19.61 versus $11.37) and immigrant food workers ($19.60 versus $11.22). These figures seem to indicate that those engaged in self-employment reap important economic benefits. The data also show that these benefits require independent business operators to work long hours and invest significantly more time in their work than salaried workers. For instance, the mean number of hours worked by self-employed people is 41.3, compared with 32.6 for other workers, with a quarter of workers putting in more than 50 hours per week and the top 10 percent working more than sixty hours—a very rare occurrence for hired labor. A small but significant number of ethnic food entrepreneurs (111, or 2.5 percent) also reported working without pay. This number is likely an undercount given that many people, including family members, who participate in a business for free might not consider themselves employed and therefore would not be counted in the workforce.

The restaurant industry is one of the most volatile, with about 7.5 percent of businesses failing in the first year and almost 20 percent closed by year five.[41] These national figures are even higher for independent ethnic restaurants, with more than half having discontinued their activities or changed ownership after seven years.[42] It is therefore not surprising that, while some ethnic entrepreneurs succeed financially, many struggle. Indeed, variations in earnings among the self-employed are very large, ranging from $0 to $275 per hour. Almost 25 percent earned less than the $11 hourly minimum wage. In addition, economic success may not be as dramatic as in other enterprises. For example, at the very top of the earning distribution, the annual income of the ninety-ninth percentile was $308,000 for ethnic and $217,000 for immigrant food entrepreneurs, well below the $493,000 earned by the top percentile of Anglo US-born entrepreneurs outside the food economy.

The interviews that I conducted with food store and restaurant operators in 2016 and 2017 also show that self-employment comes with a series of financial and personal costs unique to this type of economic activity. Many ethnic businesses struggle to be profitable, leading to a high rate of turnover and widespread self-exploitation. Indeed, numerous owners, mostly foreign-born men, told me they were working seventy to eighty hours per week, often with help from a spouse, child, or sibling. Many work every day of the week and do not count their hours. Amina, an East African woman who was working without pay in a City Heights food store, explained: "I help in my husband's store almost every day, when he needs me, sometimes in the morning when he has deliveries, sometimes in the afternoon when the store gets a little more busy. . . . My children, they come after school. They get a snack and do homework in the back. Sometimes they help too. They carry boxes and put things on the shelves. They do not like being here so much . . . well it's OK, but they want to go home. Sometimes I can take them home early, but sometimes I can't leave the store."

Unpaid work is common and likely underreported in the Census. Wives and children "help out" and siblings and extended family members "pitch in" without expectation of being paid. This is most common in immigrant-owned businesses, where family members work in exchange for support and assistance. For example, Ramsin, an Iraqi shop owner who came to San Diego as a refugee in the 1990s after the first Gulf War explained: "I just brought my brother from Germany here. He has been helping me in the shop. He is staying with me right now until he finds his own place. So, it's been a great help to have him around." When asked if his brother was an employee, Ramsin responded: "No, he is not an employee. He does not get paid directly. But he stays at my house and I help him for now. . . . He likes to come to the shop and support the family. That's how Iraqis do business; it's all family!" For Katherine Hill, who observed a similar pattern in Chinese restaurants, "ethnic networks are unwritten rules of obligation, gift, giving, and repayment."[43]

The majority of entrepreneurs I interviewed do not pay themselves a set income either, but instead bring home whatever is left after expenses are covered. In very small enterprises personal and business finances are often mixed without clear accounting; owners take money from the cash register to buy dinner or put gas in their car and rely on their own savings to maintain cash flow. Indeed, finance has been a challenge in most ethnic food businesses. Many owners reported never having borrowed money from a bank or received any type of financial or technical assistance for their business. Instead, they use their own savings and rely on contributions from family members to start or expand their professional activities. Occasionally, they use a credit card to finance unexpected expenses—an expensive alternative given the very high interest rates charged by credit card companies.

The family's economic and social integration is so deeply intertwined with the success of the business and its role in the community that the lines between those three spaces—family, business, and community—are often blurred. Owners justify their hard work and sacrifices with potential future economic gains as well as the positive role that their store plays in the neighborhood. For instance, Raoul, the Mexican owner of a small grocery store, told me how much he appreciates when "[his customers] say thank you for being here, thank you for having good produce. And I love that, when they say that . . . because we do work long and hard, put in so many hours here." Regardless of ethnicity, many immigrant business owners describe their hard work as a sacrifice they are making for their families, especially for their children. "I am doing this for my children . . . so they can have a better life: not work as hard as I did, go to college, get a good job. This is an investment in the future," Ernesto, who runs a taco shop, told me. His statement was echoed by many other shop keepers, hinting at the enduring power of the American dream despite its elusiveness.

Knowledge regarding potential sources of funding or technical assistance appeared to be limited among the business operators I interviewed, partly because of a distrust of banks and government agencies. They described themselves as being different than other businesses and therefore operated under the assumption that they would never qualify for any loan. Asked whether he was aware of a local small business loan program, Sergio, a Mexican convenience store owner, answered: "No, I don't know about this. I don't think they would lend me any money. We do not qualify for bank loans. They want too much paper. They do not lend to small businesses like us . . . immigrants, you know."

This assumption is not ill-founded. A recent analysis of loan data that commercial banks are required to provide under the Community Reinvestment Act found that, in San Diego, businesses in low-income census tracts—where most ethnic food stores and restaurants are located—were much less likely to receive bank loans than those in high-income areas (21 percent versus 62 percent).[44] The study also provided evidence that all together businesses in low-income areas received less than 5 percent of the total amount lent, while those in high-income areas took almost half. Furthermore, businesses in tracts with high minority populations were 54 percent less likely to receive loans than those in tracts with a greater proportion of white residents. The greater the proportion of Latinos in a tract, the lower the probability that businesses in that tract received a loan. These findings suggest that, despite policies to end discrimination in lending practices, historical biases against low-income and minority areas continue to negatively affect ethnic entrepreneurs today. Although these disparities may be less pronounced than during the redlining era described in chapter 2, they nevertheless contribute to food apartheid by depriving communities of hundreds of millions of dollars in loans that could have supported small ethnic food businesses.

Because of these financial constraints, owners view their business as a work-in-progress and an evolving project. They patch together funding from their personal savings, home equity loans, and informal loans and gifts from friends and family, which creates a network of social debt. Occasionally they obtain small business loans from local banks, including nonprofit community banks like Accion, but more often they rely on credit cards, online loans, and even day lenders to pay their bills and expand their business, putting them at risk of bankruptcy. Effective interest rates on these alternative loans are commonly above 100 percent.[45]

As a result, incoming revenue determines the scope and speed of ethnic business improvements—a new sign, a refrigerator, a few tables, fresh paint, or an expanded produce selection. Most of the owners I interviewed talked about their plans for the future and their desire to expand. None, however, reported having prepared specific business plans or secured financial resources. Miguel, a young Chicano man who owns a small corner store in City Heights, is excited about the future. He showed me where he plans to add a small seating area for a "mini-restaurant" where people can sit and enjoy the dishes he would prepare. The store is in disarray, with empty shelves and construction materials piled up in the corner where the future restaurant would be.

> I almost closed in October. Things were really bad. I was running out of milk because I could not pay to have inventory and customers were not happy. I just don't have the money. I tried to get a loan with the bank on University [Avenue] but that did not work out. I'd like to improve my business: add seafood . . . meat is doing really well, customers like it. I wanted to serve fruit cups but I did not get the permit from the Health Department. . . . The restaurant will take time and money. I just do not have the money right now, but next year I will put in new windows.

Later on, Miguel told me that he considered selling his store: "The neighborhood is changing. New people are coming in, moving into the new houses and apartments. They want different things. I can sell to them or I can sell my store. People are buying stores on this street because of the new people. I would like to sell, possibly. Get out of this. Stop working so hard. But then I think that there is an opportunity here." Miguel's ambivalence about newcomers and his fears about being able to meet the new demand and stay in business was echoed by several other participants—a topic to which I return in chapter 6, where I investigate the effects of gentrification.

Although gentrification brings in new customers and more purchasing power, it also threatens the livelihood of small ethnic entrepreneurs who may not be able to adapt to new demands and tastes, partly because of the financial constraints discussed in this chapter. As a result of intensified competition, earnings and working conditions in the ethnic food economy may actually worsen. Long hours, hard work, stress, earning uncertainty, lack of financial resources, and dependence on friends and family members are parts of ethnic entrepreneurship that do not fit neatly with the success stories we commonly hear. And while on average ethnic entrepreneurs earn higher incomes than hired workers, they must contend with additional costs that are rooted in racially differentiated geographies of opportunity.

"SEEING" LABOR

Those who bring us food are mostly invisible to us. While we may see the famous chef, the friendly waiter, or the colorfully clad Indigenous tortilla maker, we rarely consider the cooks, drivers, janitors, packagers, dishwashers, and others who work behind the scene. Both restaurants and supermarkets are labor-intensive operations, yet we only see the public façade. If we were to look behind this façade—as I did in this chapter—we would find exploitation, poverty, and harsh working conditions. We would also see that race, ethnicity, and gender are intimately tied to the precarity and informality that characterizes the food service and retail industry. There appears to be a dissonance between the professed desire to "eat ethically" and the working conditions of most food workers, particularly those employed in ethnic businesses and contributing to the cosmopolitan foodscape. Labor has remained marginal to the contemporary food movement, which is animated by a wide range of issues, including health, taste, environment, and animal welfare.[46]

Yet, as Sarumathi Jayaraman has put it, "no matter how locally sourced, organic, biodynamic, vegetarian, or otherwise healthy the food might be, as long as workers are too poor to be able to take care of themselves and their families, or sick while cooking and serving their food, the food cannot be healthy or sustainable."[47] This disconnect in the food movement is partly related to the invisibility of food workers who toil behind closed doors. However, as kitchens become increasingly open, both literally and figuratively, one must wonder whether the problem is not blindness on the consumers' part. Perhaps we have become so enthralled by our own eating experiences that we confuse patronizing ethnic establishments with supporting the workers involved. In fact, for many people, one of the appeals of ethnic food is that it is "cheap"—a fact that also adds to its democratic aura. There is little evidence that food workers in San Diego and elsewhere in the United States have benefited from the growing fascination with ethnic and authentic food. Despite being one of the fastest growing sectors of the economy, the food service and retail industry remains one of the most poorly paid and exploitative.

4

Coping with Food Insecurity

*Everyday Geographies of Social Reproduction
in the Ethnic Foodscape*

IN THE UNITED STATES many of the men and women who make and serve food for a living suffer from hunger and food insecurity. San Diego is no exception. Perhaps this should not be surprising in light of the prevailing low wages in food retail and service jobs described in the previous chapter. Yet it is a sad irony that those who toil in the kitchens of restaurants and the backrooms of grocery stores come home with an empty stomach and do not earn enough to feed their families. This problem is exacerbated by the fact that these workers, most of whom are people of color, often live in neighborhoods where food apartheid impedes access to life-sustaining foods. Patrons of ethnic restaurants may be surprised to learn that the cooks who make them delicious and authentic food rarely eat those dishes themselves.

At the same time, despite these economic constraints, food continues to play an important and positive role in the everyday lives of food workers, their families, and communities. In the neighborhoods where I conducted research—including Barrio Logan, City Heights, and Southeastern San Diego—food-insecure households have created their own food geographies by sharing food with neighbors and friends, relying on local convenience stores and street vendors, participating in the informal economy, using ingredients and leftovers creatively, and growing their own produce. As the vast literature on the relationship between food and ethnic identity suggests, the survival strategies of immigrants and subsequent generations are imbued with cultural meaning, memories, and emotions such as belonging and pride. Under the current political climate in which fear and shame inhibit immigrants' participation in public assistance programs, community self-sufficiency has become especially important in helping people put food on the table. Women, who remain disproportionately responsible for the social reproduction of households (including food provisioning, home making, and cultural preservation), have been especially involved in these activities. As Lois Stanford has argued, in the case of immigrant households, food security must be examined "from below . . . through the lens of family and community" rather than through the binary framework of survey variables.[1]

This means simultaneously paying attention to how food apartheid constrains food procurement activities in ethnic neighborhoods and how residents exert agency by resisting and transforming oppressive structures through everyday food activities. Conceptualizing food security broadly and through the body, as biological, political, emotional, and cultural, I investigate the role of food in everyday social reproduction, paying particular attention to the places where immigrants and people of color desire, purchase, prepare, ingest, and share food. The emphasis on geographies of social reproduction is important because it draws attention to the social relations and everyday activities underlying foodscapes and the vital role of food in sustaining communities and life itself.

"THE SHOEMAKER ALWAYS WEARS THE WORST SHOES"

Food insecurity among food workers is widespread. A recent report shows that in New York and the San Francisco Bay Area, 32 percent of restaurant workers are considered food insecure—twice the average rate for these areas.[2] Risks of food insecurity—defined as a situation in which people lack "physical and economic access to sufficient, safe and nutritious food to meet their dietary needs and food preferences for an active and healthy life"—was almost twice as high for immigrant food workers.[3] Undocumented immigrants were especially vulnerable, with more than two-thirds suffering from food insecurity. Although paradoxical, food insecurity among food workers is hardly surprising given the precarious labor conditions in the industry and the demographic composition of its workforce, which consists primarily of immigrants and people of color who disproportionately suffer from hunger.[4]

In 2016 and 2017, I conducted interviews with owners and employees of food stores and restaurants in City Heights and Barrio Logan that revealed a common concern regarding the ability to purchase food, eat regular meals, and provide for their families. Many talked about the challenges of balancing a very tight budget and providing for basic necessities, including food, especially toward the end of the month when money runs out or for those with very unstable schedules. They also discussed how the nature of their work made it difficult to eat regular meals because they were rarely given breaks and had to work long and unusual hours. Although some restaurants serve meals to their staff, either before or after their shift, this practice appears to be in decline and some workers complained that the food offered is usually not very good, consisting of leftovers and expired foods. Skipping meals or eating a quick snack instead of a balanced lunch or dinner were extremely common. By the time they got off work, it was often too late to shop for food to cook at home. Fast food was a convenient and relatively affordable option. In fact, many workers reported rarely cooking for themselves or their families. This was especially true of men who saw this as a woman's responsibility, underscoring a traditional gendered division of labor in which professional cooking was assigned to men and domestic cooking to women. Men, however, had strong feelings about their role as "providers" or being the "breadwinner," taking pride in their contributions or expressing both shame and anxiety about being unable to bring enough money home to buy desired food.

Because I purposely interviewed immigrants who worked in ethnic food stores or restaurants, I cannot compare their experience with that of the larger population. However, data from the Current Population Survey Food Security Supplement confirm that in San Diego County food insecurity is three times more common among food service workers than the overall workforce.[5] For immigrants, people of color, and Latinos the rate is even higher, especially for restaurant workers who are less likely to be unionized, have stable contracts, and earn benefits than grocery store workers.[6] Although likely underestimated, approximately eighteen thousand food workers in San Diego struggle with putting food on their family's table, adding up to almost fifty thousand people who depend on the food industry for survival and suffer from food insecurity.

Food insecurity, which can be roughly estimated by looking at participation rates in CalFresh, is concentrated in the very neighborhoods where food apartheid is most pronounced and the majority of food workers reside, including City Heights, Barrio Logan, and Southeastern San Diego. In other words, food insecurity disproportionately affects communities of color whose primary source of income is low-wage jobs in food service or other similar industries. Paradoxically, these food-insecure neighborhoods are those whose unique, diverse, and authentic food scene is currently attracting foodies, raising questions about access and power. Highlighting residents' experiences of food insecurity points out the hypocrisy of our collective obsession with ethnic food.

RETHINKING FOOD INSECURITY THROUGH THE BODY

The term *food insecurity* began replacing *hunger* in the 1990s. The switch in terminology reflected a desire for more "objective" measures of deprivation. Instead of relying on descriptions of pain and distress associated with not having enough food to eat, scholars turned their attention to the economic resources that might constrain food access. Official surveys, including the Food Security data used in the previous section, are almost entirely focused on "money," as illustrated by questions such as: "'The food that we bought just didn't last and we didn't have enough money to get more.' Was that often, sometimes, or never true for you in the last 12 months?" or "'In the last 12 months, did you ever eat less than you felt you should because there wasn't enough money for food?' Yes or No." Responses to as much as eighteen such questions are used to determine whether people are food secure or insecure. Among the food insecure, a distinction is made between those with low and very low food security. The former have little or no indication of reduced food intake but experience diminished quality, variety, and/or desirability of food. The latter show multiple indications of reduced intake and disrupted eating patterns.[7]

Lost in these surveys and measurements is the visceral and emotional aspect of hunger, which goes beyond limited access due to insufficient economic resources. If we believe that food is much more than nutrition, then food insecurity is also more than not having enough food to eat; it is the inability to gather generations together around a meal, share stories and traditions, discipline children, promote values about health, connect to place, create a home, express identities, and sustain memories. It is also the debilitating pain and visceral reaction provoked by an empty stomach—however subjective these may be. When people are deprived of nutritious, affordable, accessible, and culturally appropriate food, individual physical health certainly suffers, as evidenced by a large body of research on the effects of food insecurity on diabetes, heart disease, and nutrition-related chronic diseases.[8] But it is also the emotional health and well-being of families and communities that are threatened. Thus it is time to broaden the meaning of *food insecurity* beyond "not having enough money to buy food" and to consider the many ways in which hunger is experienced, often violently, as a threat to life itself.

The multifaceted experience of hunger is poignantly illustrated in the distinction that Mariana Chilton and Sue Booth have made between "hunger of the body" and "hunger of the mind."[9] "Hunger of the body" refers to the physical pain that one interviewee describes as "how it feels to be so hungry until you feel like you can't walk, you can't sit, you can't lay with yourself comfortable."[10] "Hunger of the mind" expresses the emotional pain—the traumatic and stressful experience of hunger that leads to anxiety and depression. Over time, like slow violence, the physical, emotional, and social pains and traumas of food insecurity exert their toll on the body, with severe consequences for health.

To those pains, I could also add the related social pain of being unable to "be oneself," meet one's potential, and fulfill social and cultural expectations—however gendered and problematic these may be. This form of suffering is particularly relevant and acute for immigrants and marginalized people for whom food often represents an important avenue for identity expression, belonging, and place-making. It is intensified among women whose identities as mothers, wives, and lovers are often wrapped up in domesticity and their ability to feed loved ones, which food insecurity confiscates.[11] Although scholars have been prone to romanticize immigrants' relationship to food by veering into nostalgia, recent work considers the complexities of food in the everyday experiences of immigrants, including experiences of hunger, intergenerational conflicts, gendered domesticity, racism, and stigmatization. This new research suggests that, for many, food is as much a source of pleasure as it is a source of tension.

I find work on the biopolitics of hunger extremely useful in thinking critically about food insecurity and conceptualizing it as the embodiment of social marginalization and denied access to resources.[12] As elaborated by Michel Foucault, *biopolitics* refers to the idea that the body and human life itself are politicized and governed by regulations, interventions, ideologies, and self-imposed disciplining.[13] Indeed, the various forms of suffering associated with food insecurity are both corporeal and political. Focusing on the body as the site of hunger's havoc draws attention to how structural and environmental factors limiting access to food become embodied or inscribed in the flesh, often violently, through symptoms such as weight loss/gain, disease, tiredness, anxiety, or depression as well as the social stigma those bring. Hunger, as a visceral embodied experience, is the expression of broad structural forces such as labor market segmentation, housing discrimination, neoliberal food policies, and food retail consolidation that create unequal access to food according to race, ethnicity, immigration status, class, and gender. In that framework, racialized and gendered bodies are political sites of control, manipulation, and/or neglect—a process that becomes obvious in the context of food assistance that shames, disciplines, and regulates poor and hungry bodies.[14]

Critical geographers have eagerly adopted the notion of embodiment as a way to connect corporeality, bodily practices, and environments. For feminist geographers Linda McDowell and Joanne Sharp the body is akin to "a surface to be mapped, a surface of inscription, as a boundary between the individual subject and that which is Other to it, as the container of individual identity, but also a permeable boundary which leaks and bleeds and is penetrable."[15] In other words, the body is always in the making, molded by interaction with an environment that it simultaneously shapes and absorbs. For Allison Hayes-Conroy and Jessica Hayes-Conroy, "individual visceral feelings are never detached from wider economic structures and systems of meaning making"—a dynamic relationship they define as "political ecology of the body."[16] Thus the body is both expressive of its singularity and reflective of its material and discursive surroundings. As such, it is a terrain of struggle—"both vehicle and victim of power."[17]

Such focus on the body should not be mistaken with an individualist or behavioralist perspective. Rather than narrowing down on individual behavior as a rational or "disembodied" response to external constraints, scholars who center their work on the body draw attention to the corpo-reality of the human experience and its relationships to the world around it, including state-sanctioned racial and economic inequality. As David Harvey has put it, "the study of the body has to be grounded in the understanding of real spatio-temporal relations between material practices, representations, imaginations, institutions, social relations, and the prevailing structures of political economy."[18] The places and spaces where bodies are materially and discursively situated are central to the idea of embodiment, which is undoubtedly why this theoretical approach is appealing to geographers.

Although the food-body-space nexus has prompted important scholarly work among geographers on obesity, nutrition, and fatness, as well as gender, and immigrant food practices, it has yet to inspire the same level of research on hunger, particularly as it relates to race and ethnicity.[19] Nik Heynen's work is a notable exception, as he has called upon geographers to acknowledge the primacy of "the material foundations of bodily survival."[20] Inspired by Marxism, he focuses on the social and discursive production of hungry bodies in an analysis of radical antihunger projects such as the Black Panther Party's food programs. He shows how capitalism and racism threatens human bodies by producing hunger in particular times and places. Although not explicitly stated, this embodied perspective of hunger meets geographer Ruth Gilmore's definition of racism as the "state-sanctioned or extralegal production and exploitation of group-differentiated vulnerability to premature death."[21] Indeed, the structural inequities manifested in hunger originate in state-sanctioned racist policies, ideologies, and practices that result in food apartheid and underlie food insecurity. As Heynen has argued, however, the visceral and life-threatening experiences of hunger can also mobilize powerful antihunger movements, underscoring the significance of the body in both experiencing and resisting the structural violence of hunger.

Outside of geography, anthropologist Megan Carney's work on food insecurity among Mexican and Central American immigrant women is a major source of inspiration for my research.[22] She uniquely focuses on the dual effects of the "biopolitics of food insecurity"—how food insecurity results from political-economic forces—and the concomitant "biopolitical project of food security"—how state and nonprofit agencies govern hunger by shifting the responsibility on individuals and communities. Teresa Mares's ethnographic research on the food strategies of Latina immigrants in Seattle is equally insightful in drawing attention to the structural violence of food insecurity and the constrained agency of women in resisting this brutality by reclaiming and reshaping their foodways.[23] Although Carney and Mares do not fully articulate the role of place in underlying these processes, their emphasis on how bodies are governed differently by being afforded or denied life-sustaining resources lends itself to exploring the uneven geographies underlying differences in chances of bodily survival.

Much can be gained by thinking about hunger through the lens of the body and biopolitics. In this perspective a starved body is more than an impoverished individual who does not have enough money to eat; it is a body that is physically and emotionally devalued and degraded by others, including employers, policymakers, public health officials, or even family members operating within racist, sexist, and classist structures. A satiated body, in contrast, is one that has ingested food that the same system has made differently available to them. Simultaneously considering the visceral feelings of hunger and the structural relations underlying them opens up new ways to examine food insecurity as a situated, embodied, and politicized experience that acknowledges the differences that race, immigration, and gender make.

By "placing" bodies and biopolitical processes in urban neighborhoods, I seek to develop an *urban* political ecology of the body in which the city and its uneven foodscape feature prominently. This orientation parallels Heynen's quest to understand hunger "by articulating the connections, interrelations, and interdependences between the metabolism of food through the human body and the metabolism of cities."[24] It also aligns with Ashanté Reese's approach that connects large-scale processes of food apartheid with the microgeographies of how residents navigate uneven foodscapes and practice self-reliance.[25]

EVERYDAY FOOD GEOGRAPHIES AND SOCIAL REPRODUCTION IN ETHNIC COMMUNITIES

For the more than sixty residents of City Heights, Barrio Logan, and Southeastern San Diego I interviewed between 2016 and 2018, including several food workers, putting food on the table is a priority—a necessity for bodily survival.[26] It is the reason they put up with harsh working conditions and often work multiple jobs. It is also why they devote so much time to food procurement, looking for deals, growing their own produce, preparing thrifty recipes, shopping in multiple places, searching for donations, and navigating food assistance programs. And in some instances, it is the motivation for grassroots organizing. Contrary to popular belief, immigrants are reluctant to seek assistance outside of their immediate social networks. Instead, they engage in a variety of place-based practices to feed themselves and their families, relying heavily on neighborhood resources and fighting for their "right to the city."[27]

Public Assistance

Because the mainstream discourse constructs food insecurity in terms of household ability to purchase food, the primary policy solution to fight hunger has been to supplement people's income with food stamps or vouchers that allow them to purchase certain foods at participating stores.[28] Since their inception, however, these programs have been under constant attack for presumably creating a culture of dependence on government handouts. Since the late 1970s, neoliberal pressures to reduce the size of government and encourage personal responsibility have exacerbated these attacks and justified various spending cuts and tightening of restrictions. This eroding of the welfare state has been accompanied by a rise in the shadow state—the large nonprofit and voluntary sector that has replaced the government in providing social service.[29]

During that period, food banks have proliferated, partly because of government contracts with nonprofits and tax benefits to private and corporate donors, but also because of the moral appeal of "feeding the hungry" among the American public that sees donating to food drives and volunteering at soup kitchens as simple ways to ease its conscience.[30] Rather than addressing the underlying causes of hunger—such as racism, poverty, and the lack of housing, good jobs, and medical care—this shift to the nonprofit sector has given policymakers a license to further dismantle the safety net of the welfare state by assuming that kindhearted individuals and communities will take care of the hungry. Thus today the primary mechanisms for dealing with food insecurity are "handouts" provided by a shrinking state and an expanding nonprofit sector in the form of vouchers or food donations.

While I certainly do not wish to diminish the hard work of volunteers and the value of both public and private assistance programs for thousands of households, I want to point out that they constitute what Carney calls the "biopolitical project of food security."[31] By doling out assistance to "deserving" citizens, who must jump through numerous hoops to prove their eligibility and receive benefits, these agencies monitor and control hungry people. Immigrants in particular are fearful and reluctant to rely on "assistance" for a variety of reasons linked to this biopolitics. In the current anti-immigrant political climate, many immigrants have stopped using or postponed applying for food stamps, known as Supplemental Nutrition Assistance Program (SNAP) or CalFresh in California, for fear that it would threaten their prospect of becoming citizens and possibly lead to deportation.[32] It is worth noting that legal immigrants who have been in the United States for fewer than five years and undocumented immigrants are not eligible for SNAP, while their US-born children are.

Maria, a Central American woman who has lived in San Diego for twelve years and has a green card, tells me that she is afraid to apply for CalFresh. Because her job recently switched to part-time, her income has been curtailed and she is having great difficulty feeding her two school-aged children who were born in the United States. CalFresh would provide much needed assistance until she finds more work, but she has been discouraged by stories of people "losing their status" because they used public assistance. She is referring to the requirement that green card applicants prove that they are not a "public burden," meaning they have not received cash assistance such as Temporary Assistance to Needy Families and Supplemental Security Income. In 2018 the Trump administration publicized a new definition of "public charge" broadening the scope of public assistance to SNAP, Medicaid, and housing vouchers for which certain immigrants, their US-born children, and refugees are eligible. In 2019, Trump issued a memo requiring sponsors to pay back any benefits that green card applicants might have received. Although this proposal has been challenged in court, no final decision had been made by the end of 2020. This uncertainty has been a major source of confusion and anxiety among immigrants and had a chilling effect on SNAP participation.[33] The notable drop in CalFresh participation among immigrants has prompted the San Diego Hunger Coalition to respond with an education campaign titled Know your Rights and a Safe Food Assistance program, but much damage has been done already.

This chilling effect comes on top of a generally negative experience most interviewees have with the "system" of public assistance. For instance, Emir, an East African convenience store clerk from City Heights, recalled how his wife had to go to the county office three times before they could get CalFresh benefits. Each time she spent almost the whole day there, waiting for her turn to meet with a representative. The first two times she was sent away because she did not have the proper documentation. Eventually she was able to prove her children's eligibility. Many would have given up, relinquishing resources that could make a difference in their lives because they do not have the time, resources, and mobility to spend a whole day or more at a Health and Human Services Agency center. Even if some applications are processed quickly, the general perception is that it is a lengthy process with no guarantee of eligibility at the end.

Some are turned off by what they describe as a humiliating experience. Patricia, a naturalized US citizen who was born in Mexico and lives in Barrio Logan with her husband and their two teenage children, told me:

> I don't like asking for handouts. I only went for my kids because
> my neighbor told me. I didn't want to go. I was embarrassed. I
> wasn't raised like that. . . . When I got there, I had to wait for a
> long time. The worker made me feel like a beggar; she asked for
> so much information I couldn't give her, like copies of bank state-
> ments and my husband's pay checks. I didn't like the way she was

talking and looking at me, like I didn't deserve [assistance] and I was trying to get something for nothing. She didn't understand how hard it was for me to even be there. I felt ashamed. I never went back. I knew I should not have gone. I don't want to depend on the government anyway.

Patricia's experience speaks to the cultural attitude that many immigrants have toward public assistance. Aside from the stigma that may come from the outside (e.g., media, social workers), there is a general perception within immigrant communities, among family, friends, and neighbors, that getting help from the government should be avoided except under extreme circumstances. Many find pride in "never having asked for help" and often insinuate that "[public assistance] is for other people, who are worse off than us." Those who used CalFresh often justify it by emphasizing their unusual and temporary circumstances, indicating that they "would have been starving or homeless without it." This perception that CalFresh is for "other people" stems in part from the experience of migration, which ultimately is a quest for survival and a better life. To many immigrants, applying for government assistance is an admission that they have failed at achieving this better life. Making do without help is a way of asserting autonomy and claiming agency in the challenging project of migration. For some, this attitude distinguishes them morally from low-income native-born Americans who they view as lazy and entitled. This narrative would often begin with "We Mexicans . . . ," "In Iraq, we . . . ," or "Somali people . . . ," suggesting that this rejection of assistance and fierce independence is a shared value tied to immigration and ethnicity.

Despite the Trump administration's rhetoric and the perception in conservative policy circles that immigrants come to the United States specifically to take advantage of welfare benefits, underutilization rates are well documented.[34] Data from the most recent American Community Survey indicate that in San Diego, when considering households with income under 200 percent of poverty thresholds, SNAP participation rates are 25 percent, with no difference between eligible immigrants and non-immigrants.[35] Since 200 percent of poverty is close to the eligibility cutoff, this rate represents significant underutilization. The experiences of the women and men I interviewed in urban San Diego are similar to those of

Mexican and Central American immigrant women in rural Santa Barbara County as recounted by Carney. They too struggled with fear, stigma, and confusion about eligibility and as a result underutilized CalFresh.

Other important federal programs include the Special Supplemental Nutrition Program for Women, Infants, and Children (WIC), the National School Lunch Program (NSLP), and the School Breakfast Program (SBP). WIC focuses specifically on low-income pregnant women, new mothers, and their infant and young children. In California, immigrants—regardless of legal status—are eligible for WIC and many women participate in the program. Like for Food Stamps, however, the new "public charge" rule (which does not apply to WIC) has had a chilling effect. In 2015 fewer than half of eligible women participated in WIC and participation rates, especially among immigrants, have dropped since then.[36] Participation in school programs is also threatened by politics that shame and stigmatize beneficiaries as witnessed in recent attention to unpaid bills. All public schools in the three study neighborhoods participate in the Community Eligibility Program that provide free school lunches for all students, given that well over 40 percent qualify for this benefit. This program too came under attack by USDA director Sonny Purdue for not being "fair" to the "American People."[37]

Private Charities

Private charities offer food assistance that might be less intimidating to immigrants. As noted above, in the past three decades, the nonprofit sector has come to play an increasingly large role in collecting and distributing food to hungry people. Daniel Warshawski has described a devolved system in which a few very large food banks, such as Feeding America, collect food from government and corporate surplus as well as individual donations.[38] These items are then sorted and distributed to community organizations that handle the delivery of food to those in need. A wide range of agencies, including faith-based organizations, schools, social service providers, soup kitchens, food pantries, and community centers, are involved in food distribution, each with their own mission, target population, and values that may influence participation. Many have contracts with government agencies, including the USDA, which donate food but impose restrictions on its use.

One would expect those employed in the food industry to have priority access to food surplus before it gets thrown away or donated to food banks. Yet many employers have strict policies about how food waste is to be handled and usually do not allow employees to take food home. Ernesto, a Mexican man who lives in City Heights and works in a famous restaurant downtown, complained: "There is always a lot of wasted food in restaurants, but we can't have it. The manager keeps track of everything and the trash cans are locked. Some guys eat food left on people's plates, but if they get caught doing that, they'll get fired. It doesn't make any sense to me." Instead, excess food goes to waste or is donated to food banks that redistribute it to communities.

There are several charitable sources of food assistance in the study neighborhoods, including a few soup kitchens that serve meals daily or weekly, community centers that distribute monthly food boxes, churches involved in outreach programs, and school-based initiatives that help families through children. Most organizations have some restrictions on hours of operation, frequency of aid, or eligibility. For instance, many places are only open once a week, every other week, or just once a month. The majority do not allow people to receive assistance more than once a month and limit these donations to six times per year. In addition, recipients must often provide proof of need and residency in the service area. Before receiving food, they may also be required to pre-register and provide personal information, which undocumented immigrants may be especially reluctant to do. Some organizations also limit services to specific populations such as seniors, homeless people, military veterans, and families with children. These restrictions create barriers for some people, especially in emergency situations. For example, there is a cluster of organizations near Barrio Logan and the northwestern edge of Southeastern San Diego, where many homeless shelters and service providers have been relocated following the development of downtown's East Village. Yet long-term residents of this area do not feel that these organizations are there to serve their needs. Instead, they worry that they are attracting a growing population of homeless individuals who suffer from chronic mental health and drug abuse issues.

Viviane, who came as a refugee from Vietnam decades ago, recounted how she turned to a City Heights church for assistance:

The church over there gives out boxes of food on the last Tuesday of the month. I have seen people waiting in line before and I saw a sign on the door about it. So I decided to go. I was there at 9:30, half an hour before they opened. It was pretty fast and people were very nice. They asked me a bunch of questions; if I lived in the neighborhood, how many children I had, if I had a job. . . . They also asked about my husband, but we are separated, you know . . . so I told them. They wanted me to register. I asked them why and they said it was to make sure I don't go and get food somewhere else.

These comments echo the sort of shaming and stigmatizing of single mothers and people of color that Rebecca de Souza observed in food pantries in Duluth, Minnesota, where the white privilege of volunteers and the prevalence of neoliberal ideas create a culture of suspicion that emphasizes the individual failures of hungry people over the systemic failures to meet basic needs.[39]

While thankful, the very few interviewees who received food assistance from nonprofit organizations indicated that the food they received was not ideal. For example, Marissa thought that the food pantry she visited in City Heights "did not have anything for us"—meaning that it did not have the type of food that her family typically consumes. In other words, the food was not "culturally appropriate"—an important and rarely acknowledged aspect of food security.[40] Marissa, who is from Guatemala, explained: "We don't eat that kind of food. There were a lot of small packages of Asian noodles in the box, I had never eaten those before. There were also granola bars, but my kids didn't like them. I ate those for lunch. . . . I don't think the food they give us is very healthy. It's hard to make a meal out of it." Samira, a young mother from Somalia, pointed out the disconnect between the nutrition advice and the content of the food package she was given at a community clinic: "They keep telling us that we should eat more vegetables, but the bag only had pasta, crackers, and snacks."

Nutritional Advice

Public and private food assistance is often accompanied by nutritional advice. In some cases, this advice is meant as a substitute for food assistance under the belief that if people were better educated on how to shop, store, and prepare food, they would not experience food insecurity. "We just need to educate people" has been a common mantra among social and health workers. Yet nutritional advice was often questioned by recipients and viewed as patronizing. As such, it presented another deterrent to seeking food assistance. Selena, a Mexican American women, put it bluntly: "I know how to make a healthy meal. I don't need to learn how to cook. I have been cooking with my mother since I was a kid. I just need food to cook with." This finding aligns with critical studies of nutrition that emphasize the lack of concern for diversity, context, and hierarchies in the mainstream principles and practices of nutrition.[41] Nutritional advice is often standardized in ideal counts of calories or servings of fruits and vegetables consumed. It rarely accounts for differences in circumstances and preferences and, as such, often seems irrelevant or unattainable to immigrant and ethnic groups whose food habits do not fit this normalized diet.

Specifically, the educational materials displayed and handed out at food pantries often present a dichotomous view of nutrition by contrasting "healthy food" with "food to avoid" based on the normalized middle-class white American diet. For example, white bread is to be rejected in favor of whole grain bread. However, most immigrants—whether from Mexico, Central America, Asia, or Africa—do not consume white bread regularly. Switching to whole grain bread may actually represent a step back from their traditional diet in terms of nutrient intake. To the extent that ethnic foods do not figure in nutritional advice, many people assume that they fall under the "bad food" category, leading to feelings of guilt or shame and resistance to mainstream nutrition. These negative feelings also contribute to the Americanization of immigrants' diet, with lower consumption of fresh produce and higher consumption of fast food and sugary drinks.[42] Once culinary traditions are lost, it is often difficult to bring back home cooking.

This emotional relationship to food is particularly poignant among teenagers, who perhaps more than anyone struggle with questions of identity and the desire to fit in. In 2015 my colleague Fernando Bosco and I conducted participatory photo-based research with high school students in City Heights in an effort to gather data on their everyday food practices and the way they negotiate contradictory foodscapes.[43] Among the thirty-eight students who participated in the study, none considered themselves white, 20 percent were born outside of the United States, and 78 percent had foreign-born parents. Through photos and interviews, we uncovered both a rejection of school food, which often ended up in the trash, and a simultaneous embarrassment about one's own ethnic food, whose look and smell occasionally garnered unwanted attention from peers. This contradictory attitude led many young people to skip meals—including free school breakfasts and lunches—and to turn to "junk" food from local shops after school, which they all understood as unhealthy. This practice of skipping meals and consuming "empty calories" is especially problematic given the prevalence of food insecurity among students in the neighborhood.[44] Yet it is understandable as a form of emotional and social resistance in which young people commonly engage.[45] For immigrants and bicultural youths these acts of identity negotiation, formation, and expression are especially important.[46]

Home Practices

For immigrants the notion of home carries a unique meaning that is deeply connected to food. In fact, "good food" is almost always associated with homemade food. In the context of conflicting messages regarding "good food," people come up with their own definitions, reflecting their knowledge, unique circumstances, cultural background, and agency. For example, the vast majority of the young people we interviewed in City Heights associated healthy food with home.[47] Although not always complimentary toward their parents' cooking, they described home-cooked meals as pleasurable and healthier than anything else they ate, even if not highly nutritious by common standards. This finding would no doubt please their mothers, who—if similar to the women I interviewed at various food stores in the neighborhood—spend much time and energy ensuring that their children have home-cooked meals regularly and learn about good food.

Several mothers deplored having to depend on highly processed or fast food because other options were not available or affordable. Indeed, mothers almost universally condemned fast food, which they view as sabotaging their efforts to promote healthy eating habits in their children and causing diseases like diabetes and cancer that disproportionately affect their communities. This was especially true of recent immigrants who were often nostalgic about the food of their birthplace. Many seemed saddened about being unable to provide this experience to their loved ones in San Diego because of financial and time constraints, unavailability of ingredients, and occasionally resistance from younger generations. Nyala, an Ethiopian mother of three, explained: "Back home, we always had a lot of vegetables: cooked greens, lentils, beans, cabbage, and other vegetables you cannot find here. We also had meat: lamb, goat, or chicken. We made injera [teff flatbread] every day. It was different. Here people do not have time to cook like that. They are always busy. My kids, sometimes they like [Ethiopian food], but sometimes they like American food. It's sad, but I don't make real Ethiopian food very often. I really wish I could, but it's complicated, you know."

I single out mothers in this section because they often brought up healthy meals in their conversations with me and seemed to be the ones socially entrusted with the responsibility of keeping their family well-fed.[48] Like young people, mothers typically conflated "healthy" and "homemade" and believed that meals cooked at home were generally better, even if somewhat simple, partly processed, and not always balanced or nutritious. "Rice and beans are better than that stuff [fast food served at a neighborhood outlet]," exclaimed Monica, a Mexican American mother. Others, like Natalia, echoed this feeling: "American food is not healthy . . . well, it depends, some people spend a lot of money. . . . But in Mexico, food is better. It's all fresh and natural. Even poor people eat better because they cook at home with fresh ingredients . . . maybe vegetables they grow themselves." Husbands and fathers expressed similar attitudes in favor of home-cooking, although they distanced themselves from the necessary labor. Of course, it is probable that these strong feelings against fast food and in favor of home-cooked meals might reflect both the dominant public heath narrative that interviewees have absorbed and their assumption that as a food researcher I might like to hear them voice such opinions.

Nevertheless, in the different immigrant communities that I studied, most meals were consumed at home, except for those taken at school or at work. My interviewees reported spending about one hour each day cooking at home and cleaning afterward. This was primarily done by women but occasionally involved men and children. They described several strategies to deal with low food supplies and limited budgets. The most common practice was to cook large quantities that would last several days and could be used in different dishes. For instance, braised chicken was served with rice one day, made a tasty filling for tacos the next day, and ended up in a soup at the end of the week. More expensive ingredients like meat and vegetables were typically combined with cheaper and more filling items like rice, beans, noodles, bread, or tortillas. Less expensive ingredients became relatively more important as budgets got tighter, especially toward the end of the month before pay day. Occasionally, dishes would literally be "watered down" to make sure there would be enough for everybody. Soups made with broth (such as Mexican caldo, Vietnamese pho, or Filipino sinigang) are typical "comfort" food that illustrate creative ways to make a meal out of few relatively affordable ingredients.

Family gatherings, including weekly dinners and birthday parties, often prompt serious cooking and grilling, with intentional leftovers being divided among guests at the end of the party. In fact, these social events are instrumental in redistributing food within social networks, with guests contributing according to their ability and those in need leaving with more than they brought. To outsiders, these gatherings where food seems plentiful might look wasteful. To participants, however, they are an occasion to get together, build community, and help loved ones in informal and caring ways. Similar potluck-style meals are also held frequently in the courtyards of City Heights's apartment complexes where many refugees live. Occasionally these become informal business platforms where plates of food are sold for a small price or donation.

Sharing food and knowledge among family members, friends, and neighbors is fairly common. For example, Danny, a Black resident of Southeastern San Diego, bought a large box of tomatoes at a farm stand near the construction site where he worked and gave a couple to each of his neighbors. "It was such a good deal, but I can't eat all of these tomatoes. I know it's not always easy for people to get food on the table. So I decided to get a whole box and give some away to my neighbors. The lady downstairs made soup and brought me some. I never had it before, but it was really good." Women often share information regarding places to shop, ongoing sales, and recipes for tasty, healthy, and affordable recipes. This sort of sharing is mostly limited to one's ethnic community and/or neighbors. Thus, contrary to popular belief that immigrants and low-income people need to be "educated" about healthy food through public health campaigns, my fieldwork suggests that both adults and children had a reasonable and contextualized understanding of healthy food that centers on home practices. More than a lack of knowledge, low access and unaffordability prevented mothers from achieving gendered aspirations of what they perceive as their responsibility toward their families.

Local Businesses

Although it is often assumed that low-income households shop at large supermarkets and discount stores where food is presumably more affordable, the vast majority of food consumed by the sixty-four residents I interviewed in City Heights, Barrio Logan, and Southeastern San Diego was purchased from local stores and prepared at home. While some have the resources to plan regular trips at larger stores in suburban areas, many rely heavily on neighborhood businesses, which they visit several times a week (3.5 times on average) and often daily for people with limited mobility and complicated job schedules.

Chapter 3 underscored the importance of ethnic food stores and restaurants in providing jobs and income to immigrants and ethnic minorities. What is less well understood, however, is the importance of these institutions in the everyday lives of residents of low-income neighborhoods. Those who struggle with food insecurity are especially sensitive to the environment in which they shop. Not only are they searching for good prices, but they are also looking for respect and compassion. In addition, they may be looking for culturally appropriate ingredients, including spices, herbs, fruits and vegetables, cuts of meat, and cheeses, to prepare familiar dishes. Small ethnic markets and convenience stores often meet those needs.[49] To learn more about the retail foodscape of the three study neighborhoods, my colleague Fernando Bosco and I worked with several undergraduate and graduate students to conduct extensive retailer audits between 2014 and 2018.[50] We canvassed the neighborhoods and visited

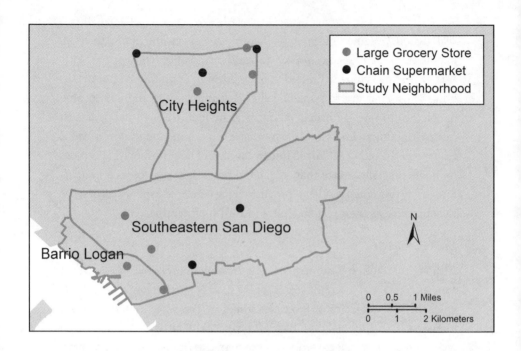

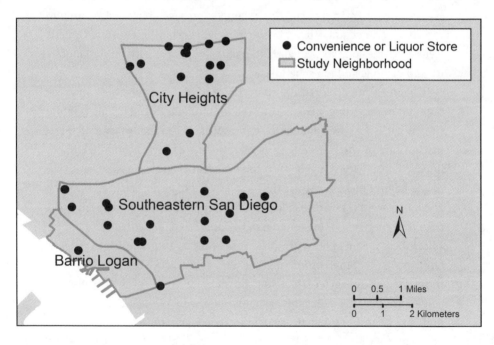

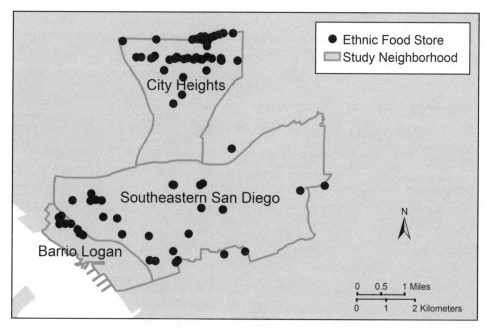

MAP 4.1 Geographic distribution of food retailers in Central San Diego, by type, 2018. Without small businesses, especially ethnic food stores, the three study neighborhoods would have very limited access to food, given the dearth of chain supermarkets and large grocery stores. Maps created by author with own audit data (2014–18), supplemented with 2016 data from the California Department of Public Health, "Communities of Excellence: Retail Food Environment."

every store and restaurant to collect detailed information on quantity, quality, and price of food, size and aesthetic of buildings, signs, advertising, and so on.

Despite being branded as food deserts and having experienced disinvestment and supermarket closures since the 1960s (described in chapter 2), City Heights, Barrio Logan, and Southeastern San Diego are home to small businesses that play an important role in the social reproduction activities of local residents (map 4.1 and table 4.1). Grocery stores, small markets, convenience stores, and discount stores, especially those with an ethnic affiliation, are well represented along the main streets and commercial arteries of the areas under consideration. There are also numerous restaurants, including a large number of independent small, casual, and fast food restaurants. In fact, independent businesses are much more

TABLE 4.1 FOOD STORES AND RESTAURANTS BY TYPE AND ETHNICITY, 2018

TYPE AND ETHNICITY	NEIGHBORHOODS			
	Barrio Logan	City Heights	Southeastern San Diego	Total
FOOD STORES	N = 13 (%)	N = 80 (%)	N = 56 (%)	N = 146 (%)
Supermarket	7.7	1.3	5.4	3.4
Grocery	15.4	27.5	23.2	24.8
Convenience	23.1	30.0	23.2	26.8
Specialty	38.5	8.8	8.9	11.4
Discount/pharmacy	0.0	10.0	12.5	10.1
Liquor store	15.4	22.5	26.8	23.5
Independent	84.6	82.5	80.4	81.9
Chain	15.4	17.5	19.6	18.1
Ethnic	53.8	60.0	48.2	55.0
African	0.0	14.6	0.0	8.5
Middle Eastern	0.0	6.3	3.7	4.9
Vietnamese	0.0	8.3	7.4	7.3
Chinese	0.0	16.7	0.0	9.8
Other Asian	0.0	4.2	0.0	2.4
Mexican	100.0	45.8	85.2	63.4
Other Latino	0.0	2.1	0.0	1.2
Soul, Southern, Caribbean	0.0	2.1	3.7	2.4
RESTAURANTS	N = 48 (%)	N = 112 (%)	N = 91 (%)	N = 251 (%)
Fast food	39.6	51.8	70.3	56.2
Casual	50.0	48.2	29.7	41.8
Upscale	10.4	0.0	0.0	2.0

	NEIGHBORHOODS			
TYPE AND ETHNICITY	Barrio Logan	City Heights	Southeastern San Diego	Total
RESTAURANTS	N = 48 (%)	N = 112 (%)	N = 91 (%)	N = 251 (%)
Independent	79.2	82.1	33.0	63.7
Chain	20.8	17.9	67.0	36.3
Ethnic	62.5	80.4	62.6	70.5
African	0.0	8.9	0.0	4.5
Middle Eastern	3.3	1.1	0.0	1.1
Vietnamese	0.0	33.3	1.8	17.5
Chinese	6.7	11.1	7.0	9.0
Other Asian	13.3	4.4	3.5	5.6
Mexican	73.3	36.7	73.7	54.8
Other Latino	0.0	3.3	3.5	2.8
Soul, Southern, Caribbean	3.3	1.1	10.5	4.5

Figures represent percentage of all stores or restaurants, except for ethnic categories, where italicized figures are the percentage of all ethnic stores or restaurants. *Source*: Author's own audit data.

common in these older urban neighborhoods than in suburban areas, representing 82 percent of restaurants and 64 percent of stores in the three areas combined. The presence of such a diverse food economy challenges the notion of food desert, which is based on supermarkets alone. Table 4.1 summarizes the number and types of food businesses in each neighborhood.

In 2020, I counted 149 stores and 251 restaurants operating within the geographic boundaries of Barrio Logan, City Heights, and Southeastern San Diego. The majority are ethnic enterprises, representing 55 percent of stores and 75 percent of restaurants. Such businesses were identified as those meeting at least two of the following three criteria: (a) ethnic name (e.g., Pancho Villa Market), (b) prominently displayed ethnic symbols (e.g., national flags, foreign language signs), and/or (c) prevalence of ingredients or items associated with a particular ethnic cuisine (e.g., spices, corn masa, halal meat). Although based on visible characteristics recorded in audits, this identification method was validated in owners' interviews.

In City Heights successive groups of refugees and immigrants have become entrepreneurs and invested in small stores and restaurants specializing in foods from their region of origin. Thus Colombian, Ethiopian, Ghanaian, Salvadoran, and Vietnamese businesses, among others, can be found on the same block, making the neighborhood one of the most diverse in San Diego. African food stores and restaurants are concentrated in the northeastern part of the neighborhood along El Cajon Boulevard and University Avenue, in an area known as Little Mogadishu. A number of Middle Eastern enterprises, managed by Iraqi and Syrian immigrants, are located in the same section of town. East and Southeast Asian businesses, mostly Vietnamese and Chinese operations, share space in an area called Little Saigon, recently designated by a colorful mural on El Cajon Boulevard. Today, many of the Vietnamese refugees who settled in the area in the 1970s have moved with their families to suburban neighborhoods such as Mira Mesa. However, they continue to own businesses in City Heights, including thirty restaurants and four food stores. Mexican stores and restaurants are the most numerous and dispersed in the neighborhood, totaling over fifty businesses. This is not surprising given the large Mexican population residing in City Heights.

In Barrio Logan the majority of stores and restaurants have a Mexican association. Fruterías, carnicerías, tortillerías, panaderías, and taquerías have historically filled the landscape and several remain in operation today, with 100 percent of ethnic stores having a Mexican identity, as do almost three-quarters of ethnic restaurants. Southeastern, a historically Black community that is quickly diversifying, contains fewer ethnic retailers and more chain businesses than the other two neighborhoods. Still, it is home to a large number of independent stores and restaurants, many of which have an ethnic affiliation. Mexican businesses are concentrated in the western half, which was separated from Barrio Logan by the construction of Interstate 5 in the 1960s. Several Soul, Southern, and Caribbean restaurants, typically ran and operated by Black residents, uniquely serve Southeastern San Diego. Despite the relatively large and growing Asian population in the neighborhood, Vietnamese and Chinese businesses remain concentrated north in City Heights and Filipino businesses are clustered south in National City.

The great majority of restaurants are considered "fast service" or "casual," with taco shops representing more than half of all restaurants. For some residents these taco shops—many open twenty-four hours a day—are a convenient and somewhat affordable option to obtain a hot meal before or after work. For many San Diegans, not just those who identify as Mexican, tacos and burritos are comfort foods that provide pleasure beyond filling an empty stomach. As we will see in the next chapters, however, the popularity of tacos and other ethnic food among outsiders is changing the role of these small restaurants in their communities. With menus changing and prices inflating rapidly, as epitomized by the sixteen-dollar taco served by a new upscale restaurant, local restaurants may not be affordable to low-income residents much longer.

It is typically assumed, especially in public health research, that food quality, diversity, and prices are less desirable in ethnic markets. Our audits uncovered no evidence of systematic price gauging, low-quality produce, or expired food, except in a few rare instances. Although food prices in small ethnic markets were occasionally higher than in large grocery stores, this was mostly due to smaller package sizes, lower sales volumes, and unavailability of generic brands. For most items, including fresh produce, prices were usually comparable or even lower.[51]

Likewise, meals at ethnic fast food restaurants were priced similarly to other fast food options. But prices and physical accessibility—convenience factors—are not the only reasons people patronize certain businesses. Having a very limited budget to shop for food, not being familiar with mainstream food items and brands, and using public food assistance are causes of anxiety that small ethnic markets may alleviate by catering specifically to ethnic and low-income customers. Clerks speak the same language, recognizable products are available, and EBT—the government-issued Electronic Benefit Transfer card used by CalFresh and WIC recipients—is accepted without judgment in many locations. Occasionally store owners even extend credit to known consumers, although that practice appears to be disappearing quickly.

Coping with food insecurity is an emotional process that may be assuaged by ethnic markets. For migrants and internationally displaced people, feelings of home and belonging are often associated with food, turning food provisioning activities into meaningful but also stressful experiences. The lack of access to familiar foods makes it difficult for people to budget properly, forcing them to limit their purchase to recognizable items or turn to high-calorie and low-nutrient "convenience" and "comfort" foods.[52] This is often further complicated by religious constraints (e.g., halal meat and kosher food). Thus access to culturally acceptable foods is essential to food security. In an urban setting where the majority of residents obtains food from local retailers, ethnic markets are places that provide more than specific ingredients; they sustain immigrant livelihoods, enable food sovereignty, respect multiple food knowledge, and allow for the expression and development of racial and ethnic identities through food practices.

The many customers I interviewed in parking lots and in front of ethnic food businesses indicated that service was a very important, if not the most significant, reason they shopped in those stores. By "service" they meant the way they were treated by store managers and employees. They enjoyed the personal experience: the fact that many merchants knew them by name, would engage in informal conversation, spoke their language, even set aside specific items for them, and made them feel welcome. Those customers were willing to accept slightly higher prices and more limited selection in exchange for a sense of belonging. For example, Berta, who is from Guatemala, explained that she visits a given store several times a week: "Sometimes I come three times in a day. I get things for breakfast, lunch, and dinner. I even send my son if we need something more. They know my family." She laughs and tells me that the store is like a family. Like other shoppers, Berta contrasts her experience at this small store with shopping at the only neighborhood supermarket: "Yes, I have gone to the new supermarket on University. My brother took me there once. I didn't like it. The security guard actually followed us when we were shopping. He was looking at us in a strange way. Did he think we were going steal something? I don't know what he was thinking. . . . It's a Mexican store and we are Mexican, but still he looked at us in a suspicious way, you know, I did not like that at all. I almost went to the manager."

In this statement Berta suggested that the security guard's suspicion was caused by her ethnicity, underscoring the everyday racism that people of color experience and pointing out the value of welcoming spaces. During my numerous visits in local ethnic shops, I observed interactions between consumers and food retail workers that exposed the significance of these spaces in creating a sense of belonging. These relationships were more than simple economic transactions, they engaged people in multiple ways, including via smells and sounds, reinforcing a sense of community and reminding them of a home left behind. In other words, these small businesses are helpful in addressing the cultural, social, and emotional aspects of food insecurity associated with the loss of agency and the inability to fulfill aspirations related to tradition, ethnic identity, or domesticity.

Ethnic entrepreneurs are very much aware of the crucial role they play in the everyday life of residents, especially co-ethnics, and view it as a way to compete with larger chain stores. Many describe their businesses using terms such as *community* and *family*. Natalia, who owns a Mexican store in City Heights, explained: "[My business] is a community. I know a lot of people here because I've been here fourteen years, so they know me and I know them, but yeah, it's like family, you know?" Good service and personal relationships with customers are business strategies that keep them afloat in a competitive environment. I asked Alfonso, the manager of small Mexican grocery store in City Heights, whether he was concerned by competition from El Super—the new supermarket that had just opened in the neighborhood. He was not worried: "My customers come here because of what we offer. We have the products they want and we treat them like family." This perception was echoed by Zhao, the owner of a Chinese grocery store: "We have loyal customers who have been coming to our store for years. They prefer shopping here than at the supermarket because of the unique products we sell and the service we provide. That's what we are known for and that's why they come. They might go to the supermarket for things like milk and toilet paper, but they'll always come to us for poultry and vegetables."

A large proportion of food retailers in City Heights, Barrio Logan, and Southeastern San Diego accept EBT. Not only does this help residents eligible for public assistance programs, but it also supports participating businesses by expanding the community's purchasing power. This is an important and rarely acknowledged benefit of these programs: the indirect subsidy to retailers and the potential multiplier effect on local spending. Store managers acknowledged that EBT represents a significant source of income for their business. Yet they are less likely to qualify than larger supermarkets, given requirements in terms of refrigeration and availability of produce, meat, and dairy. Indeed, several managers had seen their application denied by the USDA.

Ethnic markets play an important role in the fight against food insecurity, a role that could be expanded with greater public support in the form of small business loans, technical assistance, and subsidies. To deserve such support, however, ethnic markets must contend with the racial stigma of poor food selection and inflated prices. In addition, they must also shed the perception that they are sites of racial tensions and potential criminal activity. For example, conflicts between Black residents and Korean owners of convenience and liquor stores in South Los Angeles intensified during the 1992 unrest. These racial tensions, which need to be contextualized within food apartheid, appear to have been exaggerated by the media inclined to portray low-income neighborhoods as dysfunctional and crime-ridden.[53] In San Diego, Chaldean store owners, who have built an ethnic niche by investing in convenience stores in low-income neighborhoods (discussed in chapter 3), have drawn similar attention and even been the target of hate crimes.[54]

These tensions may reflect resentment against racialized "middleman minorities"—whether Jewish, Arab, or East Asian—as illustrated by a negative comments made against "Middle Eastern [businesses] taking over the neighborhood." The majority of residents, however, were grateful for these Chaldean-owned shops. Indeed, ethnic entrepreneurs in general try to serve all residents, creating multiethnic shops where Aleppo and dried Guajillo peppers can be found on the same shelf. For example, Yussef—an Iraqi refugee who became a US citizen—recently purchased a convenience store in City Heights from its previous Mexican American owner. He decided to keep the store's old name and is learning about Mexican staples. As he put it: "We are in this together." Like Koreans in Los Angeles, Chaldeans in San Diego may be unfairly blamed for a historical disinvestment and systemic neglect they did not cause but used as an opportunity to make a living in an economy where they faced many closed doors.

Informal Practices of Social Reproduction

Social reproduction—the caring, emotional, and physical labor of reproducing bodies, households, communities, and societies, which includes food provisioning—often takes place in hybrid spaces between public and private, market and home, paid and unpaid labor.[55] In low-income neighborhoods, where food apartheid means that people's needs are not fully met by formal retailers, residents often turn to the informal economy to obtain food. Recent research in City Heights reveals that nine out of ten residents purchase food outside of the regulated formal economy either always or sometimes.[56] Furthermore, 85 percent of respondents claimed to purchase their groceries within walking distance from their home, underscoring the importance of local providers. Although such data are not available for other San Diego neighborhoods, my observations in Barrio Logan and Southeastern San Diego suggest the existence of a lively informal food economy. Street vendors, in particular, provide a wide range of foods, including fruits and vegetables, prepared food like hot dogs, tamales, and tacos, and snacks such as frozen treats, churros, and tostilocos. Some use mobile carts to access underserved areas. Others set up stands in parking lots and parks. Most are immigrants who come from countries where street vending is much more common than in the United States.

Not only do these informal food businesses generate income (see chapter 3), but they also serve an important role in improving access to food, activating the streets, and enhancing the neighborhood's foodscape. These activities can be interpreted as immigrants claiming urban space and exercising their "right to the city." By avoiding or bending existing rules, informal vendors provide services that would otherwise not be available. For example, in City Heights street vendors set up shop on the weekends in the back of their cars and along the sidewalk near soccer fields used by the local youth league. There I met Alma who was buying a tamale and a drink for her son, whose team had just won their game. She explained:

> This is like Mexico. I love it! People hang out, sit together, catch up
> with friends, watch their kids play, eat some food. . . . The vendors
> help make the place interesting and safe for families. People come
> just to eat something, like hot dogs, tamales, elotes, fruits. It's not

very expensive and they don't have to cook. On weeknights, it's very different here. It's quiet. But on weekends, people come out, grandparents, aunts and uncles, big kids, little kids. . . . It really makes me appreciate my neighborhood. It's different, but it reminds me of my hometown.

Yet in many places street vendors face the risk of being fined and having their supplies and equipment confiscated for not having proper permits and licenses. Immigrant and labor advocates in California have been fighting to decriminalize street vending and reform the permitting process to encourage entrepreneurship, resulting in the 2018 Safe Sidewalk Vending Act. The state law dismisses and prohibits criminal charges against street vendors violating local ordinances and replaces those with administrative fees. However, under certain circumstances cities may choose to continue regulating street vending with their own ordinances. For example, they may ban vending in high traffic areas or demand that vendors obtain a health certificate, food handler card, and seller's permit. San Diego is considering such restrictions in an attempt "to put some order to a surge of street vendors" in response to complaints by local businesses that "vendors illegally dump trash, don't handle food hygienically and block access to restrooms, emergency lanes or mass transit."[57] Thus efforts to decriminalize street vending have led to a backlash that reproduces negative stigma around informal activities. Meanwhile, gourmet food trucks, food festivals, and public markets, which serve a higher-income clientele and fit the creative city model, are encouraged in San Diego and numerous cities across the United States.[58] Such disparate treatment reflects policymakers' racial biases against immigrant street vendors—yet another threat to social reproduction.

A similarly ambivalent attitude pervades conversations about so-called cottage food operations that market "nonhazardous" food prepared at home, such as jam, honey, baked goods, chocolate, salsas, and so on. This too is now regulated by recent state laws such as the 2013 California Cottage Food Operation law (AB1616) and the 2019 Microenterprise Home Kitchen Operations law (AB 626). Both laws impose a series of restrictions on types of food, number of employees, points of sale, training, labeling, storage, sanitations, inspections, maximum income, and so forth. They also leave room for counties and cities to authorize operations and therefore maintain control over producers. For instance, AB 626 has not yet been authorized in San Diego County, and only a few permits have been granted under AB1616. Although these laws were theoretically adopted to encourage community-based food production, the requirements to legalize home-based food operations are so strict they will unlikely help formalize informal immigrant food businesses, especially those run by undocumented immigrants. Here too racial biases about immigrants' home kitchens as unsanitary and unsafe limits their prospect. The criminalization of immigrant food survival strategies is a significant obstacle to both immigrant livelihoods and community food security.

Alternative Food Practices

With the help of community-based organizations, other informal food practices have become more acceptable to policymakers and urban planners. These include urban agriculture projects and farmers' markets, which represent the pillars of the so-called alternative food movement. Nowhere in San Diego are these efforts more visible than in City Heights, where philanthropic organizations and nonprofits have invested significant resources in transforming the food environment. The International Rescue Committee (IRC)—a refugee resettlement agency that operates in City Heights and several other locations across the United States—has been keen to develop urban agriculture as a platform for the integration of refugees. To this end, the IRC established New Roots Community Farm and a weekly farmers' market where growers can sell their produce and residents can use EBT to purchase it. These two programs have been so successful that First Lady Michelle Obama chose New Roots as a site to launch her Let's Move! campaign in 2010.

Alternative food projects have historically been associated with grass-roots organizing by immigrants and people of color and inspired by social and environmental justice agendas critical of the neoliberal, capitalist, and racist agrifood system.[59] Nonetheless, there is now ample research evidence that, more often than not, so-called "alternative" food initiatives serve the interests of white and affluent urbanites who have become increasingly interested in growing their own food, purchasing locally grown produce, cooking, curing, fermenting, baking, and brewing at home, and interacting with farmers and other like-minded individuals.[60] Once considered backward and reserved to low-income immigrants who could not afford to buy modern processed food, these activities are now a symbol of taste and a means of social distinction. As a result, they have become more common in middle-class areas where foodies reside and appear to play a role in speeding gentrification and displacement.[61]

Local governments have begun to warm up to alternative food projects as well, seeing their potential to revitalize neighborhoods while seemingly addressing food insecurity and climate change concerns without incurring much direct expenditure. For some, this reflects a neoliberalization of urban policy whereby individual and communities must step in to fill gaps left by a crumbling social welfare system.[62] Through these recent reframing of local food initiatives, their ethnic origins and radical roots have been diluted, if not erased. As a result, the type of projects advocated by many nonprofits no longer resonate with residents of the neighborhoods they wish to serve.

Rather than taking sides and assuming that urban agriculture is either liberating or reproducing the inequalities underlying food insecurity among immigrants and people of color, I suggest that we consider each project on its own. Looking at particular gardens or farmers' markets as "projects" draws attention to how places, people, and things come together to shape them.[63] Although all organizations operate in a structural context where race, class, and gender influence their ability to control land, capital, labor, and ultimately food, some adopt a more radical agenda that tackles these constraints head-on while others operate within these constraints to simply increase access to food. This is reflected in the mission, membership, and activities of each organization and underlies the distinction made earlier between food sovereignty and food security agendas.

For example, the New Roots Community Farm encourages ethnic entrepreneurship as a path to social and economic integration. The program is run by the IRC and has benefited from various sources of funding, including the USDA, that influence its top-down governance and explain its mostly apolitical stance. As a successful social enterprise, the IRC has replicated its model in other refugee resettlement locations with the goal of "developing and refining innovative business and marketing models for urban farming and micro-enterprises that can be adopted by many ethnic immigrant communities as well as lower-income residents in urban communities."[64] Most of the eighty-five plots are cultivated by Somali-Bantu refugees, many of whom were farmers in their home country. Long-time City Heights residents, including Latinxs and Asians, do not feel welcome at the garden, and some even resent the attention it has received. According to Belinda, whom I interviewed in front of a small grocery store: "There are thousands of people in City Heights who would love to grow their own food. Everybody always talks about New Roots, New Roots, New Roots. . . . Politicians come and give speeches, volunteers, students, many people. That's great, but it doesn't help us if we can't get a spot there. We need gardens for everybody, not just refugees."

In contrast, Mount Hope Community Garden is run by Project New Village, a grassroots nonprofit that aims at redressing the deep structural inequalities that have historically disenfranchised Southeastern San Diego. The garden is part of the nonprofit's People's Produce Project, which uses food as a way to energize and connect people in the neighborhood. Their agenda is clearly antiracist and inclusive. While most of the regular growers are Black, other neighborhood residents help with the collective beds, participate in volunteer days, and stop by for the weekly produce sales. Recently, however, the city put the garden's land for sale, canceling its lease agreement with Project New Village and threatening the whole operation. This threat, reflecting historical structural inequalities in land ownership that have kept people of color away from farming, has catalyzed a grassroots effort to purchase the land and create a community food hub known as the Good Food District. The project centers around the garden and adds a small cooperative food store, a community kitchen, a classroom, and a few affordable housing units for seniors. The needs of local residents, as growers, entrepreneurs, consumers, and learners shape the development of the Good Food District, which is owned in a community trust.

Despite the popularity of urban agriculture projects, they represent a minimal source of food for urban residents. There are 5 community gardens in City Heights (approximately 150 plots), 4 in Southeastern San Diego (about 75 plots), and just one small herb garden in Barrio Logan where the land is both scarce and likely to be contaminated by industrial pollutants. A quick and rough calculation, using high-yield estimates of about 1.3 pounds of produce per square foot, indicates that these ten gardens generate about 15,000 pounds of food per year—or less than 0.3 pound per poor resident.[65] Of course, to those involved in gardening, this represents a significant source of food and possibly income, as well as a way to stay active, spend time outdoors, and connect with neighbors. Nevertheless, without a concerted effort to expand urban agriculture by supporting growers and increasing access to land, it is unlikely that it will do much to alleviate rampant food insecurity among residents.

In addition, these projects must also contend with the fact that many people of color, especially immigrants, are reluctant to grow food, partly because of a lack of time due to employment constraints but also because of the trauma linked to the historical oppression of people of color in farm labor. Thus, for urban agriculture to become a path to food security, a number of structural constraints and related cultural barriers must be addressed.

URBAN POLITICAL ECOLOGY OF THE BODY

By "placing" hungry bodies and the biopolitical processes leading to food insecurity within urban neighborhoods, I have developed an urban political ecology of the body in which the city and its uneven foodscape feature prominently. In Barrio Logan, City Heights, and Southeastern San Diego, food apartheid is the background for the "life work" of social reproduction, causing a considerable amount of stress for residents. In a context where food access is limited and assistance programs are under constant attack, food-insecure people have had to devise strategies to obtain food and create their own food geographies. How people navigate food apartheid is intimately tied to identities, particularly immigrant status, ethnicity, and gender that shape the significance of food in everyday life. It is also grounded in the communities and places where immigrants and people of color live and seek to improve their everyday lives by opening shops and restaurants, selling food in the street, cooking for others, and growing produce against many odds.

Indeed, for the majority of Barrio Logan, City Heights, and Southeastern San Diego's residents, food-provisioning strategies entail patronizing local businesses that are typically small and independent, and ethnic markets and restaurants where they are more likely to experience senses of community, familiarity, and belonging. They also involve reciprocal and intergenerational relationships where food, recipes, and resources are shared within families and amongst neighbors. Often they rely on informal economies, such as street vending and home kitchen operations. Occasionally it means visiting a food pantry or soup kitchen. For a few residents, such strategies also encompass growing food in community gardens, in backyards, or on windowsills. These practices, especially when engaging the broader community, may be interpreted as forms of food sovereignty. Organizing street vendors, supporting urban agriculture, strengthening ethnic businesses, and creating collective food hubs are meaningful ways in which residents gain more control over their food.

Similar practices of self-reliance are described in Reese's *Black Food Geographies*, underscoring the significance of place-making in refusing the constraints of food apartheid.[66] Yet it is sobering to realize that the ethnic foodscape created and tended to address food insecurity is now attracting the attention of foodies. This recent and seemingly sudden interest of consumers, investors, and philanthropies in the "quaint" and "authentic" foodscape of immigrant and ethnic neighborhoods is causing displacement that once again threatens the lives of immigrants. I turn my attention to these neighborhood changes in chapters 5 and 6.

5

"Best for Foodies"

Gastrodevelopment and the Urban Food Machine

"**C**ITY HEIGHTS IS on the way up. . . . It is not quite North Park yet. . . . It will be the next Little Italy within ten years," declared the *San Diego Reader* in 2018.[1] Less than a year later, *San Diego Magazine* confirmed that "the neighborhood is more than likely the next boom."[2] Similarly, such local sources as *San Diego City Beat*, *The Coast News*, and *The Sun* have reported on an ongoing "renaissance" in Barrio Logan—one of "San Diego's next hot neighborhood[s]."[3] In Southeastern San Diego, observers from the *Union Tribune* cautiously foresee imminent change, while the *San Diego Real Estate Hunters* points to Encanto, one of its smaller neighborhoods, as a "great place to live."[4] These frequently echoed predictions of a "bright future" for some of San Diego's poorest urban neighborhoods are almost always attributed to their cultural diversity and "vibrant food scene." In Barrio Logan, "gallivanting gallery goers come for the art and stay for the craft beer, coffee, record stores, lively music and Mexican street food."[5] In City Heights, "the mix of food options is endless."[6] In Southeastern, "excellent ethnic food is easy to come by, as are delicacies from the American South."[7]

Such praises are somewhat surprising. For decades, news stories about City Heights, Barrio Logan, and Southeastern San Diego had been dominated by crime, homelessness, dog fights, and gang violence. For example, in the early 1990s, in an article titled "The Most Dangerous Part of San Diego," the *San Diego Reader* reported that "135 San Diegans were murdered in 1990. More than 100 of those deaths occurred south of Interstate 8 and were concentrated in the neighborhoods such as Barrio Logan, Southeast San Diego, City Heights, and the border area."[8] More recently, the same magazine published a "feature story" titled "City Heights Hell" in which an anonymous author described their experience growing up in the neighborhood they call "Shitty Heights." After white people left, the author wrote, "their houses were inherited by banks who rented the properties to the most despicable swine imaginable: drug dealers, molesters, abusers, prostitutes, cockfighting rooster- and pit-bull breeders, and overexcessive beer-drinking college students, just to give you an idea."[9] The place stigma promoted by this type of story is deeply racialized; it is people of color and immigrants who have "destroyed" these neighborhoods with their presumably dysfunctional lifestyle and inferior culture. Portraying urban areas as "boiling cauldrons of social decadence, moral dissipation, and national debility" perpetuates destitution and marginality by shifting our gaze away from the structural causes underlying divestment in these places.[10]

Today, in sharp contrast, cultural elites, city officials, real estate agents, and visitors are excitedly praising the authenticity of these neighborhoods' food scenes, changing the image of these places and giving them growing cultural cachet as "best for foodies" destinations. To be sure, the old narrative has not gone away entirely, but it is being countered by a new one in which food features prominently. A search for City Heights on the *San Diego Reader* website brought up 104 articles published during the past five years, between 2015 and 2019. Among these, twenty-five articles were devoted to food, including articles on Vietnamese pho and banh mi; Mexican barbacoa, birria de chivo, and ceviche; Somali odka and canjeero; Cambodian nom pang and jok; Chinese BBQ pork ribs and egg flower soup; Colombian antojitos as well as kale and radishes grown by African refugees for the City Heights farmers' market. Indeed, every single food story returned by my search focused on what is typically understood as "ethnic" food. These articles were clearly written for a broad audience, encouraging adventurous visitors and foodies—primarily affluent, educated, and white people with avid interests in food—to venture into previously disparaged neighborhoods in search of authenticity. How do we reconcile these emerging stories with the negative stigma that for decades has plagued these places? What explains this sudden interest in ethnic foodscapes? Does the "urban grittiness" of City Heights, Barrio Logan, and Southeastern San Diego contribute to their appeal?

The cosmopolitan foodscape is socially and spatially produced out of the ethnic foodscape, both materially (via urban planning and capital flows) and discursively (through new narratives about food and place). Various actors, including nonresident entrepreneurs, investors, policymakers, and consumers, play a central role in this transformation. This chapter develops the idea of "urban food machine" as a key driver of "gastrodevelopment." Influenced by the concept of "urban growth machine," this idea highlights to role of urban elites and managers in creating cosmopolitan foodscapes that are conducive to growth, rising property values, and gentrification.[11] The chapter describes how public, private, and nonprofit actors are regulating, shaping, and advertising the foodscapes of Barrio Logan, City Heights, and Southeastern San Diego.

GASTRODEVELOPMENT AND
THE URBAN FOOD MACHINE

In the 1970s, Harvey Molotch revolutionized the way urbanists look at the city by describing it as a "growth machine." For him, the city is "the areal expression of the interests of some land-based elite" for whom "the desire for growth provides the key operative motivation toward consensus."[12] Such elite is composed of local government officials, business coalitions, realtors, bankers, universities, utility companies, newspapers, and sports franchises—all of whom benefit directly or indirectly from rising population density, which increases land values, retail activity, and tax revenues. This "growth coalition" works together to facilitate investment, encourage development, and spread the idea that market-led growth is a public good.[13] As growth takes place, their wealth rises, making them increasingly powerful in shaping the future of the city by dismissing and suppressing alternative voices and more equitable models of prosperity. Thus, for Molotch, addressing the question of "who rules cities?" also sheds light on such distributive questions as "for whom?" and "for what?"

Fundamental changes have affected cities since the 1970s, including increased globalization of the economy, deindustrialization of the workforce, diversification of the population, further dismantling of the welfare state, and neoliberalization of governance. Despite these dramatic changes, urban scholars have continued to draw inspiration from Molotch's growth machine thesis. Of course there are disagreements, but most agree that urban coalitions have played a decisive role in shaping cities by presenting and creating a positive image of urban life.[14] This idea forms the basis of what became the New Urban Politics—a body of work emphasizing the increasingly entrepreneurial nature of urban governance and the role of new (often private) actors in promoting but also policing the city.[15] Place-branding projects that market neighborhoods as cultural and entertainment destinations and spaces of consumption and leisure have become the hallmark of new urban politics. Not only do waterfront districts, festival marketplaces, outdoor shopping promenades, and other venues need to be physically revamped or built, they also need to be symbolically branded as desirable as well as policed into safe, clean, and attractive— meaning white—spaces. The growing involvement of the private sector in shaping, managing, and surveilling cities makes the "for whom?" question especially relevant, with many commenting on the postdemocratic and exclusionary nature of contemporary cities and the immanent loss of public space.[16]

Today, in the urban contexts of postindustrialism, where culture has become a primary source of profit, and postmodernism, where individual experiences and lifestyles increasingly form the basis of identity, food has turned out to be an incredibly valuable and meaningful commodity. Beyond biological sustenance, food confers eaters with an opportunity to distinguish themselves, to express their identities, and to experience a sense of belonging. An interesting, exciting, and diverse food scene provides urbanites a place for self-expression, distinction, and social encounters. According to Richard Florida, food is also one of the urban amenities that make a city attractive to the creative class—the highly educated scientists, bohemians, artists, technicians, and professionals who presumably fuel the growth of cities with their talent and innovative spirit.[17] Inspired by this idea, urban elites around the world have been promoting what I call *gastro-development*, actively shaping their city's food scene in an effort to attract the creative class. A sort of "food machine" has been set into motion to draw innovative people and entice investors to particular neighborhoods through food. The ultimate goal of this food machine, however, is not to support the food industry or feed urban masses but to promote urban growth and capital accumulation.

Food has the great advantage of appearing mundane and apolitical; people of all political persuasions, ethnicities, and social classes presumably enjoy a good meal. At a superficial level, food has the potential to unite people who may otherwise have different interests.[18] For instance, a new food hall, street food festival, or rooftop garden can make a housing development project more palatable to those concerned with its impact on the community and the environment. In other words, community stakeholders often find consensus around food-related projects. Those who oppose or critique gastrodevelopment are portrayed as nonsensical, careless, and irrational. The power of the food machine is as much in the profits it generates as in the ideology it reproduces—a hegemonic ideology that legitimizes urban growth and reinforces the neoliberal model of urban governance that is based on municipal entrepreneurship, public-private partnerships, privatization of public space, and devolution of state functions onto individuals and communities.[19] Indeed, critical observers have pointed out the neoliberal nature of local food politics, even within the so-called alternative food movement.[20]

Under the guise of sustainability, community-building, workforce development, and place-making, urban leaders promote gastrodevelopment and endorse a variety of food projects that are redirecting flows of capital and reshaping the city. Because food and place are so intimately intertwined, this process has important territorial ramifications. On the one hand, specific places—such as old warehouses, public parks, historic neighborhoods, and pedestrian areas—provide attractive settings for food projects and contribute to a desirable dining experience. On the other hand, new food establishments elevate the cultural status of certain places that become exciting destinations. The aesthetic of many ethnic neighborhoods and their typically undervalued real estate market make them ideal candidates for such projects. Food becomes a tool for boosterism, with local media, government agencies, real estate brokers, community-based organizations, and nonprofits unexpectedly joining forces to produce cosmopolitan foodscapes and transform ethnic neighborhoods, redrawing the lines of food apartheid with consequences for the well-being of long-time residents.

THE PRODUCTION OF COSMOPOLITAN FOODSCAPES

Building a cosmopolitan food scene is a political place-based project whose nature is defined by the various actors involved. It requires both material investments in buildings, kitchens, and other spaces as well as discursive investments in reframing the narratives and imaginaries surrounding these places. The latter is especially important for food, which engages multiple senses. Together, the following actors play a central role in this project of gastrodevelopment: local governments, public-private partnerships, local media, and the real estate industry.

Local Governments

Municipal governments and their agencies are the most powerful public actors involved in planning and regulating the city. They make decisions regarding land use, grant permits, facilitate development through land acquisition, police the activities of residents, and provide public services. As urban governance moved from a managerial to an entrepreneurial model, however, the role of municipal governments switched from service provider to urban booster and facilitator of private investments.[21] San Diego has not been immune to this trend, embracing a mantra of public-private partnership and the idea of becoming America's finest creative city.[22]

In recent years, various city agencies have become increasingly involved in promoting lifestyle amenities believed to attract investors and an educated workforce, including the so-called "creative class."[23] More and more, such amenities include food districts, walkable neighborhoods with cafés and restaurants, farmers' markets, and street food festivals, which are now promoted in urban development projects and community plans as a way to brand cities and neighborhoods—a trend illustrative of the process of gastrodevelopment. Recent community plans pertaining to the three study neighborhoods have begun paying attention to food. In the context of promoting "mixed-use," "main street," and "pedestrian-oriented" development, food places and events (including food truck gathering, community gardens, and farmers' markets) are identified as playing a key role in improving access to healthy food, strengthening community, and creating economic opportunities. For instance, the *Mid-City Communities Plan* that encompasses City Heights suggests that "a center of ethnically oriented commercial activities should be encouraged within an 'International Marketplace' bounded by El Cajon Boulevard and University Avenue at Fairmount Avenue and 43rd Street. In addition to restaurants and retail outlets, small- to medium-scale food processing and craft-oriented manufacturing facilities should also be accommodated. Special regulations should be considered to accommodate cultural needs, such as in the processing and sales of food products."[24] Today this area is home to what has come to be known as Little Saigon and Little Mogadishu.

In 2013 a revised community plan was submitted by Barrio Logan residents and approved by the San Diego City Council. However, it was rescinded in 2014 by a citywide ballot challenge financed by industry organizations opposing land-use changes requiring a buffer between heavy industries and residences. The plan paid significant attention to family-owned restaurants that contribute to the character of the neighborhood, providing a historical list of establishments and a number of pictures. One of the main elements of the plan was a public market in the Community Village Area "planned to be a vibrant pedestrian neighborhood with enhanced connectivity that reflects the types of public spaces, structures, public art, connections, and land uses that are influenced by Latino culture."[25] Food was at the core of the public market, and the plan allowed for the following list of uses on nearby parcels: "farmers' markets, retail sales fresh and prepared foods and cooking related products, secondary food manufacturing, restaurants, cafes and coffee shops with outdoor seating, community gardens, certified kitchens, and community event space."[26]

Similarly, the 2015 *Southeastern San Diego Plan* envisioned its main commercial corridors to become "active spines in the neighborhood" with space for restaurants and retail shops serving the needs of the community. In addition, the plan also "supports local agriculture, farmers' markets, and eating locally-grown food."[27] In short, food has become part of the city's urban agenda. Yet the public resources allocated to achieving the priorities defined in community plans are extremely limited. As a result, public-benefit agencies, nonprofits, and private groups have stepped in.

Public-Private Partnerships

In San Diego, place-branding efforts, including those that rely on food, are often undertaken by so-called public benefit organizations, which embody the idea of public-private partnership. The most common forms are business improvement districts (BIDs) and maintenance assessment districts (MADs). Such organizations emerged in the 1980s as powerful actors in urban development in North American cities. Incorporated as nonprofit public benefit corporations and presumably organized to serve the general public, such organizations are typically created (or at least sanctioned) by the state and receive a significant share of funding from voter-approved special property assessments imposed on local residents and businesses. However, they do not have the same level of accountability and transparency as state agencies. Indeed, this form of financing has been criticized by urban scholars for privatizing public services by effectively giving private entities control over public resources and spaces.[28] More-over, they have been accused of contributing to urban inequality by linking development projects to local resources and devolving responsibility for services onto local communities.[29]

Business improvement districts and maintenance assessment districts are actively involved in each of the neighborhoods under consideration. Among other things, their activities include promoting existing food busi-nesses such as restaurants, advertising and hosting food-related events like street fairs and farmers' markets, and supporting other local initiatives. The capacity and mission of these organizations vary greatly, reflecting dispari-ties in property tax bases, additional resources, membership composition, and community participation. For instance, in the neighborhoods of Little Italy and North Park most activities are controlled by a single powerful agency that has come to dominate community development with the pri-mary goal of supporting local businesses and increasing property values. In other neighborhoods, such as City Heights, Barrio Logan, and Southeastern San Diego, a number of public benefit organizations are involved in shaping and branding the foodscape. However, their funding is lower and less stable, limiting their capacity to generate long-term change.

In North Park most of the food-driven development activities are sponsored by North Park Main Street (NPMS)—an organization formed in 1996 to administer the BID created by the City of San Diego in 1985. It is affiliated with the Main Street program of the National Trust for Historic Preservation. In 2016 residents voted to create a new property and business improvement district (PBID), which further increased NPMS's budget for landscaping, street cleaning, and seasonal decoration. From the very beginning, NPMS concentrated their efforts into creating a cosmopolitan foodscape. One of the main projects that helped put the neighborhood on the map is Ray at Night—a monthly art, music, and food event that was launched in 2001 on Ray Street, where several art studios and galleries were located at the time. Over the years, Ray at Night expanded to include a beer garden and many food vendors, often associated with local restaurants. The Thursday Farmers' Market has also drawn large crowds of locals for almost fifteen years. Today, NPMS continues to market the neighborhood as a destination for foodies and beer lovers:

> From world class restaurants to simple taco stands and everything in between . . . North Park is home to countless restaurants, cafes, coffee shops, breweries, tasting rooms, and more. What makes North Park a perfect place to enjoy a meal is the walkability of the neighborhood. Within a short walk you can shop at our Thursday Farmers Market, enjoy happy hour and a meal, grab a delicious craft beer, then head out for a nightcap. Your food and beverage options are nearly endless, and offered by some of the best restaurants, bars, and breweries in town.[30]

The dramatic rise in property values in North Park suggests that this entrepreneurial model has succeeded in attracting affluent residents and businesses and raising the financial resources at North Park Main Street's disposal for future projects. By the mid-2000s, however, most of the neighborhood had become unaffordable to many of its longtime residents, who began to relocate elsewhere.

The history of redevelopment in Little Italy follows a very similar trajectory. Here too, a single powerful organization controls most projects. Like NPMS, the Little Italy Association (LIA) was created in 1996 to promote the revitalization of the neighborhood. It too is financed by a business improvement district, along with a maintenance assessment district and a parking district, all of which generate revenue for the purpose of improving the business environment and property values in Little Italy. Food has been an essential component of the LIA's efforts to reinvent Little Italy into a "hip and historic neighborhood." More than half of the area's businesses are restaurants and the weekly farmers' market—the Mercato—is one of the largest in the city. In its early years, the association built up the Italian identity of the neighborhood, which was home to many traditional Italian American restaurants. Today, however, the foodscape is much more eclectic with more than a hundred restaurants lining up its two main streets, India and Kettner.

The other study neighborhoods in this book also have public benefit organizations involved in redevelopment efforts that increasingly include food-related projects. This includes The Boulevard in City Heights, the Diamond District in Southeastern, and the Barrio Logan Association. All three organizations have supported food truck gathering, street festivals, and other food-related events. By far the most successful, the monthly Barrio Art Crawl, is hosted by the Barrio Logan Association, financed by the Barrio Logan maintenance assessment district. It draws large numbers of visitors to the area with food, craft beer, music, and art.

These areas are also home to community development corporations (CDCs), such as the City Heights CDC and the Greater Logan Heights CDC, which have been created specifically to promote economic development in "blighted" areas with support from federal programs such as community development block grants (CDBGs). Although the primary focus of CDCs has been affordable housing, many have diversified their community development activities into workforce development, social services, and support of local businesses. Perhaps not surprisingly, this includes food businesses. For example, following the lead of other neighborhoods, the City Heights CDC hosted its first Annual City Heights Street Food Festival in September 2019 to "get people together around tables and food stalls to celebrate another year of community building."[31] In the words of the event organizers, street food is "a delicious, convenient, affordable community builder. . . . [It] does far more than fill bellies. Street food gets people outside, into the community, together." This inaugural festival adds to a growing list of events in the community, including the new Lantern Festival, New Year Lunar Festival, African Restaurant Week, Brazil Carnival, and Dia de Los Muertos, in which food shines a new light on the neighborhood.

Another domain where public-private partnerships have been at the forefront of promoting San Diego's food scene is tourism—San Diego's second largest industry after defense. With travelers increasingly interested in local food and culinary adventures, marketing the unique characteristics of San Diego's food culture has become increasingly important. Many tourists are turning away from chain restaurants and corporate hotels, instead seeking unique local experiences. To address this trend, the San Diego Tourism Authority—the region's most powerful mutual benefit nonprofit organization—has embarked on a neighborhood marketing campaign leveraging special assessment funds and hotel tax revenues. Recently, despite historical neglect of environmental and social issues in Barrio Logan by the city, the San Diego Tourism Authority began promoting Barrio Logan as a foodie destination:

> Fortunately for hungry visitors, Barrio Logan is where you'll find the real deal in Mexican food. In addition to the landmark Las Cuatro Milpas, where the line for the homemade tortillas can snake down the block, there's also the San Diego Taco Company, which shares space with the Border X Brewery. At the La Fachada taco shop, you'll find a parking lot grill heaped with hot chili peppers. Inside, you can get beef tongue tacos and pork gorditas that will rival anything you can get south of the border. For dessert, head to Tocumbo for homemade Mexican paleta (ice pops). Look for flavors like mango and chili, and pair them with thirst-quenching agua frescas.[32]

Indeed, Barrio Logan, City Heights, and Southeastern San Diego all appear on the Tourism Authority's list of San Diego's Nine Art Districts (along with North and South Park). This is a significant departure from the past, when tourists were typically discouraged from visiting these neighborhoods and mostly confined to downtown San Diego and the affluent coastal areas. To be sure, most advertising continues to be directed to downtown and the expanding convention center. Yet the recent shift of attention to surrounding communities reveals predictions of economic growth and significant potential returns on investment in these areas.

Local Media

Articles in lifestyle and travel magazines contribute to geographic imaginaries of foodscapes with curated pictures and exaggerated claims by food and cultural experts. Such magazines include *Sunset, San Diego Magazine,* and *Edible San Diego* that often feature articles about neighborhoods worth visiting, highlighting "best for foodies" destinations, and providing restaurant and boutique recommendations. The *San Diego Union Tribune* and other local newspapers also publish restaurant reviews and stories about particular neighborhoods that draw attention to their food scene. These publications are primarily financed through advertising and often represent the interests of local real estate, tourism, and restaurant industries.

For example, in 2015, *San Diego Magazine* published a neighborhood guide of City Heights, which it described as a "central urban nabe [that] lays claim to authentic international eats, along with live music venues, craft beer, coffee, and outdoor fun."[33] The article contained several ethnic restaurant recommendations, including one for Minh Ky with the following suggestion: "Don't let the exterior fool you; inside this hole-in-the-wall you'll find authentic Chinese-Vietnamese cuisine, including noodle soups and the much-loved roasted duck." More recently, the magazine's home buyer's guide identified City Heights as one of five "up-and-coming neighborhoods" in San Diego.[34] Again, it attributed the neighborhood's popularity to its population diversity and eclectic "culinary landscape" where "restaurants like Phó Hòa, Minh Ky, and Red Sea Ethiopian have become institutions, and Fair@44 is a thriving international food and flea market that convenes every Wednesday." The article also provided links to a concert venue, farmers' market, and beekeeping class. The themes of diversity and authenticity, which are particularly appealing to cosmopolitan eaters (see chapter 6), are recurring across reviews.

In recent years, we have witnessed the growth of online media specializing in restaurant reviews. Unlike printed guidebooks, online reviews are updated much more regularly, with new eateries surfacing and disappearing from top-rated lists quickly. For instance, *Eater, The Infatuation, Time-Out, Thrillist,* and *Zagat* provide regularly updated rankings and "best of" lists for specific cities in the United States and abroad. These lists and reviews are produced by cultural elites, who make a living by promoting consumption and being able to identify trends ahead of others. Because these websites are national and occasionally international platforms, top-rated places are becoming increasingly similar across cities, reflecting almost identical cosmopolitan aesthetics of authenticity, diversity, democracy, and—paradoxically—localism.

For example, in "Where to Eat and Drink in San Diego," *The Infatuation* recommends Corazón de Torta, a taco truck operating in Sherman Heights at the western edge of Southeastern San Diego, near Barrio Logan, and Super Cocina, a cafeteria-style Mexican restaurant in City Heights.[35] The remaining twenty restaurants on the list are located throughout the county and include a mix of upscale establishments such as Addison and Born & Raised and more casual eateries like The Crack Shack, Cantina Mayahuel, and Tita's Kitchenette. Writers establish their cultural literacy by emphasizing authenticity, multiculturalism, and democracy, combining a variety of ethnic restaurants as well as highbrow and lowbrow food. Unlike less educated consumers, they are able to tell the difference between generic Mexican food and the authentic or regional versions. For instance, Super Cocina stands out among other restaurants because of its classic dishes: "There are hundreds of Mexican restaurants across San Diego that serve everything from tacos to fajitas. But if you're looking for classic Mexican stews and platters, Super Cocina is the spot to check out. This homey cafeteria-style restaurant in City Heights serves a rotating list of specialty dishes, like chicken in cilantro sauce and pozole."[36]

Similarly, Corazón de Torta is appreciated because of its unique and authentic Tijuana-style food: "This taco truck makes some of the best Tijuana-style tacos and tortas this side of, well, Tijuana. . . . The taco and torta selection is always rotating, but make sure to try the guajillo short rib, cauliflower mole, and chipotle meatball if they're available."[37] Other websites offer similarly curated lists of recommendations that typically feature at least one or two ethnic restaurants from one or more of the three neighborhoods studied in this book, along with a series of presumably more upscale eateries in traditional dining destinations downtown or along the coast. Map 5.1 shows the location of restaurants included in the 2019 top lists from *Eater, The Infatuation, TimeOut, Thrillist,* and *Zagat* and the result of kernel density analysis used to identify culinary "hot spots" in the region.[38]

A few popular establishments—such as Addison, Trust, Wrench and Rodent, Menya Ultra, Juniper and Ivy, Kindred, Born and Raised, and Campfire—were featured on at least three lists, suggesting a sort of consensus among food experts regarding the best restaurants in the region. With the exception of a few small hot spots in Oceanside/Carlsbad, La Jolla, and Kearny Mesa, most of the hype is concentrated in and around downtown, which is San Diego's primary entertainment destination and home to more than 500 restaurants, including approximately 250 ethnic restaurants. Most tourists and many San Diegans dine downtown, especially in the Gaslamp Quarter, Little Italy, and more recently the East Village. As discussed in the previous chapter, this is also the area with the greatest concentration of food industry jobs, most of which are filled by immigrants and people of color residing in surrounding neighborhoods.

This primary hotspot is spreading northeast of downtown toward Little Italy, Hillcrest, North Park, University Heights, and City Heights and southeast toward the East Village, Golden Hill, Barrio Logan, and Southeastern San Diego. Majority-Latinx South Bay and working-class East County were almost entirely ignored by food critics, who preferred affluent coastal areas and "eclectic" urban neighborhoods. Interestingly, the three study neighborhoods of Barrio Logan, City Heights, and Southeastern San Diego are located at the boundary of the central culinary hotspot, with a few establishments beginning to draw the attention of experts. This contested zone is what I describe in chapter 6 as the "culinary frontier," borrowing the term *frontier* from Neil Smith and others who view gentrification as a territorial process of expropriation and dispossession akin to colonization.[39]

Although there is a wide range of restaurants reviewed on these websites, those in the three study neighborhoods are almost exclusively "ethnic," including several Mexican restaurants especially in Barrio Logan and Southeastern San Diego and a Chinese-Vietnamese restaurant in City Heights that received attention in multiple online guides. Indeed, reviews suggest an imaginary spatial association between immigrant neighborhoods and good ethnic food, assuming that in order to experience authentic Mexican food, one must visit places like Barrio Logan. The

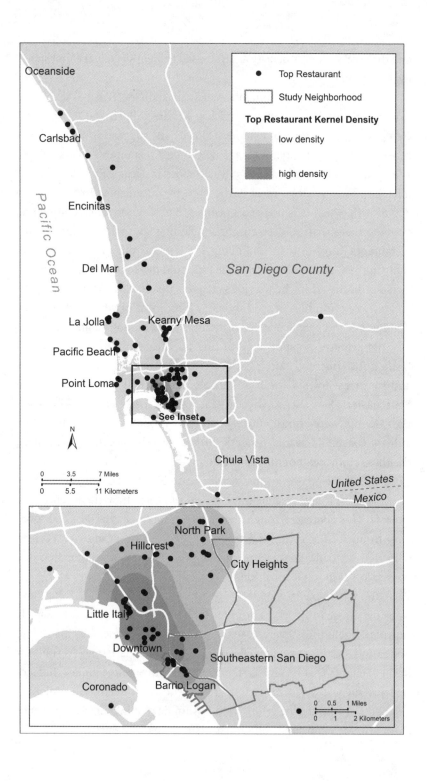

Oceanside

Carlsbad

Encinitas

Del Mar

La Jolla

Kearny Mesa

Pacific Beach

Point Loma

See Inset

Pacific Ocean

San Diego County

● Top Restaurant

☐ Study Neighborhood

Top Restaurant Kernel Density

low density

high density

N

| 0 | 3.5 | 7 Miles |
| 0 | 5.5 | 11 Kilometers |

Chula Vista

United States

Mexico

North Park

Hillcrest

City Heights

Little Italy

Downtown

Southeastern San Diego

Coronado

Barrio Logan

| 0 | 0.5 | 1 Miles |
| 0 | 1 | 2 Kilometers |

unspoken corollary assumption is that "upscale" cuisine (e.g., French, Italian, Japanese, New American) can only be found in affluent neighborhoods. In other words, place gives food cultural capital.

Real Estate Industry

The real estate industry is driven by population growth and rises in property values. To the extent that an exciting food environment contributes to the attractiveness of an area, it increases demand for properties and raises values, benefiting real estate agents and developers. Today, real estate agents often use food as a way to advertise properties in Barrio Logan, City Heights, and Southeastern San Diego. A May 2019 search on the online real estate database Zillow for properties for sale in these neighborhoods revealed thousands of entries featuring such terms as *food, restaurant, café,* and *farmers' market.*[40]

Property descriptions are clearly written to convince potential buyers to invest in an "up-and-coming neighborhood" where they could "walk to the city's best restaurants and cafés," "shop at the local farmers market," join "summer food truck festivals," and even participate in "community food drives"—an ironic benefit of moving into a place where food insecurity is common. A particular ad justifies the $600,000 price tag of a 700-square-foot studio in Barrio Logan by describing it as "poised perfectly in the path of the fastest gentrification and revitalization project in all of San Diego. Extensive redevelopment currently underway throughout the community for the first time in 30 yrs. . . . Unique coastal climate, fabulous walkability to restaurants, coffee shops, yoga and workout studios, close to freeways." Other ads urge buyers to "become part of the

MAP 5.1 "Best" restaurants and regional culinary hot spots. The majority of restaurants highly reviewed by experts in the food media are concentrated in and around downtown and in wealthier communities along the coast. Very few top restaurants are found in low-income neighborhoods of color such as Barrio Logan, City Heights, and Southeastern San Diego. Map created by author with data compiled from Eater, "Essential San Diego Restaurants" and "The Hottest Restaurants in San Diego Right Now"; The Infatuation, "Where to Eat and Drink in San Diego"; TimeOut, "The 18 Best Restaurants in San Diego"; Thrillist, "The Best Restaurants in San Diego Right Now" and "Fifty Things You Need to Eat in San Diego before You Die"; and Zagat, "Best Restaurants in San Diego" and "Hottest Restaurants in San Diego."

Barrio Logan Art District while you still can" and "enjoy craft beers, award-wining dining and nightlife" or "walking to restaurants, park, gym and markets, such as Chicano Park, Northgate Gonzalez Markets, Iron Fist Brewing, Mercado del Barrio shopping center."

Space for gardening, markets, or restaurants are often incorporated by developers in "mixed-used" development plans, making them more attractive to "creatives" and more palatable to the community. For instance, in Mission Hills a developer worked with a private company to start a weekly farmers' market around the time its fifty luxury condominium units became available for sale. A year later, once most of the units were sold, the farmers' market closed and never came back. In the East Village a community garden and outdoor gathering space with food stands were incorporated into Makers' Quarter—a large multiblock tech-oriented development project that broke ground in 2016 after years of planning. Both spaces appear as central features in the early drawings used to obtain community support and approval. A number of such events as "Beers & Bites," "Tacos, Tequila & Beer," and urban agriculture fairs were hosted at the Silo open space between 2014 and 2016, during the planning and early construction phases. After a few years, however, the garden and outdoor meeting space no longer exist; they have been removed to accommodate "co-working spaces" and parking for owners and tenants. Today such events as kombucha tastings are reserved for members only.

Real estate agents, contractors, and developers are important advertisers in local magazines and heavily fund these publications. One of the primary objectives of *San Diego Magazine* is to promote real estate through a variety of special issues, blogs, and articles, such as its annual *San Diego Homebuyer's Guide, Hot Blocks' Real Estate Gossip and News,* and *Best Places to Live in San Diego.* The emphasis that has recently been placed on food in these articles suggests that good food contributes to appreciation of the housing stock and benefits the real estate industry.

A COSMOPOLITAN FOODSCAPE WITHOUT IMMIGRANTS?

Given the powerful interests involved in gastrodevelopment projects shaping neighborhoods, blocks, and streets, it is difficult to argue that the result embodies the democratic and inclusive values of cosmopolitanism.

The voices of immigrants and low-income residents are often lost in this urban food machine where influential actors work together to maintain control over the city and direct flows of capital. The urban foodscape that emerges from the interaction of government agencies, public-private partnerships, and media interventions reflects the desires of property owners and investors who are set to benefit most from targeted branding and marketing of particular neighborhoods. It is therefore ironic that the most trendy and popular food projects are being described in terms emphasizing diversity, authenticity, inclusion, and community. In that contest, *cosmopolitanism* appears to be a façade for furthering capital accumulation and a way to control the terms of engagement with diversity. Because the cosmopolitan foodscape is fabricated by economically powerful actors, it reduces encounters with difference to tolerance and appropriation. In other words, the urban food machine defines and normalizes the "us" to which cosmopolitan citizens belong.

Meanwhile, at the margins, small business owners try to keep their operations afloat and low-income families continue to struggle to put food on the table. Yet these activities remain mostly invisible. In some cases, longtime residents join forces with the urban food machine in transforming the ethnic foodscape. In fact, many local businesses and residents participate in the food fairs and street markets organized by business improvement districts and other nonprofits. Some have organized and promoted such events under the assumption that it would strengthen the local economy and community. Others are joining the expanding alternative food movement, engaging in urban agriculture and local food networks, hoping to gain more control over food production, distribution, and consumption. Unfortunately, so far these efforts appear to contribute to the cosmopolitan foodscape, rather than stop its expansion. Alternative food spaces such as community gardens and farmers' markets have become mainstream and attract young, affluent, and educated urbanites. As a result, the ethnic foodscape no longer serves the needs of residents but becomes a gentrified cosmopolitan "white space." I turn my attention to this process of racialization and gentrification in the next chapter.

6

The Taste of Gentrification

Appropriation and Displacement in the Cosmopolitan Foodscape

"AN URBAN SANCTUARY" is how Jenny Niezgoda described her future Barrio Logan juice bar, La Gracia. In the promotional video that launched her Kickstarter fundraiser in October 2017, she explained that her goal was to "build a plant-based café that nourishes community, conversation, respect, positive thinking, and togetherness."[1] The young white entrepreneur from Texas who described herself as the "Barefoot Bohemian" selected Barrio Logan for her venture after "spending the last couple of years searching the world for the most vibrant, history-rich, artistic, and food-centric neighborhood." As she explained to viewers, Mexico had "stolen [her] heart," but she "found it here, in San Diego, two blocks from Chicano Park." Niezgoda envisioned her "modern frutería" as "much more" than a frutería; it would be "an integral thread to this neighborhood fabric." She urged viewers to contribute to her project to "help us improve San Diego, help us bring variety, and a healthy option to the barrio." The video showed Niezgoda leisurely walking through the sun-drenched streets of Barrio Logan, past the colorful Chicano Park murals, seemingly oblivious to the struggles they depict and the conflicted history of the neighborhood.

Tweets, hashtags, and other social media reactions were quick to follow, expressing both shock and indignation from neighborhood residents.[2] At the heart of the community's outrage were the dual threats of gentrification and cultural appropriation. For instance, hours after Niezgoda's video went live, one Facebook user aggressively asked: "Can someone pull this Guereja [blondie] by her bleached hair and shove some of her fruteria bullshit up her pilates toned ass and show her where Barrio Logan ends so she can set up her culturally appropriated fruit stand somewhere else." Her video was retweeted with comments such as "gentrification at it's [sic] finest" and "this is what #Gentrification looks like." Some turned to humor, renaming her project "La Desgracia" (the disgrace) or responding with "No Gracias" (no thank you). Others described it as "Columbusing," suggesting that, like Columbus, Niezgoda was claiming to have discovered something that already existed and was an important part of everyday life for many people. As critics pointed out, the neighborhood was already home to several Mexican-owned fruterías. Residents seemed particularly offended at the fact that the entrepreneur, despite her repeatedly stated desire to build community, had not reached out to them, did not have any personal connections to the neighborhood, and seemed to ignore its history and geography. Under this wave of criticism, the video was taken offline and the project was canceled just a few days after being launched.

No other cases rival La Gracia in illustrating the social tensions surrounding "taste" in the changing foodscapes of low-income communities of color like Barrio Logan, City Heights, and Southeastern San Diego. Few store or restaurant openings in these neighborhoods generate this much attention and debate. In fact, for some residents this sort of change is welcome and interpreted as neighborhood improvement or revitalization. More often, however, the transformation of the ethnic foodscape is gradual and ignored by locals who are too busy to consider the implications of a new shop or eatery until they begin to feel "out of place" in their own neighborhood. By then, it is often too late to go back: old stores have disappeared, the demographic mix of consumers is different, the aesthetics of buildings has changed, and even the smells of food are not the same. Soon, rents and food prices start going up, making life increasingly unaffordable for long-term residents.

I use the concept of taste in its multiple senses to shed light on the process of gentrification as one that remakes neighborhoods to cater to the desires of newcomers, privileging their lives and bodies over those of longtime residents. Socially and spatially contingent notions of "good food" are linked to a set of aesthetic values that are used to draw boundaries and establish hierarchies between "us" and "them," reinforcing distinctions based on class, race, and ethnicity. Under the guise of cosmopolitanism, ethnic food spaces and practices are successively devalued, rediscovered, appropriated, elevated, and erased, such that immigrants and people of color no longer belong in the new foodscape. The systemic erasure of ethnic foodscapes and their reinvention into cosmopolitan foodscapes draws attention to the social and cultural aspects of gentrification that marginalize immigrant and ethnic ways of life and produce a loss of place, even as people stay put.[3] As the gradual erosion of longtime residents' geographies of social reproduction, gentrification represents a violent and racist project of dispossession, displacement, and erasure.

After presenting in this chapter a brief overview of gentrification patterns in San Diego, I elaborate on the role of food and taste. Relying on social media data, I map San Diego's ethnic/cosmopolitan borderlands where the "taste of gentrification" is produced as authentic, democratic, and ethical. I examine how these notions are used to redefine ethnic food in ways that elevate gentrifiers while simultaneously devaluing, excluding, absenting, and ultimately displacing immigrants and people of color. Documenting the effects of these changes on longtime residents and their physical, social, cultural and emotional food geographies, I stretch the notion of displacement.

THE GEOGRAPHY OF GENTRIFICATION IN SAN DIEGO

In one of the most expensive real estate markets in the nation, the pressure to redevelop and rebrand low-income neighborhoods into upper-middle-class areas is extremely high. Since the 1980s, San Diego has experienced multiple waves of gentrification with an evolving spatial pattern. Map 6.1 uses US Census tract data from 1980 to 2017 to summarize more than three decades of gentrification, starting in Little Italy, downtown, Hillcrest, and

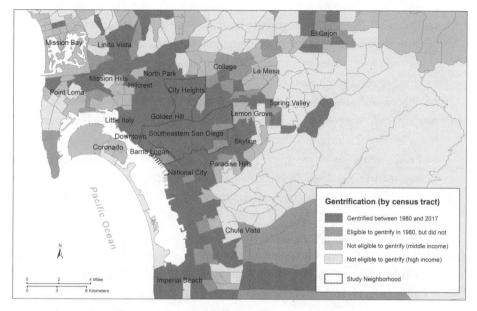

MAP 6.1 Gentrification in Central San Diego, by US Census tract, 1980–2017. Since the 1990s, gentrification has spread out of downtown, first moving north and today heading east and south. By 2018 most of the urban core of San Diego had undergone some level of gentrification, except for a few tracts at the fringe. Note that suburban tracts are too affluent to be eligible for gentrification. Map created by author with data compiled from the Longitudinal Tract Data Base of the American Communities Project at Brown University (2019); Summary File Data from the US Census, "American Community Survey Five-Year Estimates, 2008–2012" (2014), and "American Community Survey Five-Year Estimates, 2013–2017" (2019).

the western edge of North Park in the 1980s and spreading further east and south in the subsequent decades, moving through downtown's East Village toward Barrio Logan, through North Park into City Heights and Rolando, and through Golden Hill into parts of Southeastern San Diego and National City.[4] Except for a few clusters in Oceanside, San Marcos, Imperial Beach, and El Cajon, gentrification in San Diego is concentrated within that expanding urban core.

Some of these neighborhoods—such as Golden Hill, Little Italy, and North Park—have been in the process of gentrifying for several decades and specific tracts are now considered middle class or affluent. Property values in all three neighborhoods have increased rapidly and are now nearing or surpassing the county median of $483,997. Rents have gone up faster than in the county as well, doubling in real terms since the 1980s in North Park and Golden Hill and rising fivefold in Little Italy. These neighborhoods also became whiter despite the fact that, in the county, white people have seen their share decline consistently and have been the minority for almost a decade. Between 2000 and 2017 the share of white residents increased from 48 percent to 78 percent in Little Italy, 54 percent to 60 percent in North Park, and 30 percent to 42 percent in Golden Hill. "Creatives" have also moved in, as reflected in the above average and rising percentage of adults with college degrees, growing from 5 percent to 74 percent in Little Italy, 20 percent to 53 percent in North Park, and 14 percent to 39 percent in Golden Hill.

Barrio Logan, City Heights, and Southeastern San Diego began gentrifying more recently and remain in transition, with several tracts experiencing little change. Among these neighborhoods, Barrio Logan is at a more advanced stage of gentrification, with property value increasing by 67 percent in the past seven years alone. Yet despite sharp increases, housing cost remains relatively lower than elsewhere in the city, making these neighborhoods prime targets for further gentrification. Although white and college-educated households are slowly moving in, these neighborhoods continue to be home to many low-income and working-class people of color and immigrants. These inhabitants, however, are finding it harder to stay put. Monthly rents have risen by about 30 percent in real terms since 2000, nearing or surpassing $1,000 and quickly catching up with the county average of $1,640. These three neighborhoods are the "borderlands" where gentrification pressures, negotiations about belonging, and threats of displacement are most intense. They have in common a proximity to downtown, a large ethnic and immigrant population, an older housing stock including quaint cottages and historical homes, and a long history of neglect and abandonment by policymakers and investors. They also share a foodscape marked by food apartheid, where community survival strategies have created ethnic restaurants and unique food spaces to be "discovered." The cultural cachet that ethnic food brings to these communities—along with art, music, and architecture—plays an important role in attracting investors, consumers, and potential residents.

FOOD, RACE, AND ETHNICITY
IN GENTRIFICATION THEORY

Much has been written regarding urban gentrification—the transformation of previously devalued neighborhoods into middle- and upper-class areas and the associated displacement of longtime residents. Until very recently, reputable urban scholars would have never considered food as a critical element of this process, which was first understood as driven by the economic forces of capital accumulation. However, the recognition that gentrification is not just an economic but also a cultural phenomenon has drawn attention to the significance of lifestyles, consumption, and identities in shaping cities. Because food is intimately connected with these notions, it eventually surfaced in gentrification studies.[5] Today, many observers agree that food is a symbol of gentrification, with the arrivals of coffee shops, fancy fruterías, and expensive taco stands signaling changing demographics.[6] I go beyond this claim by positing that food actively produces gentrification, as restaurants, food halls, farmers' markets, and street food festivals draw people with significant disposable income into previously ignored neighborhoods. Intersecting the study of food and gentrification opens up new ways of looking at the remaking of cities.

Gentrification became a serious topic of urban scholarship in the United States in the late 1980s and early 1990s, when investors began pouring capital into "inner-city" neighborhoods under the banner of urban revitalization and renewal.[7] Investors were attracted to older urban neighborhoods by the historical character of the housing stock, which was undervalued but could be restored to its previous grandeur with some investment. The difference between the market value of real estate and the potential return of investment in the form of higher rent is known as the "rent gap" and viewed by some as the primary driving force behind gentrification.[8] As multifamily units became single-family homes or luxury condos, tenants were either evicted or left unable to pay rising rent. Urban governments facilitated this process by first contributing to urban decline and deflating property values through redlining and other racially biased policies and subsequently promoting redevelopment through a series of neoliberal strategies to subsidize investors, sponsor evictions, and police changing neighborhoods.[9] In this approach, gentrification is primarily conceptualized as a political-economic phenomenon tied to capitalism and neoliberalism.

At the same time, other researchers have been paying attention to the cultural aspects of gentrification. Beyond the favorable real estate market, they have argued, newcomers are often attracted by the unique cultural experiences that older urban neighborhoods seem to provide.[10] In contrast to the dreary predictability of suburbs and upscale quarters, low-income urban neighborhoods are perceived as bohemian, unique, gritty, multicultural, authentic, sociable, and community-oriented—cultural attributes that have become attractive to urban elites, especially in a postmodern era of increasingly fluid identities. In this research, gentrification is often attributed to changing individual preferences for urban living rather than to a political-economic structure that encourages an inflow of capital in particular areas. Consumption is prioritized over production in explaining the changing character of urban neighborhoods. Although this perspective has been criticized for minimizing the negative effects of gentrification and "deliberately gut[ting] the concept of its inherent class character," it has contributed to a rich debate in urban studies and ultimately a more nuanced understanding of gentrification in which both production and consumption interact to produce change.[11]

Considering the role of food in encouraging gentrification helps move this debate forward by intersecting cultural and political-economic explanations. Like housing, food is produced through monetary investments in the physical spaces of restaurants and retail shops as well as the hiring of food workers. However, food also acquires value through its cultural and symbolic significance as a social experience and a marker of identity. Food has become an integral part of the urban imaginary of gentrifying areas in which adventurous, cosmopolitan, and enlightened eaters see themselves mingling with each other at newly discovered "neighborhood gems"—one of the most overused terms in restaurant reviews. This sort of cosmopolitan urban imaginary facilitates capital accumulation and vice versa. Urban elites, including developers, public officials, leaders of cultural economies, and the media, work hand-in-hand to create cultural representations of urban places and lifestyles that reward investors and favor white middle-class residents. Restaurants, public markets, gardens, food festivals, and breweries are increasingly important components of "gastrodevelopment"—efforts deployed by urban place-makers to maximize symbolic value and minimize the risk of investing in neglected neighborhoods. Despite the stated intention of the urban food machine to preserve and uplift the ethnic character of gentrifying neighborhoods through these initiatives, the emerging spaces are effectively "white spaces" that enable new middle-class white residents to experience and exhibit the sort of cosmopolitan taste and lifestyle attributed to foodies.

Race has always loomed large in gentrification studies but has not always been theorized carefully, especially when it comes to ethnicity and migrancy. Although scholars have recognized that racial minorities are disproportionately vulnerable to displacement, gentrification has primarily been viewed as a class-based process of dispossession affecting the poor, which only indirectly means people of color.[12] However, racial differentiation is not just the outcome of gentrification; it is also a prerequisite for it. Gentrification relies on race to first devalue and pathologize urban neighborhoods as inhabitable ghettos—a process Katherine McKittrick has called "urbicide"—and then justify revitalization projects that suppress and make disappear unwanted racialized people, practices, and narratives.[13] Similarly, race underlies the production of food apartheid and the deployment of food desert narratives to warrant targeted reinvestment. Thus racism both paves the way for food gentrification and ensures that nonwhite people are excluded from the opportunities it creates.

In recent years, several authors have turned to the notion of racial capitalism developed by Cedric Robinson to stress the centrality of race in the making and remaking of urban space, including processes of gentrification.[14] In this perspective, racism is the primary structuring logic of capitalism whose expansion is predicated on racial inequality and exploitation. Specifically, "racial banishment" leads to the erasure, dispossession, containment, and/or displacement of racialized people to manage cities under capitalism.[15] Thus gentrification is interpreted as a "whiteness project" designed to remove working-class people of color from particular neighborhood to benefit white newcomers.[16] Within this new body of work, some conceptualize gentrification as a form of settler colonialism: a spatial process of acquiring control over a territory, occupying it with white "settlers," pushing out racialized current residents, and erasing historical traces of their existence for the purpose of accumulating capital.[17] Although the settler-colonial metaphor is problematic in assuming commensurability between Indigenous expropriation, displacement, and alienation, and other forms of social injustice, it draws attention to gentrification as a violent uprooting of racialized communities that is premised on their dispossession.[18] It is a "spatial complement to theories of racial capitalism."[19] As such, it draws attention to the "borderlands" where gentrification is lived and the boundary between those who belong and those who do not is negotiated.[20]

Metanarratives about the racial capitalist nature of gentrification, which often focus on anti-Blackness, are complicated by ethnicity and migrancy. First, the diversity of racial experiences, including the participation of Black and Latinx people in gentrification projects, points to the importance of acknowledging historical and geographic differences in the coformation of race, ethnicity, and place.[21] Second, the contemporary currency of ethnicity, especially ethnic food, in marketing urban neighborhoods for reinvestment indicates that it may be deployed in gentrification projects in different ways. Here too, the scholarship on settler colonialism is helpful for thinking about gentrification as a structuring process that sustains capital accumulation over time by racializing and dispossessing increasingly heterogenous racial groups in new ways. Rather than being erased, the ethnic identities of places may instead be misappropriated and curated to serve redevelopers and assuage the guilt of white folks in a multicultural context. Far from being fixed, the boundaries of race and ethnicity are being redrawn in the borderlands of gentrification, in taco shops, ramen bars, and other ethnic eateries and markets.

Indeed, foodscapes are microcosms in which the relationships between place, race/ethnicity, and capital are lived and embodied. In gentrifying neighborhoods, foodscapes are contested terrains where longtime residents (mostly people of color) and newcomers (mostly white) compete for survival, social distinction, and belonging, redefining ethnicity in the process. Ethnic foodscapes have been fashioned over time by racially biased policies that underlie food apartheid and residential segregation. Abandoned by corporate retail capital, ethnic communities have turned to formal and informal food businesses and practices to fill the gap, creating an alternative foodscape that enables social reproduction. The resulting ethnic foodscape is both a spatial expression of racism and a platform for the enactment of ethnic foodways that have suddenly become intriguing to middle-class white consumers enthralled by their authenticity but blind to the struggles from which such foodways emerge.

Ironically, the interest of outsiders in authentic ethnic food is once again threatening the food provisioning mechanisms of low-income people of color. By prioritizing the consumption habits and cosmopolitan tastes of white middle-class newcomers, gentrification produces a curated version of ethnic foodscape that destabilizes the food practices of longtime residents and alters the rhythms of neighborhood life. Although seemingly bringing people together, ethnic food is experienced differently along ethnoracial lines: what looks like an incredible bargain to an outsider might be out-of-reach for longtime residents; "exotic and unusual" to some might be commonplace to others; "upgraded and improved" becomes insulting and demeaning; "hip and trendy" might also be exclusive and obnoxious; and "authentic" is meaningless. Focusing on the politics of everyday life and the power tensions surrounding taste in gentrifying neighborhoods reveals the multiple, banal, and subtle ways in which gentrification works to value or devalue particular ways of life and displace people.

THE TASTE OF GENTRIFICATION

What does gentrification taste like? Do the flavors and aesthetics of food in gentrifying neighborhoods differ from those in other places? The millions of photos uploaded by cultural "influencers" on social media capturing horchata latte, kimchi tacos, matcha donuts, and endless variations of avocado toasts consumed in "neighborhood gems," "holes in the wall," and other urban "hangouts" around the world suggest that there is indeed a taste to gentrification.[22]

At the most basic level, *taste* is about the intensity, quality, and hedonics of food—the ways it feels in the mouth and whether it is pleasurable or not. To some, it is the result of a chemical and biological reaction between food and receptor cells known as taste buds. For others, taste is not an intrinsic property of objects but an affective response to them shaped by social and cultural conventions. Indeed, taste is constructed through social and biological relations. Just like an appreciation of bitterness may be acquired though repetition, the enjoyment of gourmet and exotic foods may be gained through education and refinement. In *Distinction*, Pierre Bourdieu contends that taste provides the upper class with a way to distinguish itself from lower socioeconomic groups by exhibiting their cultural superiority.[23] In the world of food, which is loaded with symbolism, distinction can be achieved in many ways: extravagant settings, luxurious dinnerware, prized ingredients, complicated recipes, proper table manners, unique combinations of flavors, timing of meals, and sophisticated presentation. These allow the upper class to distance itself from the working class for whom necessity—the affordability, caloric value, and familiarity of food—is presumably more important, underlying its lack of "taste." Thus gustatory preferences and aesthetic notions of "good food" are not objective or universal but instead influenced by income and cultivated through continuously evolving social norms.

The focus on social class, however, overlooks the role of race in producing taste. Haute cuisine, just like fine art and classical music, is typically associated with European culture and white consumers. The food, art, and music of people of color are often racialized as folkloric, primitive, cheap, or simple, until they are "discovered" and misappropriated by white elites, like jazz and sushi. In the context of gentrification, where the class and race composition of neighborhoods is being remapped, gentrifiers come to redefine what good food is in ways that reproduce their racial and economic privilege by creating boundaries between them and ethnic others through taste.

Place is an important contributor to taste; it can impart a certain level of sophistication and cultural capital to food and the eating experience itself that is denied to those with limited mobility. For instance, eating pozole at Pujol—a Michelin-starred restaurant in Mexico City—or Corazón del Tierra—a highly rated restaurant in the Guadalupe wine valley just south of the Tijuana–San Diego border—confers a different status than doing so in a less exclusive location. Aside from the exorbitant price tag of these dishes, accessing these places is an insurmountable obstacle to many. Simply knowing that such places exist and being able to talk about them authoritatively with others is in itself a form of distinction. Even within one's city, food places can be exclusive because they are only accessible to customers "in the know" with sufficient disposable income, wearing the appropriate attire, and feeling like they might belong there. While "creatives" do not seem to mind traveling all over the city (and beyond) in search of particular food or dishes, less privileged people operate within more confined spaces; mobility is a privilege.

Place is central to creating and validating notions of good food; to be fully appreciated, certain foods must be consumed in specific places. For example, lobster rolls must be tried in New England, chile verde in New Mexico, deep-dish pizza in Chicago, and so on. While consuming these dishes in the "right place" may not necessarily generate a superior reaction on the tongue, it may produce different affective impacts. Powerful geographic imaginaries shape the eating experience, such that eating food in the "wrong place" would both taste bad and be in poor taste. Geographer Doreen Massey has stressed the role of food in place-identity when she describes how visitors to Paris find "the *real* France" in cafés with "the smell of Gauloises, the taste of good coffee and croissants"—not in fast food restaurants.[24] Such food-place associations are created over time through social interactions and institutionalized—at least temporarily— through magazines, cookbooks, and social media.[25] These geographic imaginaries work at a variety of scales—from culinary regions to cities, neighborhoods, streets, homes, and restaurants—to racialize place and food. For instance, City Heights is the right place to sample Vietnamese or Somali food, and Barrio Logan is the best destination for tacos. However, they may never be the right place for upscale French, Italian, Japanese, or "new American" food, which are deemed better in La Jolla or Little Italy.

In today's era of global consumerism, "good taste" may be more elusive than ever. International migration has made cities increasingly diverse and refashioned their foodscapes. Experts love to claim that Filipino, Mexican, Thai, or other "ethnic" foods have "finally" reached the status of high cuisine—itself a testimony to racist biases. For instance, a recent magazine article announced that "Mexican food [had] enter[ed] the fine-dining realm" and, a year later, another predicted that "Filipino food [was] becoming the next great American cuisine."[26] Until then, white and formally educated consumers had presumably misunderstood such cuisine and equated it with unsophisticated, unhealthy, and cheap food—that is, until "enlightened" experts took notice and prestigious awards, along with inflated prices, followed, granting these cuisines taste and credibility.

In this multicultural context, foodies have become "omnivorous," rejecting "highbrow" food, broadening their food repertoire, and espousing cosmopolitan and democratic values. In order to maintain their social and cultural superiority, however, white cultural elites continue to distinguish themselves by controlling knowledge about and access to "good food." Once something becomes mainstream, mass-produced, and accessible to most, it also becomes vulgar and is no longer appealing to cultural elites. Thus "good food" must be constantly rediscovered or reinvented in order to confer status. One of the ways to achieve distinction is to attach particular moral values to food, including democracy and colorblindness. For example, consuming an "authentic" taco at Las Cuatro Milpas in Barrio Logan conveys that one is colorblind, open to "foreign" cultures, supportive of local economies, unfazed by simple settings and "dangerous" places, appreciative of authentic food, and comfortable among people of all social status and origins. It is therefore not surprising that this restaurant, which has existed since 1933, has recently earned rave reviews from foodies and experts alike. That act of consumption, however, does not confer the same status to Latinx residents of Barrio Logan for whom eating at Las Cuatro Milpas is presumably less self-conscious and intentional.

To the extent that mostly white cultural elites venture into ethnic neighborhoods to enjoy superior food experiences, the process of racial distinction through gustatory taste is inherently spatial and linked to gentrification. It involves mobility and the ability to access the right places, which is not afforded equally to all. It also involves negotiation about what and who belongs in these places where the everyday survival of longtime residents increasingly clashes with the desires of middle-class and primarily white newcomers. To meet the needs of gentrifiers, the foodscape must embody their desired lifestyle and professed values of democracy and cosmopolitanism. Too much visible poverty, food insecurity, and urban decay undermine gentrifiers' ability to express these values and distinguish themselves, creating pressure to erase the past and replace it with a carefully curated image of cosmopolitanism built on decontextualized, flattened, and inoffensive symbols of ethnicity. In that sense, the taste of gentrification is rather insipid.

THE GENTRIFYING
ETHNIC/COSMOPOLITAN FOODSCAPE

Where do foodies go in search of unique eating experiences? How do foodie destinations correlate with gentrification trends in San Diego? Data from social media present an opportunity to answer these questions and examine changing foodscapes from the perspective of privileged consumers. With foodscapes becoming increasingly aestheticized and taste changing quickly, what was a popular spot yesterday can fall out of fashion today and be out of business tomorrow. This process has been exacerbated and sped up by information technologies and social media that play a key role in the dissemination of ideas regarding the "right places" to consume "good food." Although capital investments remain essential in shaping the physical foodscape, blogs, online reviews, and user-generated content serve as a "megaphone" to draw attention to particular establishments and neighborhoods.[27] These platforms, in addition to attracting the young and fairly educated, also draw people with strong positive and negative opinions as well as "influencers" looking to be noticed and followed by other viewers. Yelp's own data indicate that contributors are "disproportionately young, white, childless, wealthy, and highly educated," aligning them closely with creatives and gentrifiers.[28] These very biases make Yelp a relevant source of data to explore perceptions of ethnic restaurants and neighborhoods among relatively privileged consumers who resemble today's gentrifiers.[29]

In December 2019 there were 5,763 restaurants reviewed on Yelp in San Diego, from which I extracted 451 "ethnic" restaurants to analyze.[30] Map 6.2 shows the location of these restaurants, with the top fifty uniquely identified. Not surprisingly, there is a high concentration of reviewed establishments in the downtown area, mirroring both the actual distribution of restaurants and the "best of" lists described in the previous chapter. However, ethnic restaurants in surrounding neighborhoods, including Barrio Logan, North Park, and City Heights are receiving considerable attention and some of the highest ratings from "Yelpers," despite being ignored by professional food critics. Kearny Mesa and Mira Mesa are "ethnoburbs" worth mentioning for their concentration of highly rated

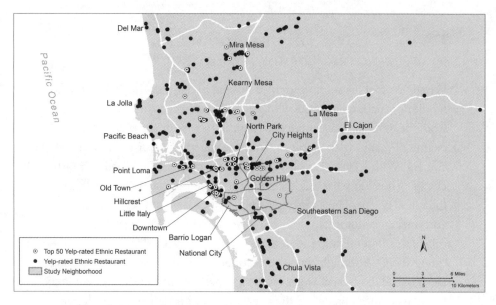

MAP 6.2 Ethnic restaurants reviewed on Yelp, including "Top 50." Yelp-rated ethnic restaurants are more evenly distributed in the region than those rated by experts as illustrated in map 5.1. Ethnic restaurants with the best Yelp rating, however, are concentrated in gentrifying areas such as Little Italy, North Park, City Heights, Southeastern San Diego, and Barrio Logan. Map created by author using 2019 data compiled from Yelp.

Asian restaurants.[31] Escondido and the South Bay are home to a number of highly rated Mexican restaurants, reflecting these areas' demographic composition.

Much can be learned by analyzing Yelp restaurant reviews separately for the three gentrifying neighborhoods of Barrio Logan, City Heights, Southeastern San Diego and the three comparison neighborhoods of Little Italy, North Park, and Golden Hill, which are now considered highly gentrified. First, Yelpers are clearly more engaged in gentrified neighborhoods as reflected in the number of reviews. For instance, restaurants in Little Italy received over seven times more reviews than those in Southeastern San Diego. Second, ethnic restaurants are more often and more highly rated in City Heights and Barrio Logan than other restaurants, indicating that these are the types of places consumers appreciate and associate with these areas. This also occurs to a lesser extent in Southeastern San Diego.

Third, in the most gentrified neighborhoods, ethnic restaurants do not stand out from other establishments. Although they still have more reviews, they are not rated as highly. Here it is authenticity that draws attention. Indeed, the proportion of restaurants considered "authentic" according to Yelp's classification, which is based on descriptions provided by businesses and consumer reviews, increases with gentrification and is the highest in hypergentrified and now increasingly white Golden Hill. The disconnect between authenticity and ethnicity suggests that the former, like the latter, is socially constructed based on aesthetic and symbolic factors such as décor and presentation, rather than on the people who cook ancestral food from their homelands. Indeed, the idea of authenticity seems to reflect an outsider's perspective of what is presumably original. It cements otherness and denies self-identification and fluidity. The percentage of restaurants described as authentic is lowest in Southeastern San Diego—the least gentrified neighborhood in this study and one that is often viewed as lacking character and sense of place.

Contrasting map 6.2, showing the location of highly rated ethnic restaurants from Yelp, with the culinary hot zone map based on food experts' ratings presented in chapter 5 (see map 5.1) reveals the existence of an ethnic/cosmopolitan borderland at the edge of the central consumption zone, where foodies venture in search for cultural capital and distinction. The majority of ethnic restaurants rated 4 or above are located in this borderland, which spreads out of downtown and extends both northeast (through North Park and City Heights) and southeast (toward Barrio Logan and the western edge of Southeastern San Diego). It is on this "culinary frontier" between ethnic and cosmopolitan—where food apartheid and flourishing food economies coexist—that gentrification pressures are currently intensifying and that racial and ethnic boundaries are being redrawn through notions of authenticity.

AUTHENTICITY, SOCIAL DISTINCTION, AND ETHNIC BOUNDARIES

Yelp reviews are helpful to understand the taste of gentrification, including the shifting meaning of "authenticity." Through descriptions of excitement, discomfort, and disgust, reviewers reveal the racist and classist biases they carry with them while eating in neighborhoods such as Barrio Logan, City Heights, or Southeastern San Diego. I analyzed twenty-four hundred recent reviews of sixty ethnic restaurants in these three gentrifying neighborhoods.[32] As I have done for other social media sources, I purposely do not provide the names of Yelpers who posted their reviews publicly but did not expressly consent to participate in my research.

Two related narratives emerge from my analysis. The most common story is that of "holes in the wall" being discovered in "sketchy neighborhoods" where customers must set aside their fears to enjoy "authentic" food prepared by "home cooks" and served by "not-so-friendly" people who "don't speak a word of English" in a "simple" and unsanitary setting. Paralleling this narrative is a more positive one of "hidden gems" where "authentic" food is "prepared to perfection" by "innovative young chefs," attracting an "eclectic and diverse crowd" that is "eager to support a vibrant community." Both narratives embrace the idea of authenticity; the first does so through ethnicity while the second emphasizes cosmopolitanism. There is a spatial pattern to these two stories, which not only describe food and restaurants but also neighborhoods. The first story applies primarily to highly rated restaurants in neighborhoods like City Heights and Southeastern San Diego, where gentrification is still in an early stage. The second story is much more common in Barrio Logan, where gentrification is more advanced and the foodscape is becoming more cosmopolitan than ethnic.

Place descriptions feature prominently in Yelp reviews, along with the notion that "amazing finds," "hidden gems" or "holes in the wall" have to be discovered by adventurous foodies to gain value. Many Yelpers marvel at the fact that such trendy and fashionable restaurants serving tasty and well-prepared food would actually be in the study neighborhoods, underscoring their biases and the enduring stigma of these places. By presenting "good restaurants" as exceptions, reviewers both question and reproduce negative place stigma. This is illustrated in comments such as: "Wow this place is such a wonderfully foodie spot. It is in [Barrio] Logan which can be a little rough around the edges, but damn it's worth the trip. Really a hidden gem"; "I must say I didn't have high expectations when cruising through the neighborhood [City Heights] trying to find this place . . . but you can't go wrong"; "Wow! What a surprising spot in an unlikely location"; or "This is literally the cutest place in the middle of a very unseemly neighborhood."

Another important and related theme is the neighborhood *sketchiness*. Indeed, "sketchy" is a heavily racialized term that is used by numerous reviewers to describe "must-go" places and occasionally people in the area. For example, a reviewer warns of a restaurant in City Heights: "This place was a little far and sketchy, but we decided what the heck. Best decision I've made in a long time when choosing restaurants." Similarly, another urges people to go to a café in City Heights "for legit Vietnamese coffee. It's sketchy from the outside and there are guys smoking and gambling inside." These characteristics seem to be part of the appeal and should not deter visitors. As one Yelper puts it: "Don't let the sketchy neighborhood scare you away." Numerous reviewers advise online readers to ignore "offensive" surroundings. For example, there is a suggestion that "visitors should not be deterred by the wrought-iron bars on the windows or the back-alleyway atmosphere. There's an experience both delicious and humble to be found inside." A particular reviewer is explicit about her fears regarding a Mexican restaurant in Barrio Logan, which she sets aside to enjoy the food:

> I am scared! Scared of a lot of things about this place. Going there
> by myself. Sitting at a table. Touching anything. But I am not scared
> of the food. And that is why, I am giving this place in Barrio Logan
> 4 stars despite the . . . ummm . . . unsavoriness of the surround-
> ings. . . . A little sketchy but the food is GREAT! . . . Better than
> great. Hands down the best Carnitas and best Tortillas I have EVER
> had. . . . We all left with full bellies and happy smiles. But we rushed
> to our car . . . didn't want to be caught hanging around.

For some, however, these safety-related fears are too strong to warrant further visits: "I probably will not come here again due to the location. The food quality isn't worth the risk to be harassed by homeless or to get my car broken into. . . . The bars on the windows of this restaurant seems to be needed because there are random people loitering around. . . . I was going to come back for the Banh Xeo, but my experience here was scary and sub-par, it's not worth another visit." Others had related complaints about another establishment: "Cashier doesn't speak English and it's cash only. Tables are dirty. Floor is dirty. Bathrooms are filthy. Place is packed and seats are hard to find. Between the poor quality and the dump-like ambiance I was not able to enjoy or finish my food. Put it in a box and tried to give it to the homeless guy on the street corner sitting next to my car. Even the homeless refused this food. I totally understand why. Do not waste your time or risk your health going to this dump." The term *dump* is in fact quite common among dissatisfied reviewers, who use it as an umbrella word to describe multiple aspects of the environment, including cleanliness, décor, safety, food, and service. Such labels contribute to the devaluation of ethnic foodscapes as dirty, unhealthy, rough, and tasteless—a process described in chapter 2 as constitutive of food deserts and a precondition for gentrification.

In addition to focusing on the physical environment and safety of the neighborhood, many reviewers describe food workers and "locals" as "other." They often do that by objectifying their bodies and interpreting their performance through racialized notions that tie particular behavior with race, ethnicity, or immigrant status. Comments abound in which poor service is attributed to workers' ethnicity and culture. Yet they are typically countered with advice to set those aside as part of the experience—along with the tacky décor—as exemplified in the following review:

> Nha Hang Chay Hoa Tu Bi Tam is your stereotypical hole-in-the-wall Asian eatery where one goes strictly for the food and price and nothing else. Don't expect great service or ambiance because, well, they practically don't exist in any commendable way. . . . This is one of the diviest [*sic*] restaurants I've been to in a long time. Makeshift tablecloths were made with metallic gold wallpaper hastily wrapped around tabletops. Plates were chipped and nearly paper thin. My tea was stale and cold. Half the menu lacked English names, although English ingredients are provided. . . . My "server" [quotation marks in original] didn't seem to speak a lick of English so I placed my order by pointing to items 10 and 11 on the menu. . . . I received item 9 instead. When I tried to explain the error in my alien language, my server silently took the plate away, presumably understanding

the confusion. . . . One must be determined to dine here to not be discouraged by the tacky decor and apathetic service.

A Mexican restaurant in Barrio Logan was the object of a similar complaint: "the service is the worst I have experienced in a long ass time, not even in Mexico (Tijuana) is the service this bad"—implying that bad service is common in Mexico and therefore to be expected from people of Mexican ancestry. Other reviewers, however, go out of their way to praise the "charming," "sweet," and "super-friendly" service provided by "no hipster Hispanics [who] look like your abuelita" or "a very attractive girl with great vintage tattoos" who takes your order "with a heart melting sexy accent." These comments are often counteracted with descriptions of Mexican cooks as "gang-bangers" or "some lady who looks like Griselda Blanco." Whether seemingly positive or clearly negative, these comments emphasize the stereotyping and racialization of food workers' bodies.

The importance of sociality in taste is obvious in many comments regarding interactions with owners and customers. A diner is thrilled that his party "got to meet both owners and they are great! What a fantastic husband wife team . . . down to earth, humble, kind souls that just want to make your day a little brighter with some damn good food." The diversity of customers and the presence of locals are often described positively. For instance, the attraction to a Mexican restaurant in Barrio Logan is due to the fact that "people from all walks of life love to eat here." Indeed, authenticity seems to be proportional to the number of local and ethnic consumers, as when a Thai restaurant in City Heights was described as "legitimate" because "there were a lot of actual Thai people there, so you know it has to be good." Will these "authentic" places lose their appeal as locals can no longer afford to eat there?

Throughout these reviews one can read Yelpers' attempts to distinguish themselves using different strategies. Many begin their reviews by establishing their credibility as food experts, emphasizing their knowledge of good food through discussion of authenticity, legitimacy, preparation techniques, and regional origins. This authority has typically been acquired through international travel and extensive dining experience in some of the world's best restaurants, underscoring the importance of mobility. For example, one Yelper writes: "Having been to Italy and tasting local dishes, . . . my tongue has yearned for an authentic tasting and explosion of Italian-ness when back in the US." Similarly, another explains: "This place took me back to my travels in Thailand. We got the chicken rice and chicken krapow. Both were so impeccably flavorful. Everything just tasted so authentic and the heat was definitely there." Being close to the Mexican border, one does not need to travel far to learn about authenticity—although such travel is highly restricted and not possible for those without proper visas. For example, a restaurant in Barrio Logan "is the BOMB! They aren't joking when they say coming here will save you going south of the border!! The pastor tacos are the same if not better than TJ [Tijuana] tacos." Indeed, many Yelpers seem to be "transported south of the border" by their eating experiences.

Another common way for reviewers to distinguish themselves is to assert their knowledge of particular food by emphasizing cooking techniques and regional differences, as exemplified in a review of a Mexican restaurant in City Heights:

> The "Lamb Barbacoa" is slow-cooked for 8 hours, and available as a taco, on sopes, or piled onto a plate. As opposed to the "Texcoco-style" barbacoa served at that other popular barbacoa place in Chula Vista, El Borrego's lamb barbacoa is "Hidalgo-style," where the lamb is cooked without any chilies or pastes. . . . In Mexico, it is legal for restaurants to pit-roast lamb over coals underground. . . . Rosario's lamb barbacoa has been adapted to comply with local fire safety code. . . . Pit-roasted barbacoa is smokier. . . . When cooked underground, it picks up more of the flavor of the earth itself and the soil around it.

Rich and detailed descriptions of ingredients and flavors abound on Yelp. For instance:

> At Pho Hòa, the broth has a deep beef flavor from many hours of extraction from beef bones, yet it is virtually clear. Any impurities have been removed, leaving us lucky diners with only the juices extracted from meat and bones concentrated in a thick, gelatin-rich stock with charred onion and ginger, fish sauce, star anise,

and cloves. This is not the usual pho broth you find all over San Diego, but something indeed on a different level. The flavor of the beef is more intense, the salinity is better balanced against the rest of the seasonings, and the cloves and ginger are more fragrant.

Distinction also comes from the adventurous attitude of reviewers who take significant pride in having "discovered" a "new" place, despite the fact that it might have existed for decades. This "pioneer spirit" is on display as Yelpers describe their willingness to brave "sketchy" neighborhoods and put up with a subpar environment in exchange for an exotic adventure: "The atmosphere here is fantastic, from the people at the counter who will take your order in English or Spanish, to the plastic letter board menu, to the rather loud hum of the mixers and machines. There's no indie lifestyle music or plush seating here, and the building is definitely not getting nominated for an orchid. All you'll find at LCM is vinyl tablecloths and authenticity. Definitely my idea of a special destination."

Reviews are often infused with a sense of moral superiority in which consumers portray themselves as ethical to the extent they "bring attention to a part of town that needs a little TLC," support local immigrant-, family- and minority-owned businesses, intermingle with economically and racially diverse staff and customers, and eschew corporate and elitist establishments. For instance, readers are urged to "support immigrant entrepreneurs, [because] they truly make America great" and to patronize "one of the few Black-owned restaurants" in Southeastern San Diego or "one of the only non-corporate coffee shops in the area that is owned and operated by a San Diego native who grew up in the neighborhood," for "there is no feeling like being able to support a local business." Multiculturalism and colorblindness are common themes in these reviews in which cultural diversity is valued and celebrated in ways that ignore deep-seated racial disparities. Enlightened consumers are viewed as heroes who "help" local businesses and "improve" the neighborhood through their consumption choices.

Aesthetic elements are also important in allowing reviewers to establish their "wokeness." Some highlight the unique style of cosmopolitan restaurants, such as "junk yard garage ambiance," "clean, modern with a hint of dive," or "very chill, authentic and homey." Attention to details such as "cafeteria-style ordering up front, picnic table seating on the sides, and a tortillería in the rear" and "old-school menu still written on a changeable letter board" help distinguish reviewers by revealing their eclectic, unfussy, and on-trend sense of style. Again and again, the knowledge, sense of adventure, laid-back attitude, and colorblindness that Yelpers display in their reviews reveal their privilege, which is tied to their mobility and ability to enjoy the most desirable elements of ethnic food for their own benefits while ignoring the life-sustaining significance of this food for the immigrant and ethnic groups who live and work in the cosmopolitan/ethnic borderlands.

ADAPTATION AND APPROPRIATION OF ETHNIC FOOD

The arrival of new coffee shops, organic food purveyors, wine bars, and farm-to-table restaurants in a neighborhood is a clear sign of social change. The opening of new ethnic—or rather authentic—eateries and the sudden "discovery" of old ones are similar predictors of neighborhood transformation. To Barrio Logan residents, La Gracia frutería was an unmistakable symbol of gentrification and harbinger of cultural appropriation and displacement. Yet it is more than a symbol of change; it is an integral and constitutive part of the transformation process that threatens the social reproduction of low-income and immigrant households who have called the neighborhood home for some time. In the midst of these changes, ethnic entrepreneurs are often pulled into different directions and struggle to keep their business profitable. Do they continue to serve local residents, or do they adapt to the new clientele? Do they keep selling the same food, or do they change menus and selections to meet the taste of newcomers? The choices they make are likely to have profound impacts on both the economic viability of their business and the well-being of longtime residents.

Ethnic entrepreneurs' ability to capitalize on changing tastes and the popularity of ethnic food is complicated by limited access to financial resources and heightened competition from outsiders who have deeper pockets. Work in the food economy is extremely precarious, and ethnic entrepreneurship rarely generates high profits. Indeed, according to interviews I conducted in City Heights, Barrio Logan, and Southeastern San

Diego, managers of small shops and restaurateurs often struggle to pay suppliers and workers on time, and the vast majority do not use mainstream credit, relying instead on informal sources of financing such as payday lenders, credit cards, and loans from family and friends. Under these circumstances, updating the décor, adjusting the menu, and investing in other "improvements" to attract a broader clientele may not be financially feasible. Furthermore, many entrepreneurs feel a certain sense of community and loyalty toward longtime residents who have supported their businesses through the years. Over time, some have developed intimate relationships with customers and are not necessarily willing to abandon them to cater to newcomers.

The data I gathered from interviews, online reviews, and field observations in Barrio Logan, City Heights, and Southeastern San Diego, as well as in a few comparative neighborhoods that are further along in the process of gentrification, point to two primary strategies for ethnic businesses to respond to the influx of white and affluent customers and use "authenticity." On the one hand, they could take the "ethnic" route and offer what Yelpers describe as a "hole-in-the-wall" experience in which "classic" and "cheap" dishes are prepared by "immigrant cooks" and served by "boorish waiters" in "simple settings" that "barely meet the lowest health rating." To succeed, these restaurants must serve food judged good and cheap enough to outweigh the negatives of service, setting, sanitation, location, and/or safety. Cheapness can only be achieved by keeping costs down, including labor costs. "Goodness," however, is primarily determined by online reviews, social media attention, and foodie word-of-mouth, with some restaurants reaching cult status and catching the attention of experts. In other words, these holes-in-the-wall must be "discovered" by outsiders to gain recognition.

Alternatively, business operators can take the "cosmopolitan" route by "reinventing" ethnic food. This is typically accomplished with support from the "urban food machine" (see chapter 5), including outside investors who advertise their chef's superior culinary skills, revamp menus to recreate traditional dishes "with flair," and redecorate to match the geographic imaginaries of educated and well-traveled consumers. Unlike ethnic "cooks" who presumably lack creativity and sophistication, "chefs" can "elevate" ethnic food by reinterpreting and reinventing classic dishes. In these restaurants certain ingredients become fetishized objects of authenticity, at least temporarily. A decade ago, sriracha sauce became a symbol of authentic Vietnamese food, showing up on restaurant tables and menus everywhere, until its growing popularity and ubiquity made it lose its appeal. Wasabi had experienced a similar fate a few years earlier. Today, condiments such as harissa, gochujang, fish sauce, Calabrian chili paste, miso, and tahini are making their way onto menus everywhere. Unusual and creative uses of such ingredients are highly valued by customers. For example, trendy cafés in City Heights and Barrio Logan now serve horchata coffee—giving the drink a Mexican flair. Tacos, ceviches, and moles are reinvented in myriad ways, giving us the sixteen-dollar surf-and-turf taco. So are curries, ramen, and pho. Yet they remain "authentic" in the eyes of gentrifiers because of aesthetic factors and prized ingredients.

As noted, the taste of gentrification goes beyond the gustatory properties of food; it is intimately connected to place and the social experiences it enables. Rewriting menus is only one aspect of pleasing foodies. To broaden their consumer base and increase profits, restaurants must embrace new aesthetics. This might begin by changing the décor and service style of individual restaurants, but eventually it leads to a revamping of the whole neighborhood. At the scale of the restaurant, communal tables, industrial vibes, reclaimed building materials, eclectic music, vintage political posters, imported dinnerware, and other features help create curated places in which selected elements of the past are appropriated and reinvented. These changes appeal—at least on the surface—to contemporary values of democracy, authenticity, and cosmopolitanism that foodies embrace and use to distinguish themselves. It is ironic that authenticity is more likely to be attributed to these aesthetic characteristics that please outsiders than to the ethnic origins and experiences of those who have a personal connection to this type of food.

At the street, block, or neighborhood scale, the "bustling energy" and "colorful vibrancy" of the community must outweigh the discomfort and concerns for safety that lessen visitors' enjoyment of food and diminish their overall dining experience. Evidence of poverty and food insecurity undermine the sense of democracy, populism, and cosmopolitanism professed by foodies. Bars on windows, security guards, surveillance cameras, peeling Formica tables, plastic chairs, rusty refrigerators, mismatched cups, and overflowing trash cans are not-so-subtle reminders of the daily struggles of residents. So are homeless people asking for a handout, frugal shoppers counting their cash before ordering food, consumers who simply look different, and waiters too tired, hungry, and underpaid to be friendly. Such reminders of the historical and continuing struggles of residents are discomforting and could literally leave a bad taste in the mouth of gentrifiers. Thus neighborhoods must be cleansed; the past must be erased and replaced with a carefully curated cosmopolitan image built on decontextualized, flattened, and inoffensive symbols. Restaurant owners, and the "urban growth machine" (see chapter 5), are key players in this transformation process.

As neighborhoods gentrify, traditional businesses are progressively replaced by cosmopolitan ones. Entrepreneurs who cater to the taste of gentrification thrive, while those who appear old-fashioned and out of touch with current sensitivities slowly disappear. Between 2015 and 2020 numerous restaurants closed and many more opened in the three study neighborhoods, indicating a period of "creative destruction." The overall net rate of entry, which measures the difference between openings and closings as a proportion of existing restaurants, correlates with gentrification: it was highest in Barrio Logan and lowest in Southeastern San Diego. Using audit data to distinguish between ethnic and cosmopolitan restaurants based on the type of aesthetic factors just described reveals that positive net entry rates were driven primarily by "cosmopolitan" restaurants, which opened in large numbers in all three neighborhoods. In contrast, "ethnic" restaurants had a negative net entry rate in both Barrio Logan and Southeastern San Diego where there were more closures than openings. Even in City Heights, where local organizations support refugee entrepreneurs, cosmopolitan restaurants opened at a higher rate than ethnic ones.

Restaurants and cafés in Barrio Logan provide a poignant illustration of this transition from ethnic to cosmopolitan. Longtime establishments like Rolando's, El Golosito, and Las Cuatro Milpas have been serving "humble" dishes such as burritos, tacos, tortas, tamales, and menudo (figure 6.1). A few mismatched chairs and tables furnish each place, and walls are hung with pictures of popular dishes and historical scenes of Mexico

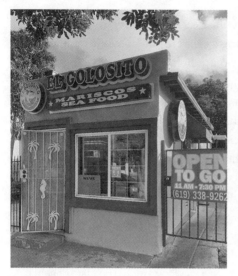

FIGURE 6.1 The ethnic foodscape f Barrio Logan: (clockwise from left) El Golosito, Las Cuatro Milpas, and Rolando's. Photographs by author.

and Barrio Logan. Colorful signs and storefronts draw the attention of passersby. Although online reviews are mixed, the customers I interviewed said they enjoyed the food and appreciated the relatively low prices and quick service. Most were local residents who ate at those neighborhood places regularly. Although they did not use the word *authentic*, they described the food as *traditional*, *typical*, and *homestyle*.

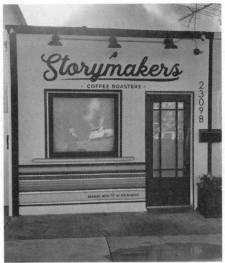

FIGURE 6.2 The cosmopolitan food-scape of Barrio Logan: (clockwise from left) Por Vida Café and Art Gallery, Storymakers Coffee Roasters, and Barrio Dogg. Photographs by author.

These older establishments are now surrounded by new businesses such as Por Vida, Barrio Dogg, and the soon-to-be-open Storymakers (figure 6.2). Their curated and Instagram-friendly décors are striking in their similar combination of Mexican and Chicano cultural symbols, including lowrider cars, Virgin de la Guadalupe, Frida Kahlo, and colorful murals, with an industrial vibe created by concrete floors, reclaimed wood counters, cinderblock façades, and iron gates. Most of these double as art galleries featuring local artists and exacerbating the artistic vibe. The food and drink they serve embody a similar hybridity and creativity, combining traditional and new ingredients and reinterpreting old recipes with new sensitivities. For example, Por Vida is known for its unique drinks such as the spicy mango lemonade served in a Tajín-rimmed cup and the mazapan latte, served hot or cold and topped with De La Rosa crumbles. Barrio Dogg offers "a taste of Chicano comfort food, with the emphasis of using high-quality ingredients, and to express the artistic flavor that comes from our neighborhood."[33] And Storymakers has been "schooling its crew" to prepare "the world's finest coffees," "made with love in the barrio" using "aeropress, beehouse, kalita, chemex, moka pot, and French press."[34] In these cosmopolitan places, aesthetics convey authenticity while allowing for creativity. To some, this sort of reinvention is a form of creolization that has always existed; to others, it is a form of appropriation.

The claim of appropriation is a loaded one: who is appropriating what and from whom? At the most basic level the story goes like this: outside entrepreneurs are appropriating the cuisines of local residents for profit, diverting resources away from historical businesses, and depriving immigrants and people of color from the opportunity to benefit from their own culture. The reality is a little more nuanced, as not all entrepreneurs are outsiders, new businesses may create jobs for local residents and provide an opportunity for the neighborhood to tell its own story and shape its future. In Barrio Logan some of the most successful new businesses are owned by locals who work with residents and help create a sense of place rooted in the history of the neighborhood and its Chicano identity. Ultimately, appropriation is about taking something from someone else without permission. Thus consent is at the core of this issue. Yet such consent is difficult to conceptualize when thinking about a culture, neighborhood, or community. Investors are not required by law to ask residents' consent to open a restaurant and serve ethnic food, whether reinvented or not. One way to think about consent at the community level is to consider whether longtime residents are supportive of the new businesses. This assumes that residents have the opportunity to participate in the community-planning process, to voice their concerns, and to shape the outcome. In reality, residents are excluded from most decisions and have very limited input into the planning process.

Another way to think about consent is to consider whether residents benefit from the neighborhood transformation linked to new restaurants and retailers. If these new businesses provide exciting and affordable dining options, create job opportunities, improve safety, beautify the built environment, and enhance community cohesion for the benefit of current inhabitants, it may be problematic to talk about appropriation. However, if they end up displacing longtime residents and benefiting newcomers instead, it is difficult to believe that consent was given.

DISPLACEMENTS

The transformation from ethnic to cosmopolitan foodscape is accompanied by several forms of displacement that hurt longtime residents—and to which they probably would not have consented if they had been consulted. This seriously challenges the legitimacy of the moral claims made explicitly or implicitly by outside investors and consumers who so vehemently wish to "support the community." It is therefore not surprising that people most directly impacted by these changes are beginning to resist them.

Most of the scholarship on gentrification emphasizes displacement through the housing market.[35] As outside investors pour capital into undervalued neighborhoods in an effort to capitalize on their newfound desirability, property values, rents, and property taxes begin to rise, pushing out low-income renters. Data presented earlier in this chapter describe gentrification trends in the study area, including a rapid rise of property value between 2000 and 2017. Even after taking into account inflation, property values rose by 85 percent in Barrio Logan, 82 percent in Southeastern, and 80 percent in City Heights, well above the 47 percent average increase in the county of San Diego.[36] Meanwhile, households in the bottom 20 percent of the income distribution—the majority of longtime residents of Barrio Logan, City Heights, and Southeastern San Diego— saw their real income drop by 6 percent to an annual average of $14,500.[37] For those households that earn income below or near poverty, housing in these neighborhoods has become unaffordable. As a result, they must make difficult choices: forgoing other basic necessities such as food, medicine, or utilities to pay for housing; doubling up and living in crowded conditions; or moving to more affordable areas typically farther from work. The demographic changes, including a slow rise in the proportion of college-educated and white residents, suggest that the most vulnerable longtime inhabitants are being displaced to other neighborhoods.

The effects of gentrification, however, are not limited to residential evictions. Another group being displaced consists of ethnic businesses that cannot compete with newcomers. Cosmopolitan restaurants are progressively replacing ethnic ones. Catering to the taste of gentrification is expensive and ethnic entrepreneurs typically lack the resources and knowledge to mold their businesses to these ever-changing contemporary sensitivities. Outside investors, having accumulated wealth, reputation, and prior experience in more affluent neighborhoods, are better able to capitalize on this opportunity by appropriating and reinventing authentic food, culture, and surroundings to match the taste and geographic imaginaries of affluent consumers. Although a few older businesses stand out in their appeal to cultural elites, it is often new or seriously remodeled establishments like Por Vida that attract the most business.

The influx of investors seeking to lease or purchase commercial properties puts pressure on the real estate market and raises rents for all, paralleling the residential market trends. Suddenly faced with higher operating costs, long-term tenants must adapt or quit. For instance, as I am writing this chapter, Wrigley—one of the few supermarkets in the greater Southeastern San Diego—just announced its closing due to rising rents. As an independent market started in the late 1970s by Chaldean immigrants, it has been a beacon in a community struggling with food apartheid, meeting local consumer demands for affordable and culturally appropriate food and building particularly strong ties with the Black community. The closing is a major loss for the community and yet another step toward reproducing food apartheid. It is unknown at this time what new tenant—if any—would replace Wrigley, but residents are already debating the potential impacts of having a Whole Foods or Trader Joe's move in.

Food-insecure households are deeply affected by foodscape changes that raise the cost of food. First, shop owners transfer at least part of the rent increases onto customers through higher prices. Second, the increased demand, caused by the influx of visitors in search of authentic food and the changing demographics of the neighborhood, is also contributing to price increases. In addition, as organic, artisanal, homemade, and authentic foods begin to replace more basic items, food simply becomes more expensive. As the three-for-five-dollar taco deal is replaced by the sixteen-dollar taco, it is more difficult for low-income residents to find affordable food, exacerbating widespread food insecurity (see chapter 4). A tweet about a new restaurant in the Los Angeles neighborhood of South Gate resonated with Barrio Logan residents who retweeted it heavily, revealing their frustration: "You blame the lack of healthy eating in my community on food deserts as if your $9 açaí bowls and $4 avocado with salt on it don't contribute to said food deserts. healthy food has always been available for purchase here, it just isn't affordable and your restaurant proves it."

The customers I interviewed at various ethnic food stores in City Heights and Barrio Logan echoed this resentment against many new businesses, suggesting a lack of consent. Neighborhood change was a universal theme in our conversations. Although some viewed the openings of new businesses favorably and welcome neighborhood revitalization, the majority deplored the fact that these businesses did not serve their needs. They were often disappointed by what they offered and offended by the prices they charged. Yolanda, a longtime Latinx resident of City Heights, illustrated this feeling when she described her experience at a new coffee shop in her neighborhood:

> I was excited when I saw the construction workers renovating the building. I heard they were going to open a food store. We need better shops for food in this part of the neighborhood for simple things, you know . . . not just fast food or liquor stores . . . a place where we can get basic things like fruits and vegetables, milk, tortillas . . . these are important. We don't always want to go to the supermarket.
>
> When I realized it was a café, I was disappointed. . . . I went to check it out. I could not believe it. It was so expensive. Truthfully, I did not know what to order. I could not just get a regular coffee. It was all fancy and stuff. . . . Let the rich white people spend their money there if they want.

Like Yolanda, many agreed that the new businesses appearing in their neighborhoods are not meant for them but for new residents or outsiders—"rich white people." This changing foodscape disrupts the fragile food provisioning and social reproduction strategies of low-income and immigrant families (see chapter 4). In particular, the closing of small ethnic shops and restaurants, where they might have been regular customers, means that they have to familiarize themselves with other vendors and may lose access to culturally appropriate food. When these options disappear, households are more likely to turn to unhealthy, familiar, and comforting foods such as fast food and other high-caloric and low-nutrient foods.[38] They are also less likely to be able to use EBT cards, request special items, receive temporary credit or discounts, or get compassion from a new shopkeeper they do not know.

This insecurity is exacerbated by the displacement of food pantry, soup kitchen, and community gardens. Illustrating Neil Smith's notion of urban revanchism, social service providers are often under attack by new residents who view them as magnets for undesirable others (e.g., criminals, drug addicts, the disabled).[39] The San Diego Police Department is overwhelmed with calls from people concerned about "suspicious" individuals "loitering." In many neighborhoods private watches and social media platforms like Nextdoor have emerged to monitor the movement of people who look "out of place"—most of whom were there before gentrifiers arrived. Any proposal for new social service providers or affordable housing is met with fierce opposition by new residents concerned for their safety and property values. The criminalization of poverty is a racialized process in which poor Black and Brown people are blamed for neighborhood dysfunction and targeted for removal from a landscape in which they no longer belong.

When the value of land begins to rise, nonprofits that operate on tight budgets struggle. Community gardens are particularly vulnerable to this trend and find themselves at risk of eviction when landlords discover more profitable uses for their land. This was the case of Mount Hope Community Garden in Southeastern San Diego, where a "For Sale" sign was discovered by gardeners early one morning in January 2018. After sitting vacant for at least two decades, the land had been rented by Project New Village at a low cost and turned into a community garden. Thirty-six raised beds and several community plots provided an important source of food and camaraderie for residents of all ages. Thanks to the perseverance of its members and their connections with funders, advocates, policymakers, and academics, Project New Village was able to obtain a loan and several grants to purchase the land and keep the garden in the community. Soon, however, it will need to generate enough income to start reimbursing the loan. Although this presents an opportunity to engage in social entrepreneurship and new activities, it threatens to displace growers who simply want a small plot of land to grow food for their families.

It is not just the built environment and amenities that are transformed by gentrification. The rhythm of everyday life—how bodies interact with time and place—is altered. As Henri Lefebvre has argued, cities have rhythms shaped by capital and its imperatives.[40] Fashioned by the classed and raced lives of residents, these rhythms emerge from repetitions and patterns of movement: when, where, and how people go to work, go home, walk their dog, exercise, entertain themselves, eat, and sleep. As neighborhoods gentrify, the temporality and spatiality of food practices change: residents stay out later, work in coffee shops, take lunch breaks in restaurants, meet friends for drinks at night, go to brunch on weekends, order takeout or food deliveries regularly, and shop at the farmers' market once a week. This new rhythm of everyday life often clashes with that of longtime residents who occupy neighborhood places such as shops, restaurants, sidewalks, homes, public spaces, and streets at different times and in different ways.

Leslie Kern's work on gentrification in the Junction neighborhood of Toronto highlights how the refashioned urban landscape "privileges new rhythms and tempos of everyday life."[41] She focuses specifically on the temporal landscape of gentrification and its aesthetic characteristics. Simulacrum of the past—what she describes as "vintage timespaces"—support particular forms of socialization that favors white, middle-class, and young residents. For example, events such as flea markets, art crawls, farmers' markets, summer festivals, and walking tours allow newcomers to imprint their temporalities on neighborhood life. The "urban growth machine" has sponsored similar events in Barrio Logan, City Heights, and Southeastern San Diego, often in collaboration with new restaurants and with the goal of attracting outsiders and encouraging consumption. Yet long-term residents rarely participate in these events for a variety of reasons related to a lack of financial resources or leisure time and social exclusion. Their absence in these "community events" becomes "a barrier to recognition, belonging and representation, one that both hides and enables the 'slow violence' of gentrification."[42] Similarly, I argue that the absence of ethnoracial people from cosmopolitan restaurants, sidewalk terraces, beer gardens, and gourmet food shops that presumably celebrate their heritage reflects a form of displacement linked to the devaluation of their needs and experiences.

Memories are lost too. For longtime residents some restaurants and food stores hold powerful memories, such as shopping for snacks with friends after school, celebrating birthdays, or simply enjoying family meals. When these places close, change ownership, or get renovated, former patrons experience a sense of loss and a devaluation of their way of life. Indeed, the residents I interviewed often described restaurants and shops that have shut down in nostalgic ways, revealing a longing for and perhaps idealization of the past. Talking about a recently closed taco shop in Barrio Logan, Javier, a Mexican American man in his fifties, explained:

> This place was not fancy, but it was full of memories. I don't know how many times I took my kids there for tacos, when they were little. My son lives in LA now, but when he comes down to visit, we would always go for tacos. His favorites were tacos de lengua— tongue tacos. He was sad when I told him that the shop had to close. . . . It held great memories for us. . . . There is no other place like this now. The new places, they are completely different, I don't even know what food that is, but that's not Mexican!

This loss of meaningful and familiar places is often accompanied by a common feeling of being "out of place" and not belonging in one's own neighborhood. Some urban scholars conceptualize the city as an archive—a sort of repository for the past.[43] The selective removal of unwanted bits from the past and their replacement with carefully curated elements effectively rewrites the history of neighborhoods and produces a sort of amnesia that marginalizes certain groups and deprives them of the possibility of living and expressing their place-based identities and telling their own stories in the future.

The multiple exclusions, erasures, and dispossessions of longtime residents relate to the whiteness of cosmopolitan foodscapes. Elijah Anderson had defined white spaces as "settings in which Black people are typically absent, not expected, or marginalized when present."[44] Many critical observers have described alternative and trendy foodscapes as "white spaces."[45] Yet this characterization seems contradictory and ironic when ethnicity, authenticity, and diversity are parts of the attraction of new restaurants, food stores, and street festivals. Indeed, people of color are there, but mostly for the benefit of white middle-class people, as cook, servers, and occasionally part of the "incredibly diverse crowd" that gives a place distinction. In other words, they are part of the "background"—objects in a multicultural experiment in which white citizens are the subjects.[46]

The unique assemblage and visibility of white bodies in cosmopolitan spaces brings whiteness to the foreground. This phenomenon is what Arun Saldanha has described as "viscosity"—the sticking together and impermeability of collectives of human bodies that define social space and belonging.[47] Thus whiteness is not just a function of the count of white bodies in a given place, but of "what whites do in these places" that leads to the exclusion of others.[48] Despite the presence of people of color in cosmopolitan foodscapes, the thickening white viscosity makes these spaces uncomfortable or unapproachable to nonwhite bodies. Although perhaps less visible and dramatic than housing evictions, these claims to space are no less powerful in *dis*-placing people—causing them to leave their home against their will even if staying put.

In 2012, Tyler Cowen (who described himself as a frugal economist and a foodie) articulated six rules for eating out in an article for *The Atlantic*.[49] One of these rules is to "get out of the city into the strip mall" in search of authentic and first-rate ethnic food. He explained: "It is especially common to see good ethnic restaurants grouped with mid-level or junky retail outlets. When it comes to a restaurant run by immigrants, look around at the street scene. Do you see something ugly? Poor construction? Broken plastic signage? A five-and-dime store? Maybe an abandoned car? If so, crack a quiet smile, walk through the door, and order. Welcome to the glamorous world of good food."

This quote exemplifies the attitude of many white, educated, middle-class consumers who over the past decade, like "urban pioneers," have ventured into Barrio Logan, City Heights, and to a lesser extent South-eastern San Diego in search of authenticity without much consideration of the impacts of their "discoveries" on these neighborhoods. Their forays into immigrant and ethnic neighborhoods both express and trigger a broader transformation of foodscapes where heritage, culture, and ethnicity are aesthetically reproduced and reimagined through a selective process. The resulting cosmopolitan foodscape—a caricatured, decontextualized, and whitewashed version of ethnic foodscapes—provides the young, educated, and affluent opportunities to distinguish themselves. Some just visit once in a while—to "try something different"—but others, attracted by the urban lifestyles on offer, move in. The carefully curated, quaint, vintage, artisanal, industrial, and cosmopolitan aesthetic that celebrates ethnicity and diversity, however, hides the displacement of longtime residents who see their way of life threatened by rising rents and food prices, disappearing familiar places, lost memories, and changing rhythms.

7

Reclaiming the Ethnic Foodscape

Food Sovereignty

S I WRAPPED up this book and organized my concluding thoughts, I was "distracted" by a new series on Netflix. Instead of writing, I sat in front of my television, binge-watching *Gentefied* and feeling guilty for procrastinating.[1] Quickly though, my guilt turned into amazement and my mind raced as I realized how relevant this new series is to my work. Although I am concerned about the normalization of gentrification and the fetishization of antigentrification that a show like this might produce, I acknowledge that it illustrates with wit and humor some of the main arguments of this book and confirms the timeliness of my research topic. Watching three Chicano cousins struggle to save their uncle's taco shop in the gentrifying East Los Angeles neighborhood of Boyle Heights reminded me of the many people I interviewed for this book—the first-, second-, or third-generation immigrants who live in places similar to Boyle Heights, work in the food economy, and struggle to belong and stay put.

Gentefied does a particularly good job at showing the complexity of gentrification; while the main characters grapple with their changing neighborhoods and lament the influx of "westsiders," they also contribute to these changes by investing in their communities, challenging traditional cultural norms, and expressing their identities as young people caught between two worlds. For example, in the fifth episode, Ana—an underpaid artist—is commissioned by Tim—a white queer man who has been buying properties in the neighborhood—to paint a mural on the outside wall of a small convenience store he recently acquired. Tim is extremely pleased with the oversized painting of two men in luchadores masks kissing passionately that he believes will "completely beautify the location," attract "people from all walks of life who share [their] passions," and bring "mucho dinero—lots and lots of business." As a queer woman, Ana is proud of her artwork and the political statement it makes but questions Tim's motives. Meanwhile, Ofelia, the Mexican immigrant woman who rents and manages the store (and was not asked permission for the mural) is troubled by the discomfort the mural causes her longtime customers and the negative consequences it might have on her business. When she complains, Tim tells her: "It's my building and I am making it better *for you!*" As he later tells Ana, he believes that "she [Ofelia] does not know what is good for her." To "save the store" and protect the mural, Ana and her cousins organize a "cash mob" using social media to encourage friends and acquaintances to shop at the store. Against their expectations, this generates the ire of Ofelia, who explains: "I don't need your help. What I need are my regulars who come every day."

These tensions between serving the community and adapting to attract outsiders are also evident in the cousins' ongoing debates regarding the best approach to catch up on late and rising rent payments for their uncle's shop, whether it is sticking to the classics that loyal customers expect, giving out free tacos to local kids in hopes of attracting their parents, charging for chips, adding specials such as curried duck tacos, or participating in the "Bite into Boyle Heights" foodie tour organized by the *LA Weekly* newspaper. For Ana's girlfriend, Yessika, most of these options seem like "selling out the community" and "welcoming outsiders en masse with open arms and pushing people out of their homes," but to her cousin, Chris, they are opportunities to create something of their own.

The term *gentefication*, which combines *gente*—the Spanish word for *people*—and *gentrification* captures these tensions and contradictions. It has recently emerged as a way to describe a trend in which middle-class Latinxs engage in "self-gentrification."[2] For some, it is a proposal to have the *gente* take control of their communities and shape the process of gentrification for themselves and not for outsiders. Guillermo Uribe, who owns the successful Eastside Luv bar in Boyle Heights's Mariachi Plaza, put it this way in a *Los Angeles Times* interview: "If gentrification is happening, it might as well be from people who care about the existing culture. . . . It would be best if the *gente* decide to invest in improvements because they are more likely to preserve [the neighborhood's] integrity."[3] In another interview, Uribe explained: "If we want to preserve the cultural integrity, the pride we have, the only shot we have is to do it ourselves."[4] Marco Amador, who grew up in Boyle Heights and runs a radio program out of a rented storefront near Eastside Luv, agreed: "We're not trying to get out of the barrio, we're trying to bring the barrio up."[5]

Not surprisingly, most sites of *gentefication*—whether fictional or real—in Los Angeles, San Diego, Chicago, or elsewhere, are food businesses: restaurants, bars, coffee shops, bakeries, and small markets that are owned and operated by immigrants and more recent generations. The most successful among them embody notions of authenticity, diversity, and democracy that are associated with the aesthetics of cosmopolitanism (described in chapter 6). Some are worker-owned, hold workshops on important community issues such as policing and gentrification, exhibit art from local artists, serve dishes named after their grandmothers, experiment with ingredients and recipes rooted in their cultures, and charge "pay-what-you-can" prices.

The idea of gentefication raises interesting questions in light of the trends described in this book—mainly the cosmopolitanization of ethnic foodscapes as a racial project with devastating consequences for the working-class immigrant and ethnic communities it exploits and displaces. How do we create local food economies that not only meet the basic needs of urban dwellers but also enable them to engage with food in ways that sustain livelihoods, promote healthy lives, encourage civility, and positively affirm difference? Do gentefication and antigentrification efforts seeking to reclaim the ethnic foodscapes run the risk of refetishizing ethnicity and obscuring the power inequalities that caused gentrification in the first place? In short, how do immigrant communities stem the tide of rising property values and displacement that seem to accompany any efforts to revitalize, support, or enhance ethnic foodscapes?

I believe that this is a question of *food sovereignty*, which would presumably be enhanced with greater participation from la gente. I do not mean just Latinx communities here, but all communities of color that have historically inhabited segregated and neglected neighborhoods in the fullest sense—dwelling in them and weaving connections to and through them. That includes immigrants who have made a new home away from home by patronizing local shops and restaurants, making acquaintances and friends, opening businesses, growing food, cooking, vending in the streets, or sharing meals with others in the midst of food apartheid—creating foodscapes that are now being appropriated and threatened by outsiders under the guise of cosmopolitanism. Food sovereignty dictates that ethnic foodscapes ought to be produced *for, with,* and *by* such people.

FOOD SOVEREIGNTY

At first, food sovereignty might appear to be ill-suited to describe and address the conditions of immigrants and people of color in cosmopolitan foodscapes. The concept emerged in the Global South in the 1990s to frame peasant struggles and motivate a social movement that unites small farmers in dismantling the global, corporate, and industrial food system. In 2007 more than five hundred representatives of landless peasants, pastoralists, fisher-folks, and urban farmers from eighty countries cosigned the Nyéléni Declaration, which defines *food sovereignty* as follows:

> Food sovereignty is the right of peoples to healthy and culturally appropriate food produced through ecologically sound and sustainable methods, and their right to define their own food and agriculture system. It puts those who produce, distribute and consume food at the heart of food systems and policies rather than the demands of markets and corporations. . . . It ensures that the rights to use and manage our lands, territories, waters, seeds, livestock and biodiversity are in the hands of those of us who produce food. Food sovereignty implies new social relations free of oppression and

inequality between men and women, peoples, racial groups, social classes and generations.[6]

The notion of food security emphasizes the need to eradicate racism, sexism, classism, and other forms of inequality inherent to capitalism to ensure that peoples are able to exercise their rights to live free of hunger and shape food systems and policies impacting them. By *peoples*, this implies communities rather than individuals. This notion gained significant traction among Indigenous farmers in the Global South whose control over land, resources, food, and knowledge has been eroded by imperialism, neoliberal capitalism, and the globalization of food and agriculture. Over the past decade, food activists and scholars in the United States have begun adopting the idea of food sovereignty to address a wide range of food-related issues facing low-income communities of color, including uneven access to food, which I have described as food apartheid.[7] Urban agriculture in particular has received significant attention as an autonomous community response to counter the withdrawal of retail capital. By growing food together, low-income urban residents and people of color can potentially reclaim land and regain control over the production, distribution, and consumption of food.[8]

Food sovereignty, however, has not yet been used productively in research or activism addressing gentrification and the exploitation and displacement of immigrants and people of color in cosmopolitan foodscapes or contemporary urban consumption landscapes in general. This might be due to the priority that food sovereignty proponents tend to put on food production, especially urban agriculture, and exchange, including alternative local networks, over consumption, particularly if it pertains to the urban lifestyles of affluent consumers in the United States. This omission may also reflect an innate bias against retailers and entrepreneurs who presumably operate within the logic of capitalism and are therefore seen as part of the problem that, according to most proponents of food sovereignty, ought to be addressed by "alternative" schemes that carve out autonomous space outside of the racist capitalist system.

The framework of food sovereignty has often been discarded by scholars in the United States who have found that it does not resonate with activists and academics, who prefer the term *food justice*.[9] The notion of food justice has inspired much academic and activist work in the United States in the past two decades, especially in the context of cities where poverty and racism shape food systems.[10] I do not wish to rehash the debates between food sovereignty and food justice here.[11] In reality, there is significant overlap between food sovereignty and "radical" food justice perspectives: both view food insecurity, labor exploitation, and environmental degradation as the product of systemic injustices that disproportionately affect the most vulnerable members of society.[12] Rasheed Salaam Hislop's often-cited definition of food justice as "the struggle against racism, exploitation, and oppression taking place within the food system that addresses inequality's root causes both within and beyond the food chain" puts it squarely in the camp of food sovereignty.[13]

For me, *food sovereignty* emphasizes the need to address the structural causes of food apartheid, whether it is manifested in uneven food access or in dispossession linked to appropriation and gentrification, and the importance of self-determination—that is, the ability to determine the what, how, and where of food procurement. Thus it straddles the political boundary between radical change and everyday practices of resistance. I also use the term to distance what I propose from increasingly mainstream understandings of food justice that describe all sorts of initiatives to increase food access without addressing underlying class and race power differentials. That includes so-called alternative food projects, such as farmers' markets, community gardens, and community supported agriculture that prioritize the values and lifestyles of white, middle-class volunteers and consumers with the means to participate in such projects and "vote with their forks."[14] The faith placed on the ability of consumers and nonprofits to reform the food system locally is symptomatic of neoliberal capitalism to the extent that it emphasizes market-based solutions and shifts responsibility onto individual and communities.[15] This sort of project may be called food justice, but it certainly is not food sovereignty.

Sadly, we seem to know a lot more about what food sovereignty is *not* than what it actually *is*. We know that food sovereignty is not colorblind or parochial. It is also not charity, education, or redemptive action. And it is not led by foodies. Achieving the goals of food sovereignty requires that we get past bemoaning the impacts of the current food system and the pitfalls of alternative food initiatives. Rather, we must get involved in the messy and imperfect politics of building something different: opening spaces for new social relations, experimenting at different scales, engaging unexpected actors, making new alliances, and working on multiple fronts to fight gentrification.

Food sovereignty provides an opportunity to think seriously about how we might address food apartheid—the various forms of food-related dispossessions that immigrants and people of color experience in neighborhoods like Barrio Logan, City Heights, and Southeastern San Diego. As I have documented throughout this book, these dispossessions include the withdrawal of food retail capital form ethnic neighborhoods and their stigmatization as food deserts, economic hardship and labor exploitation in the food economy, hunger and assaults on social reproduction through the dismantling of place-based food procurement and survival strategies, and cultural appropriation and multifaceted displacement through food gentrification. Today, these interrelated, overlapping, systemic, and embodied forms of oppression come together in the cosmopolitan foodscape. These seemingly unrelated deprivations are shaped by state-sanctioned, capital-driven, and spatialized processes that successively devalue, appropriate, and displace the labor, cultural practices, places, bodies, and lives of immigrants and people of color to maintain the economic and cultural superiority of those in power. Thus the agenda of food sovereignty to increase control over food production and consumption by those who have been marginalized in the contemporary capitalist, neoliberal, and racist food system seems especially relevant in the context of gentrification.

THE IMPERFECT POLITICS OF RECLAIMING THE ETHNIC FOODSCAPE

Enacting food sovereignty in the cosmopolitan foodscape entails reclaiming ethnic foodscapes *for, by,* and *with* immigrants and people of color. It is not a neat process and there is much disagreement about how this can be done, as illustrated by debates about gentefication. The suggestions I offer here are directed at pushing back against racism and capitalism to create healthy, diverse, livable, and sustainable foodscapes that uphold people's right to stay put and flourish. They emphasize the geographic nature of resistance, which consists of "occupying, deploying, and creating alternative spatialities than those defined through oppression and exploitation," and draw attention to everyday practices of resistance and place-making without naively losing sight of the bigger battles against racism and economic inequality.[16] These suggestions are not new; they are inspired by the mostly unacknowledged past and ongoing work of people of color in resisting food apartheid and bringing about food sovereignty.

In *A Postcapitalist Politics*, J. K. Gibson-Graham has argued that there is more than one way to exercise power and resist oppression through seemingly small, disconnected, and partial acts of resistance.[17] Rejecting a priori judgments of what is possible or transformative widens the imagination of possible food futures beyond the neoliberal agenda of "consumer choice, entrepreneurialism, localism, and self-improvement."[18] Such openness recognizes that the politics of food sovereignty are imperfect, ambiguous, situated, contingent, negotiated, conflicted, and always and already in the making. With this notion of "imperfect politics" in mind, I outline possible ways of reclaiming the ethnic foodscape and building on what is already there to stop the appropriation, stigmatization, and displacement of immigrants and their foodways; increase community control over resources and decisions on how to meet multidimensional food needs; preserve food places, practices, and identities; and support local food-based livelihoods through fair wages and working conditions. This consists of restoring and uplifting the ethnic foodscape with and for immigrants and longtime residents without turning it into a cosmopolitan foodscape for outsiders—an imperfect process similar to the "just green enough" idea put forward by those concerned that green projects in low-income neighborhoods lead to gentrification.[19]

Strategies can be distinguished based on the *scale* of intervention, from the body to the globe; the *actors* engaged, including consumers, producers, community-based organizations, local, state and national governments as well as those most directly concerned and typically excluded from decisions; the *focus* of intervention such as food, labor, housing, and economic development; the *visibility* of resistance, from contentious politics to everyday practices; and the *scope* of demands from "commonsensical" incremental change to "impossible" visions.

Toward Empathic and Careful Eating

Much has been written about the role of consumers in alternative food movements, including the serious limitations of ethical consumerism in tackling the root causes of food insecurity. In many different ways, critical scholars have shown that food sovereignty cannot be purchased by enlightened, affluent, and primary white consumers of organic, local, and authentic food. More often than not, such strategy contributes to gentrification and displacement. But must foodies automatically be gentrifiers? Is there a role for those who "appreciate" ethnic food in preventing gentrification while supporting immigrant-owned businesses?

Those attracted to immigrant neighborhoods might presumably want to preserve the culture, authenticity, and diversity they found so attractive, including the local foodscape. Yet white privilege translates into an unwillingness and inability to think outside white or colorblind frames that normalize whiteness or erase racial differences. As a result, middle-class white consumers tend to ignore the desires, lives, and struggles of people of color and imagine their consumption as benevolent acts that lift up marginalized people. Thus "supporting the community" often means supporting projects that commodify and whitewash ethnic food into a profitable enterprise, like buying a $16 taco, turning the ethnic foodscape into a cosmopolitan foodscape without realizing that this transformation might have negative consequences for longtime residents.

Until recently, gentrification research has paid little attention to gentrifiers, emphasizing instead the experience of victims observed from some scholarly distance. In *Gentrifier*, John Joe Schlichtman, Jason Patch, and Marc Lamont Hill's autoethnographic work illustrates the importance of "placing ourselves in the story of gentrification."[20] As consumers, we need to consider the implications of our consumption practices and reflect on our privilege. Food sovereignty ought to be a reflexive effort in which privileged participants, including activists, consumers, and researchers like myself, consider how their own doings might have contributed to reproducing inequality. Alison Hope Alkon, Yuki Kato, and Joshua Sbicca have made a similar point in *Recipe for Gentrification* in which they argue for greater reflexivity in food activism and encourage "well-meaning food activists, particularly white ones, to be aware of macro-level processes of economic exploitation and racism that imbue them with privileges while constraining the lives of low-income people and people of color."[21] Appreciating ethnic food and a romanticized version of the immigrant stories behind it does not do enough to promote food sovereignty. Although ethnic food has long been seen as a vehicle for celebration of difference and a symbol of tolerance, we need to go further than "celebrating" and "tolerating" others; we need empathy and care.

In 2016, on Cinco de Mayo, President Trump tweeted about his appreciation of taco bowls—"the best [ones] are made in Trump Tower grill"—as evidence that he "loves Hispanics." The president is not the only one professing his love of ethnic food; according to surveys by the National Restaurant Association, ethnic cuisine, ingredients, and spices are on the "hot trend list" with a growing number of Americans ordering ethnic food at restaurants.[22] In 2016, 88 percent of Americans consumed at least two "ethnic category" foods per month. In San Diego, there is a powerful "food machine" consisting of real estate agents, public officials, developers, and food experts who boast about the ethnic diversity of local food (see chapter 5). These love declarations are not unlike the "I have a Black friend" statements frequently used to attest colorblindness. They mask racialized assumptions about ethnic food and those with whom it is associated. Trump's declaration of love for taco bowls and Hispanics does not negate the effects of the anti-immigrant and racist language and policies he and his administration have promoted. Similarly, middle-class consumers' growing interest in ethnic food does not necessarily equate to greater acceptance and respect of ethnic people. Neither does paying $16 for a taco.

Of course, we should continue to eat ethnic food; many businesses depend on it. However, we need to engage in more reflexive and empathic eating. Appreciation of ethnic food needs to translate into a recognition of the cultural and emotional significance of these foods for immigrants and subsequent generations and its life-sustaining meaning through livelihoods and social reproduction. This must also lead to an acknowledgment of the labor involved in producing it and a willingness to pay for it. We need to reject the common and restrictive belief that "if it is not cheap, it is not authentic." We could make an effort to learn about the history of ethnic restaurants, their owners, and workers. Based on this information, we could decide to patronize those that are owned by immigrants and people of color, hire local residents, pay living wages, and resist the pressures of catering to outsiders. Finally, we must refrain from privileging notions of authenticity that trap ethnic food and restaurants in stagnant definitions of culture and rigid hierarchies of taste that constraint opportunities. Ditching the term *ethnic food* might be a step in that direction but is unlikely to do much to fight structural inequalities underlying displacement.

Community-based Organizing: Resisting Displacement Together

In the uneven landscape of cities, where social injustices are solidified in and by spatial disparities, collective action and resistance often originates at the scale of the neighborhood, where communal reliance is built through cooperation, trust, and solidarity. Food sovereignty amplifies the practices of self-reliance that Ashanté Reese witnessed in the Black neighborhood of Deanwood in Washington, DC, and that I have observed in three ethnic neighborhoods of San Diego.[23] Across the United States, communities of color are engaged in place-making projects that challenge food apartheid by practicing self-determination and strengthening community control. They have organized to increase access to healthy, affordable, and culturally appropriate food, reclaim land, and reject the mainstream food system that has historically failed to meet their needs. Among various initiatives, community farms and farmers' markets have been by far the most common means to achieve these goals.

In San Diego, although the majority of community gardens are located in middle-class and affluent communities, a few gardens have sprung up in low-income neighborhoods to fight food insecurity and strengthen community (see chapter 4). For example, New Roots Community Farm in City Heights, Mount Hope Community Garden in Southeastern San Diego, Mundo Garden in nearby National City, and several others have provided spaces where residents—mostly immigrants, refugees, and people of color—come together to grow food. The organizations behind these initiatives had to work persistently to secure land, raise funds, endure a burdensome permitting process, organize volunteers, and build soil and infrastructure, fighting against decades of racially biased planning decisions and policies. Although "community-based," these organizations often struggle to engage the community and achieve the sort of self-determination or self-governance that food sovereignty requires. Some, like New Roots, followed a top-down approach in which educated professionals employed by the International Rescue Committee (IRC) took up leadership positions in organizing and managing the farm, while immigrants and refugees—mostly Somali-Bantu—farm the land as they had in their home country. New Roots is often touted as a success story of refugee integration through urban agriculture and has received significant media attention, especially since Michelle Obama's visit in 2016. It has inspired other "New Roots" farms in San Diego, Salt Lake City, Sacramento, Baltimore, and dozens of other cities in the United States. The IRC has been able to lead this initiative because of government contracts and grants, large infrastructure and institutional capacity, and connections with organizations such as AmeriCorps, Urban Corps, and local schools and universities that supply volunteers. As such, it is hardly a grassroots community-based effort.

In contrast, at Mount Hope the community is involved in every decision. However, poverty, along with a lack of trust and a reluctance to farming ingrained in intergenerational trauma, has made it challenging to attract residents to grow year-round, take leadership positions, shop at the farm stand, or even join community events such as the Martin Luther King Jr. day of service, the Fannie Lou Hamer celebration, or regular gardening classes. Project New Village, the organization that started the garden in 2011, is committed to a social justice and antiracist agenda and sees food as a means to accomplish these larger goals. Although they welcome outside help and resources, including my meager contribution in preparing reports and advocacy materials, they are careful to keep control within the community.[24] In spite of these struggles, Mount Hope has been a source of strength in the community, particularly for African American residents, and has played a transformative role beyond addressing food insecurity. Threatened by eviction, the organization was able to lean on its members and partners to purchase the land, which is now owned as a community trust and being used to build a community store and kitchen as part of the Good Food District project, catalyzing food for social justice.

Farmers' markets have been the other arm of localized food justice efforts in San Diego. Indeed, in City Heights and Southeastern San Diego, the same organizations that have spearheaded community gardens—the International Rescue Committee and Project New Village—have also created farmers' markets where growers can sell their produce and residents can access locally grown and organic food. These two farmers' markets were the first to accept EBT and remain exceptions in that respect among the more than sixty farmers' markets now operating in San Diego. The People's Produce Market, run by Project New Village in Southeastern San Diego, is a different kind of farmers' market. It is purposely small and focused on providing opportunities to local residents as growers and small entrepreneurs. Vendors come and go over the seasons and produce selections vary from week to week based on what can be harvested. The location, day, and time had to be changed several times in the past years. Yet there is a palpable sense of community that is visible in the way neighbors interact with each other, including occasional dancing.

As transformative as these new spaces can be in terms of providing economic opportunities, culturally appropriate, healthy, and affordable food, as well as a sense of community, they must contend with the constraints imposed by the neoliberal capitalist system and the commodification of food, land, and labor as noted by critical observers. Paying for the land and supporting their activities requires that they become financially sustainable by marketing to a larger audience willing to pay a premium for local produce. Catering to consumers' demands might jeopardize their ability to serve low-income residents first.

Other elements of local food economies have received much less attention from food activists at the neighborhood level, revealing the dominance of urban agriculture in food justice work and its privileged position in the imaginary of alternative food practices. As shown in chapter 4, ethnic businesses play an important role in promoting community food security and some are clearly embedded in the community fabric. Reese makes a similar observation regarding Deanwood's Black-owned Community Market, which she describes as operating "within a moral economy tinged by racial solidarity, pride, and collectivism."[25] Yet, despite their significance in ethnic neighborhoods, small business owners, street vendors, caterers, "cottage food operators," and food service workers in San Diego have rarely engaged in community-based efforts to gain more control over their activities and challenge ongoing threats to their livelihoods.

They certainly have not received the same kind of philanthropic and volunteer attention as urban agriculture projects have. For instance, there are no community-owned grocery stores in any of the low-income and food-insecure neighborhoods investigated here, although plans have been discussed in City Heights and Southeastern San Diego. Mandela Marketplace in Oakland, the Ujaama Food Co-op in Detroit, and the Village Market Place in Los Angeles provide models for community-owned and community-led food enterprises that prioritize the needs of residents, provide wholesome and affordable food, keep purchasing power in the community, create jobs, and reinvest profits locally.

In San Diego a number of social enterprises with a food justice focus have recently been created, including Kitchens for Good and BrightSide Produce. The former is a culinary apprenticeship program that trains people who suffer from high unemployment (e.g., adults who were formerly incarcerated, are transitioning from foster care, or dealing with domestic violence, mental health disorders, or a history of substance abuse) and provides prepared meals to food-insecure children, seniors, and unsheltered individuals. These training and food assistance programs are partly supported by a catering social enterprise. BrightSide Produce works with small stores in underserved areas of National City to increase the supply of fresh produce by acting as a distributor and allowing them to buy the quantities and varieties that are most appropriate for them. The organization operates out of San Diego State University, where it is incorporated in service learning, recruits volunteers, and raises fund through the sale of produce. Although both organizations create spaces for people who have typically been excluded from food justice initiatives, they do so through a top-down approach that is funded by more affluent consumers.

A few community-based organizations are also working to support the livelihoods of street vendors and home-based food entrepreneurs through a combination of advocacy and training that would help them formalize their activities. In City Heights the Community Development Corporation has begun organizing street vendors against a potentially devastating city ordinance that would ban street vending on busy sidewalk, depriving vendors of their livelihoods and residents of a common source of food. Ironically, the proposed ordinance has been prompted by a new California law (SB 946) meant to decriminalize and formalize street vending by streamlining the permitting process. Yet vendors in immigrant neighborhoods have not been included in city deliberations, which have been influenced primarily by dissatisfied property owners in wealthy beach areas. San Diego could take inspiration from Los Angeles, where immigrant communities in East Los Angeles have been engaged in a grassroots movement to protect their livelihoods and support the larger Los Angeles Street Vendor Campaign. In National City—just south of Southeastern San Diego—Mundo Gardens, Olivewood Gardens, and the Kitchenistas are working together to support food microentrepreneurs, most of whom are immigrant women and Latinas. They are advocating for the County to adopt a new California law (AB 626/377) that would allow homemade food operations and create opportunities for small businesses that do not have access to commercial kitchens.

The fight against gentrification has similarly involved grassroots and neighborhood organizations working to preserve affordable housing and protect tenants from impending evictions. Rarely, however, have antigentrification and food sovereignty efforts been combined into a coherent agenda. In fact, antigentrification advocates often target food community projects as symbols—if not causes—of neighborhood changes leading to displacement. This has been the case in Barrio Logan, where the community has eyed most food projects with suspicion, including those sponsored by government agencies and nonprofits. There is no farmers' market in Barrio Logan and only one small community garden—the Chicano Park Herb Garden described by its founders as a "collective community herbal garden for healing, restoring, learning, praying, meditating and grounding."[26] The biweekly San Diego Public Market, which opened in 2012 in one of Barrio Logan's old factory buildings, closed less than two years later for reasons that remain unclear. According to residents, the market did not serve the community. Instead of increasing access to affordable and culturally appropriate food, it hosted "community events" and food fairs that showcased regional celebrity chefs, brought in vendors from all over Southern California, and attracted affluent consumers from other neighborhoods. Operated by the company that also runs the Little Italy, North Park, and Pacific

Beach farmers' markets, it was a large-scale commercial enterprise aspiring to create San Diego's version of San Francisco's Embarcadero or Seattle's Pike Place. It was not a community-based project in any sense of the term, and its closure was not mourned by many residents.

In contrast to other gentrifying neighborhoods of San Diego, residents of Barrio Logan have been more organized and vocal in their antigentrification stance, building on decades of resistance against environmental racism and a tight network of community organizations like the Chicano Park Steering Committee and the Environmental Health Coalition.[27] The Chicano Park Steering Committee was created in 1970 when the community took over the land under the newly built Coronado bridge after the city reneged on its plan to create a park and began clearing the area for a parking lot and highway patrol station. This peaceful takeover is a landmark moment in the Chicano movement and the park, which is adorned by a growing collection of murals depicting the lives and struggles of Chicano people, is a sacred space to many. The Environmental Health Coalition has been working in Barrio Logan for almost forty years, fighting against environmental racism by restricting pollution and addressing the racial inequities underlying problematic land uses. These organizations are still very active today and have been working with other local groups to hold informational events and antigentrification workshops in Chicano Park, participate in city politics, produce and disseminate educational videos, and use social media to draw attention to troublesome developments like La Gracia frutería (see chapter 6).

Together, these community efforts have resulted in some victories in shaping a community plan update, increasing the production of affordable housing, bringing in a new grocery store, contesting police brutality, and addressing a wide range of interrelated issues affecting the neighborhood. Activists in Barrio Logan have been inspired by the work of others in places like Boyle Heights in Los Angeles and the Mission District in San Francisco, where Latinx people face similar threats of displacement through cultural appropriation. In these neighborhoods, gentefication is increasingly advocated as an alternative and more benevolent form of gentrification to the extent that it is driven by the community.[28] Latinx business owners and "Chipsters"—a colloquial term for Chicano hipsters—describe it as a way to regain control of the process of revitalization. As critics point out, however, gentefication does not reject the consumerist logic of urban renewal projects and asks Latinx people to commodify their own culture in order to stay put.[29]

In City Heights and Southeastern San Diego, where community organizations have been involved in a number of food justice projects, gentrification has not generated as much attention and resistance. This might be because they are at an earlier stage of gentrification; property values have not risen as fast and displacement has been less dramatic than in Barrio Logan. But another explanation is that these neighborhoods, which are larger and much more demographically diverse, do not have the same history of community organizing for social and racial justice. In Southeastern, community-based organizations often work in silos to meet specific needs for a subset of the population or a small section of the neighborhood. In City Heights, the past ten years have seen an unusually high level of attention from nonprofit actors interested in economic revitalization and community health, resulting in more than $400 million invested in the past two decades.[30] Although certain organizations like the IRC have been empowered by these recent developments, it has led to the homogenization and depolitization of ongoing projects that increasingly align with the goals of the urban food machine coalition described in chapter 5. The successes and limitations of community-based organizations in creating food sovereignty point to the need for increasing participation, rethinking leadership, scaling-up efforts, creating alliances, and making demands on the state.

Involving the State in Preventing Displacement

The state—including federal, state, and local levels of government and their various agencies—has enabled both gentrification and food apartheid through policy decisions that have contributed to the racial and economic inequality underscoring the precarity of life experienced by immigrants and people of color. From redlining to public housing to urban renewal policies, the state has sponsored the spatial segregation of cities along the lines of race, depriving nonwhite urbanites from the financial benefits and stability of home ownership and laying the groundwork for gentrification. Labor and immigration policies have created a highly segmented labor market in which many Latinx, Black, and immigrant workers are trapped in low-wage and informal jobs—often in the cultural urban economy of food. Through crop subsidies, agricultural policy has supported large agrifood corporations at the expense of small farmers, labor, and consumers. By putting faith in the market and removing regulations and protections that supposedly hinder its operation, the neoliberal state has unleashed growing inequality and increased large corporations' ability to expand their wealth and power. It might therefore be utopian to imagine that the state would become an ally in creating social and racial justice. Indeed, distrust of the state is what has driven food sovereignty activists to seek justice within communities and advocate for localized solutions.

Yet without challenging the structure of the neoliberal state, it is likely that these community-based solutions will reproduce the inequalities they seek to address and the subjectivities they hope to destabilize, as the critical literature on localism, alternative networks, and social entrepreneurialism suggests.[31] Despite its abysmal historical record, the state has the ability to redistribute wealth, reallocate resources, and adopt new policies that would redress past injustices and forge a more equitable path forward. There are examples of progressive policies, however partial and imperfect they may be, in the not-so-distant past. With political will, the state could accomplish more for food sovereignty than localized self-improvement projects. However, many potentially transformational options are foreclosed because they are coded as unrealistic, impossible, unreasonable, and unthinkable.[32] As a result, we lower our expectations from the state, do not demand enough of it, and fail to hold it accountable. We end up with a "thoroughly depoliticized imaginary" in which capitalism is seen as inevitable and the role of the state is limited to managing markets in an apolitical, technocratic, consensual, and colorblind manner.[33] Bringing the "political" back into policy and working with the state to address social injustices require organizing, strategizing, debating, demonstrating, scandalizing, and protesting—that is, the exercise of democracy—to call out and demand an end to the differentiated ways in which the state values human life.

In recent years the food movement has called upon the state to take some responsibility in addressing the social inequities inherent in the contemporary industrial food system it helped create. Similarly, affordable housing advocates have been pushing for more state involvement in ensuring that people can afford to stay in their home. Most of these demands have been directed at state and local governments that are in charge of many decisions directly affecting local economies and appear to be more responsive than the federal government. As with most community-based initiatives, state responses have been piecemeal, addressing one issue at a time and failing to provide a comprehensive approach to uplift food livelihoods in ways that would guarantee food and housing security.

In San Diego, the City Council has passed a number of ordinances to facilitate urban agriculture. Facing significant hurdles in establishing the New Roots Community Farm, the IRC spearheaded a social movement demanding that the City of San Diego relaxed its zoning regulation and permitting process for urban agriculture. In 2011, the City Council passed an ordinance incorporating many of these demands. More recently, it adopted an ordinance to implement California's 2013 Urban Agriculture Incentive Zone Act (AB551), allowing property tax reductions on "blighted" parcels converted to community gardens. These measures are helpful to remove bureaucratic hurdles and lower the costs of growing food for organized groups that have identified available land. However, they do little for those that lack institutional capacity and access to land.

After years of advocacy by street vendors, including grassroots organizations led by immigrant women in Los Angeles, the State of California passed the Safe Sidewalk Vending Act (SB946) in 2018 to decriminalize street vending and streamline the process of obtaining a license. The City of San Diego has yet to pass an ordinance determining how the law will be enforced locally. Current drafts are not promising for street vendors who would see their mobility reduced as greater restrictions are being considered in exchange for the formalization of their activities. This is likely to have a negative effect in ethnic communities where street vending provides an important service and a source of income. Meanwhile, trendy food trucks that sell gourmet food to middle-class consumers have been exempt from permits in most locations and have been issued permits as needed for special events. Such differential treatment reveals a bias in how the City of San Diego treats immigrant food entrepreneurs. A similar bias has been observed in Chicago, Los Angeles, and other cities.[34]

At the county level, the Department of Health and Human Services has undertaken a number of projects to address food insecurity and improve food access. Particularly noteworthy is the LiveWell Community Market Program designed to encourage small food retailers in low-income area to increase the availability of fresh produce through technical assistance and small grants. A number of ethnic markets in City Heights and Southeastern San Diego (such as the African-Caribbean Market, Bruno's Market, Dur Dur Market, and Minnehaha Food Market) have benefited from the program, which has helped them redesign their space and renovate their store front to attract customers and increase the consumption of healthy fresh foods. CalFresh and WIC are now allowed at several farmers' markets, making them more affordable to low-income people who often find the produce too expensive. Yet only about 20 percent of markets participate in these programs. The county could make this an option at all farmers' markets.

Local governments have also been active in creating a more inclusive food environment. For instance, the San Diego Unified School District, under pressure from community organizations such as United Women of East Africa and Mid-City CAN, is offering halal school lunches at Crawford High School, where many students are Muslim. The program is an acknowledgment of the ethnic diversity of the student body and the different paths to healthy nutrition. As noted in chapter 5, local governments, in partnership with nonprofits, have also sponsored street fairs, food festivals, and other events that celebrate the ethnic food heritage of places like City Heights, Barrio Logan, and Southeastern San Diego.

To some, these state, county, and municipal government interventions are signs that policymakers are paying attention to issues of food equity. To others, however, these initiatives reveal the boundaries of our imagination and limits of neoliberalism. Passing ordinances to facilitate urban agriculture, supporting school gardens and farmers' markets, and sponsoring multicultural food events requires very little commitment from governments. These initiatives are often part of larger urban revitalization projects that do more to encourage gentrification than they do to address economic and racial inequality. In that sense, the state remains a central actor of the urban food machine (see chapter 5).

We need to demand more from the state to guarantee that society has the tools and resources necessary for establishing food sovereignty.

This means broadening the agenda to ensure that people can live in neighborhoods where they enjoy affordable, healthy, and culturally appropriate food, have access to land in order to grow food, are able to earn a decent income with dignity while contributing to a vibrant food economy, and get to partake in meaningful food practices that strengthen their health and sense of belonging. In other words, food policy ought to be broadened to incorporate labor and housing. Fair labor and higher wages have not been a major focus of the alternative food movement that has prioritized individual consumption choices and entrepreneurial solutions, as Joshua Sbicca's work has illustrated.[35]

Rather than demanding better regulation of the labor market, such as safety standards and minimum wages, food activists typically ask for better information such as fair-trade labels and organic certificates, assuming that it would lead consumers to make better choices. State and local governments have the ability to pass and enforce living-wage ordinances that would lift up the income of most food workers who often earn poverty wages (see chapter 3). Such ordinances have been adopted in cities like Los Angeles, San Jose, and San Francisco. Despite popular fears, studies have shown that minimum wage increases have not resulted in job losses and have instead stimulated local economies.[36] Unions and labor organizations like the Food Chain Workers Alliance, the United Food and Commercial Workers International Union, the Restaurant Opportunities Centers United, and the Los Angeles Alliance for a New Economy have been instrumental in advocating for restaurants and grocery store workers by putting pressure on state and local governments to raise minimum wages, while negotiating better wages with companies and large employers. Since January 2020, San Diego has a minimum wage of $13 per hour, which is above the mandated minimum wage but below that of cities like Los Angeles and San Francisco, where the cost of living is equally high. In addition to demanding state-mandated wage increases, it is important to ensure that these regulations are properly enforced. This is crucial for immigrant workers, who are more vulnerable to abuse, and those employed in small businesses operating at the margins of informality.

"Good food" purchasing programs, like the one adopted by the city of Los Angeles in 2012 through the efforts of the Los Angeles Food Policy

Council, are a powerful tool to mandate that public agencies such as school districts purchase food that meets agreed-upon criteria related to health and nutrition, labor standards, animal welfare, local provenance, and environmental sustainability.[37] Although they might have a limited direct impact on ethnic food businesses like restaurants and grocery stores, these programs indicate that "good food" is more than tasty food. San Diego has yet to adopt a good food purchasing agreement.

Governments can also take direct action to ensure that small businesses and immigrant entrepreneurs have the resources they need to take the high road of paying their workers fair wages through a successful business strategy rather than the low road of building a business on the back of labor, frequently including their own. One of the most important barriers faced by ethnic entrepreneurs is access to credit, which could be remedied through targeted lending programs for small "minority-owned" businesses. Street vendors also need protection from the state, including the decriminalization of their activities. As noted, California recently passed a law to this end, but many local governments have yet to adopt ordinances determining how the law will apply in their jurisdiction to support vendors and help them formalize.

Housing is another area where governments have the power to enact change and thwart gentrification. There have many policy options in their toolbox, such as inclusionary housing ordinances, including caps on the number of condominium and single-family conversions and requirements to include affordable housing units in new projects, rent control, property tax increases indexed to income, and better tenant protections. Yet they often lack the political will to support new policies or even enforce existing ones, partly because wealthier residents oppose them. Demanding change requires community organizing that may be encouraged through horizontal networks between organizations working toward similar goals in other cities like Los Angeles, Oakland, and San Francisco. An important aspect of resisting displacement, including its cultural aspect, is to change the narrative underlying it—mainly the idea that consumer appreciation of ethnic food will create economic opportunities and raise the social position of immigrants—and replace it with a different story that stresses and elevates the significance of food beyond its market value.

Telling a Different Story

Eating locally is not a new practice in communities of color. Latinx, Asian, and African immigrants and subsequent generations have often relied on food to make a living and "grow roots" locally. They have developed creative and innovative strategies and food-centered relationships as gardeners, caretakers, vendors, cooks, and entrepreneurs to provide their families and communities with healthy and comforting food despite significant structural obstacles. The food practices of immigrants may actually be more "alternative" than those prescribed by participants in the so-called "alternative food movement" to the extent that they embody a different relationship to food that circumvents some of the strictures of the contemporary food system, as Julian Agyeman and Sydney Giacalone have suggested.[38]

Yet these practices have been stigmatized, dismissed, attacked, and more recently appropriated. As Monica White has argued, they have also been erased from the food movement.[39] Immigrants, and people of color in general, are often portrayed as uniformly powerless, poor, and uneducated. Therefore it is unconceivable that they would be able to make healthy, sustainable, and ethical food choices without guidance from those who know better. For example, in the public health literature it is often assumed that immigrants are ill-informed about nutrition, especially Latina mothers who allegedly lack the necessary knowledge to feed their children properly. Such racialized conceptions about immigrant foodways underly much of what passes as food justice: initiatives led by "enlightened" white, middle-class, and mostly female volunteers. It also underlies entrepreneurial approaches in which white and affluent consumers "support the community" through their purchases.

This recognition that ethnic foodways have been eradicated, trivialized, and constrained has led such authors as Luz Calvo and Catriona Rueda Esquibel to argue for a "decolonization of diets"—a project that aligns closely with the goals of food sovereignty as understood by Indigenous people around the world.[40] An important aspect of this effort is for immigrants and subsequent generations to reclaim ethnic food and retell its story. It means putting the perspectives, aspirations, and stories of people who suffer from food insecurity, labor exploitation, and displacement at the center of food sovereignty work. In that sense, food sovereignty is a process of knowledge creation that produces counternarratives based on the concrete experiences of those struggling and working in the food economy.[41] The responsibility to tell different stories also falls on academics like myself who must listen to people living food apartheid, reflect on our own privilege, and embed our work into critical scholarship on food and race.

"Better" stories would highlight the long-lasting cultural, social, and economic significance of food for ethnic communities. For instance, in San Diego they could shed light on the Mexican grocers who operated stores along Logan Avenue in Barrio Logan, the Japanese farmers who grew fruits and vegetables before being sent to internment camps during World War II and losing their farms, the Black residents who grew food and shared recipes in Southeastern San Diego, the Vietnamese refugees who opened restaurants after spending years in camps eating bland donated food, and the Italian and Portuguese women who worked in Little Italy's tuna canning factories. They would show that today's ethnic food economies are a continuation of these rich cultural heritages—not a trend discovered by foodies. They would present immigrants and people of color as innovators, creators, contributors, and transformative agents in the food economy—not just victims or recipients.

If told truthfully, these counternarratives would also inevitably reveal a long history of racism: gardens replaced by condominiums, restaurants gone bankrupt, grocery stores closed after many years, street vendors harassed by the police, farms lost following forced relocation, workers underpaid and hungry, and children chastised for bringing unusual lunches to school. They would tell the struggles and trauma that people of color experience in procuring food. These stories are harder to digest. We often prefer the shorter and cleaner versions that celebrate ethnic diversity and praise immigrants for their hard work and resilience, while congratulating affluent consumers for their open-mindedness, colorblindness, and cosmopolitanism. Failing to tell these uncomfortable and inconvenient stories will simply reproduce romanticized and exoticized notions of ethnic food that are divorced from the everyday realities of those who produce it. Counternarratives ought to be centered in the everyday life and the multiple practices through which immigrants contest oppression and stigmas and assert the value of their neighborhoods, communities, cultures, and livelihoods.

My wish is that this book has produced the sort of counternarrative I advocate and challenged benevolent notions of cosmopolitanism by revealing the complex entanglements between ethnicity, food, place, and gentrification. By documenting the production of food apartheid, making visible the labor involved in producing cosmopolitan foodscapes, and shedding light on the place-based impacts of cosmopolitan consumerism on immigrants and people of color, I hope to have contributed to efforts to reclaim ethnic foodscapes as places where ethnic people can live free of hunger and flourish.

NOTES

INTRODUCTION

1 Hannah Lott-Schwartz, "Barrio Logan: A Thriving Hub of Chicano Culture Emerges from the Shadows," *Hemisphere* (March 2018): 20.

2 Tariq Jazeel, "Spatializing Difference beyond Cosmopolitanism: Rethinking Planetary Futures," *Theory, Culture & Society* 28, no. 5 (2011): 75–97.

3 Jason Hackworth and Neil Smith, "The Changing State of Gentrification," *Tijdschrift voor Economische en Sociale Geografie* 92, no. 4 (2002): 464–77; Loretta Lees, Tom Slater, and Elvin Wyly, *Gentrification* (New York: Routledge, 2008); and Neil Smith, "Gentrification and Uneven Development," *Economic Geography* 58, no. 2 (1982): 139–55.

4 David Ley, "Artists, Aestheticization and the Field of Gentrification," *Urban Studies* 40, no. 12 (2003): 2527–44; Sharon Zukin, *The Cultures of Cities* (Cambridge, UK: Blackwell, 1995); and Sharon Zukin, *Naked City: The Death and Life of Authentic Urban Places* (New York: Oxford University Press, 2009).

5 Fran Tonkiss, *Space, the City and Social Theory: Social Relations and Urban Forms* (Malden, MA: Polity, 2005), 82.

6 Alison Hope Alkon, Yuki Kato, and Joshua Sbicca, eds., *A Recipe for Gentrification: Food, Power, and Resistance in the City* (New York: New York University Press, 2020).

7 Leslie Kern, "Connecting Embodiment, Emotion and Gentrification: An Exploration through the Practice of Yoga in Toronto," *Emotion, Space and Society* 5, no. 1 (2012): 27–35; Leslie Kern, "Rhythms of Gentrification: Eventfulness and Slow Violence in a Happening Neighbourhood," *Cultural Geographies* 23, no. 3 (2016): 441–57; and Leslie Kern, "From Toxic Wreck to Crunchy Chic: Environmental Gentrification through the Body," *Environment and Planning D, Society & Space* 33, no. 1 (2015): 67–83.

8 Kern, "Rhythms of Gentrification."

9 Neil Brenner, Peter Marcuse, and Margit Mayer, *Cities for People, Not for Profit: Critical Urban Theory and the Right to the City* (New York: Routledge, 2012); Henri

Lefebvre, "The Right to the City," in *Writings on Cities*, ed. Henri Lefebvre, 108–23 (Oxford: Blackwell, 1996); Don Mitchell, *The Right to the City: Social Justice and the Fight for Public Space* (New York: Guilford Press, 2003); Giorgio Hadi Curti, Jim Craine, and Stuart C. Aitken, eds., *The Fight to Stay Put: Social Lessons through Media Imaginings of Urban Transformation and Change* (Stuttgart: Verlag, 2013); Chester Hartman, "The Right to Stay Put," in *The Gentrification Reader*, ed. Loretta Lees, Tom Slater, and Elvin K. Wyly, 531–41 (Abingdon: Routledge, 1984); and Loretta Lees, Sandra Annunziata, and Clara Rivas-Alonso, "Resisting Planetary Gentrification: The Value of Survivability in the Fight to Stay Put," *Annals of the American Association of Geographers* 108, no. 2 (2017): 346–55.

10 Anna Brones, "Karen Washington: It's Not a Food Desert, It's Food Apartheid," *Guernica*, May 7, 2018; Leah Penniman, *Farming While Black: Soul Fire Farm's Practical Guide to Liberation on the Land* (White River Junction, VT: Chelsea Green Publishing, 2018); and Ashanté M. Reese, *Black Food Geographies: Race, Self-Reliance, and Food Access in Washington, D.C.* (Chapel Hill: University of North Carolina Press, 2019).

11 Daniel Martinez HoSang, Oneka LaBennett, and Laura Pulido, *Racial Formation in the Twenty-first Century* (Berkeley: University of California Press, 2012); Patricia L. Price, "At the Crossroads: Critical Race Theory and Critical Geographies of Race," *Progress in Human Geography* 34, no. 2 (2010): 147–74; and Rogelio Sáenz and Karen Manges Douglas, "A Call for the Racialization of Immigration Studies: On the Transition of Ethnic Immigrants to Racialized Immigrants," *Sociology of Race and Ethnicity* 1, no. 1 (2015): 166–80.

12 Price, "At the Crossroads," 154.

13 Michael Omi and Howard Winant, "Racial Formation Rules: Continuity, Instability, and Change," in *Racial Formation in the Twenty-first Century*, ed. Daniel Martinez HoSang, Oneka LaBennett, and Laura Pulido, 302–31 (Berkeley: University of California Press, 2012).

14 Ruth Wilson Gilmore, "Fatal Couplings of Power and Difference: Notes on Racism and Geography," *Professional Geographer* 54, no. 1 (2002): 15–24; Audrey Kobayashi and Linda Peake, "Racism out of Place: Thoughts on Whiteness and an Antiracist Geography in the New Millennium," *Annals of the Association of American Geographers* 90, no. 2 (2000): 392–403; George Lipsitz, *How Racism Takes Place*, ed. Ebrary (Philadelphia: Temple University Press, 2011); Laura Pulido, "Rethinking Environmental Racism: White Privilege and Urban Development in Southern California," *Annals of the Association of American Geographers* 90, no. 1 (2000): 12–40; Laura Pulido, "Geographies of Race and Ethnicity II: Environmental Racism, Racial Capitalism and State-Sanctioned Violence," *Progress in Human Geography* 41, no. 4 (2017): 524–33; and Arun Saldanha, "Reontologising Race: The Machinic Geography of Phenotype," *Environment and Planning D: Society & Space* 24, no. 1 (2016): 9–24.

15 Reese, *Black Food Geographies*.

16 Alison Alkon and Julie Guthman, eds., *The New Food Activism: Opposition, Cooperation, and Collective Action* (Berkeley: University of California Press, 2017); Alison Hope Alkon and Julian Agyeman, eds., *Cultivating Food Justice: Race, Class, and Sustainability* (Cambridge, MA: MIT Press, 2011); Robert Gottlieb and Anupama Joshi, *Food Justice* (Cambridge, MA: MIT Press, 2010); and Joshua Sbicca, *Food Justice Now* (Minneapolis: University of Minnesota Press, 2018).

17 Alison Hope Alkon and Christie Grace McCullen, "Whiteness and Farmers Markets: Performances, Perpetuations . . . Contestations?," *Antipode* 43, no. 4 (2011): 937–59; Julie Guthman, "Neoliberalism and the Making of Food Politics in California," *Geoforum* 39, no. 3 (2008): 1171–83; Margaret Marietta Ramírez, "The Elusive Inclusive: Black Food Geographies and Racialized Food Spaces," *Antipode* 47, no. 3 (2015): 748–69; and Rachel Slocum, "Whiteness, Space and Alternative Food Practice," *Geoforum* 38, no. 3 (2007): 520–33.

18 Pascale Joassart-Marcelli, Fernando J. Bosco, and Emanuel Delgado, *Southeastern San Diego's Food Landscape: Challenges and Opportunities* (San Diego, CA: San Diego State University, 2014). Pascale Joassart-Marcelli and Fernando J. Bosco, "Contested Ethnic Foodscapes: Survival, Appropriation, and Resistance in Gentrifying Immigrant Neighborhoods," in *The Immigrant-Food Nexus: Borders, Labor, and Identity in North America*, ed. Julian Agyeman and Sydney Giacalone, 59–80 (Cambridge, MA: MIT Press, 2020); Pascale Joassart-Marcelli, Jaime S. Rossiter, and Fernando J. Bosco, "Ethnic Markets and Community Food Security in an Urban 'Food Desert,'" *Environment and Planning. A* 49, no. 7 (2017): 1642–63; Fernando J. Bosco and Pascale Joassart-Marcelli, "Spaces of Alternative Food: Urban Agriculture, Community Gardens and Farmers Markets," in *Food and Place: A Critical Exploration*, ed. Pascale Joassart-Marcelli and Fernando J. Bosco, 187–205 (Lanham, MD: Rowman and Littlefield, 2018); Pascale Joassart-Marcelli and Fernando J. Bosco, "Alternative Food Projects, Localization and Neoliberal Urban Development: Farmers' Markets in Southern California," *Métropoles*, no. 15 (2014); and Pascale Joassart-Marcelli and Fernando J. Bosco, "Alternative Food and Gentrification: How Farmers' Markets and Community Gardens Are Transforming Urban Neighborhoods," in *Just Green Enough*, ed. Winnifred W. Curran and Trina Hamilton, 92–106 (New York: Routledge, 2017).

19 Fernando J. Bosco, Pascale Joassart-Marcelli, and Blaire O'Neal, "Food Journeys: Place, Mobility, and the Everyday Food Practices of Young People," *Annals of the American Association of Geographers* 107, no. 6 (2017): 1479–98.

20 Pascale Joassart-Marcelli and Fernando J. Bosco, eds., *Food and Place: A Critical Exploration* (Lanham, MD: Rowman & Littlefield, 2018).

21 Wendy Luttrell, "'Good Enough' Methods for Ethnographic Research," *Harvard Educational Review* 70, no. 4 (2000): 499–523, 500.

22 Luttrell, "'Good Enough,'" 515.

1 FOODSCAPES

1 Carl Sauer, "The Morphology of Landscape," *University of California Publications in Geography* 2 (1925): 19–54.

2 Denis E. Cosgrove, *Social Formation and Symbolic Landscape* (London: Croom Helm, 1984).

3 Don Mitchell, "Imperial Landscape," in *Landscape and Power: Space, Place and Landscape*, ed. Don Mitchell, 5–35 (Chicago: University of Chicago Press, 2002).

4 Mitch Rose, "Landscape and Labyrinths," *Geoforum* 33, no. 4 (2002): 455–67.

5 Stephen Daniels, "Marxism, Culture, and the Duplicity of Landscape," in *New Models in Geography*, ed. Richard Peet and Nigel Thrift, 212–36 (New York: Routledge, 1989), 206.

6 Arjun Appadurai, *Modernity at Large: Cultural Dimensions of Globalization* (Minneapolis: University of Minnesota Press, 1996), 96.

7 Josée Johnston and Shyon Baumann, *Foodies: Democracy and Distinction in the Gourmet Foodscape* (New York: Routledge, 2010), 3.

8 Gisèle Yasmeen, "Bangkok's Foodscape: Public Eating, Gender Relations and Urban Change," PhD dissertation, University of British Columbia, 1997.

9 Thomas Burgoine, "Collecting Accurate Secondary Foodscape Data: A Reflection on the Trials and Tribulations," *Appetite* 55, no. 3 (2010): 522–27, 522.

10 Susan Parham, *Food and Urbanism: The Convivial City and a Sustainable Future* (Boston: Bloomsbury, 2015).

11 Johnston and Baumann, *Foodies*.

12 Doreen B. Massey, *For Space* (London: Sage, 2005).

13 Yi-Fu Tuan, "Space and Place: Humanistic Perspective," *Progress in Human Geography* 6 (1974): 211–52.

14 Steve Harrison and Paul Dourish, "Re-place-ing Space: The Roles of Place and Space in Collaborative Systems," in *Computer Supported Cooperative Work* (Cambridge, MA: ACM, 1996), 1 and 3.

15 Edward Relph, *Place and Placeness* (London: Pion, 1976), 123.

16 Doreen Massey, "Landscape as a Provocation: Reflections on Moving Mountains," *Journal of Material Culture* 11, no. 1–2 (2006): 33–48, 46.

17 Lewis Holloway and Moya Kneafsey, "Reading the Space of the Farmers' Market: A Preliminary Investigation from the UK," *Sociologia Ruralis* 40, no. 3 (2000): 285–99.

18 Michael K. Goodman, Damian Maye, and Lewis Holloway, "Ethical Foodscapes?: Premises, Promises, and Possibilities," *Environment and Planning A* 42, no. 8 (2010): 1782–96.

19 Guthman, "Neoliberalism and the Making of Food Politics in California"; and Josée Johnston, Andrew Biro, and Norah MacKendrick, "Lost in the Supermarket: The Corporate-Organic Foodscape and the Struggle for Food Democracy," *Antipode* 41, no. 3 (2009): 509–32.

20 Julie Guthman, "'If They Only Knew': Color Blindness and Universalism in California Alternative Food Institutions," *Professional Geographer* 60, no. 3 (2008): 387–97; and Julie Guthman, *Weighing In: Obesity, Food Justice, and the Limits of Capitalism* (Berkeley: University of California Press, 2011).

21 Pascale Joassart-Marcelli and Fernando J. Bosco, "Food and Gentrification: How Foodies are Transforming Urban Neighborhoods," in *Food and Place: A Critical Exploration*, ed. Pascale Joassart-Marcelli and Fernando J. Bosco, 129–46 (Lanham, MD: Rowman and Littlefield, 2018).

22 Zukin, *Cultures of Cities*; and Zukin, *Naked City*.

23 David Bell and Gill Valentine, *Consuming Geographies: We Are Where We Eat* (London: Routledge, 1997).

24 Ian Cook and Philip Crang, "The World on a Plate: Culinary Culture, Displacement and Geographical Knowledge," *Journal of Material Culture* 1, no. 2 (1996): 131–53, 140.

25 Katharine Bradley and Ryan E. Galt, "Practicing Food Justice at Dig Deep Farms & Produce, East Bay Area, California: Self-Determination As a Guiding Value and Intersections with Foodie Logics," *Local Environment* 19, no. 2 (2014): 172–86; Reese, *Black Food Geographies*; and Joshua Sbicca, "Growing Food Justice by Planting an Anti-Oppression Foundation: Opportunities and Obstacles for a Budding Social Movement," *Agriculture and Human Values* 29, no. 4 (2012): 455–66.

26 Alkon, Kato, and Sbicca, *Recipe for Gentrification*. Isabelle Anguelovski, "Healthy Food Stores, Greenlining and Food Gentrification: Contesting New Forms of Privilege, Displacement and Locally Unwanted Land Uses in Racially Mixed Neighborhoods," *International Journal of Urban and Regional Research* 39, no. 6 (2015): 1209–30; Derek S. Hyra, *Race, Class, and Politics in Cappuccino City* (Chicago: University of Chicago Press, 2017); Joassart-Marcelli and Bosco, "Alternative Food and Gentrification"; Joassart-Marcelli and Bosco, "Food and Gentrification"; and Sharon Zukin, Valerie Trujillo, Peter Frase, Danielle Jackson, Tim Recuber, and Abraham Walker, "New Retail Capital and Neighborhood Change: Boutiques and Gentrification in New York City," *City & Community* 8, no. 1 (2009): 47–64.

27 Jessica Hayes-Conroy and Allison Hayes-Conroy, "Visceral Geographies: Mattering, Relating, and Defying: Visceral Geographies," *Geography Compass* 4, no. 9 (2010): 1273–83; and Robyn Longhurst, Lynda Johnston, and Elsie Ho, "A Visceral Approach: Cooking 'at Home' with Migrant Women in Hamilton, New Zealand," *Transactions of the Institute of British Geographers* 34, no. 3 (2009): 333–45.

28 Leslie Kern, "Connecting Embodiment, Emotion and Gentrification: An Exploration through the Practice of Yoga in Toronto," *Emotion, Space and Society* 5, no. 1 (2012): 27–35.

29 Hayes-Conroy and Hayes-Conroy, "Visceral Geographies."

30 Stuart Hall, "New Ethnicities (1988)," in *Writing Black Britain 1948-1998: An Interdisciplinary Anthology*, ed. James Proctor, 265-274 (New York: Manchester University Press, 2000).

31 Michael Omi and Howard Winant, *Racial Formation in the United States*, third edition (New York: Routledge, 2014).

32 Omi and Winant, "Racial Formation Rules," 307.

33 Kobayashi and Peake, "Racism out of Place"; and Pulido, "Rethinking Environmental Racism."

34 Stuart Hall, *The Fateful Triangle: Race, Ethnicity, Nation*, ed. Kobena Mercer (Cambridge, MA: Harvard University Press, 2007), 100.

35 Hasia R. Diner, *Hungering for America: Italian, Irish, and Jewish Foodways in the Age of Migration* (Cambridge, MA: Harvard University Press, 2001); Donna R. Gabaccia, *We Are What We Eat: Ethnic Food and the Making of Americans* (Cambridge, MA: Harvard University Press, 1998); and Monica Janowski, "Introduction: Consuming Memories of Home in Constructing the Present and Imagining the Future," *Food and Foodways* 20, no. 3-4 (2012): 175–39.

36 Mannur Anita, "Culinary Nostalgia: Authenticity, Nationalism, and Diaspora," *Melus* 32, no. 4 (2007): 11–31; and Krishnendu Ray, *The Migrant's Table: Meals and Memories in Bengali-American Households* (Philadelphia: Temple University Press, 2004); and Anita Mannur, *Culinary Fictions: Food in South Asian Diasporic Culture* (Philadelphia: Temple University Press, 2009).

37 Pierre L. van den Berghe, "Ethnic Cuisine: Culture in Nature," *Ethnic and Racial Studies* 7, no. 3 (1984): 387–97, 395.

38 Rachel Slocum, "Race in the Study of Food," *Progress in Human Geography* 35, no. 3 (2011): 303–27.

39 bell hooks, "Eating the Other: Desire and Resistance," in *Black Looks: Race and Representation*, ed. bell hooks, 21–39 (Boston: South End Press, 1992), 21.

40 Ghassan Hage, "At Home in the Entrails of the West: Multiculturalism, Ethnic Food and Migrant Home-building," in *Home/World: Space, Community and Marginality in Sydney's West*, ed. Helen Grace, 99–153 (Sydney: Pluto Press, 1997), 118.

41 Jon May, "'A Little Taste of Something More Exotic': The Imaginative Geographies of Everyday Life," *Geography* 81, no. 1 (1996): 57–64.

42 Lisa M. Heldke, *Exotic Appetites: Ruminations of a Food Adventurer* (New York: Routledge, 2003), 154.

43 Jennie Germann Molz, "Eating Difference: The Cosmopolitan Mobilities of Culinary Tourism," *Space and Culture* 10, no. 1 (2007): 77–93, 77.

44 Sylvia Ferrero, "Comida Sin Par. Consumption of Mexican Food in Los Angeles: Foodscapes in a Transnational Consumer Society," in *Food Nations: Selling Taste in Consumer Societies*, ed. Warren Belasco and Philip Scranton, 194–219 (New York: Routledge, 2002).

45 Ferrero, "Comida Sin Par," 198.

46 Ferrero, "Comida Sin Par," 214.

47 Ferrero, "Comida Sin Par," 215.

48 Jean Duruz, "Adventuring and Belonging: An Appetite for Markets," *Space & Culture* 7, no. 4 (2004): 427–45.

49 Duruz, "Adventuring and Belonging," 437.

50 Krishnendu Ray, *The Ethnic Restaurateur* (Boston: Bloomsbury Publishing, 2016), 11.

51 Hage, "At Home in the Entrails of the West."

52 Ray, *Ethnic Restaurateur*, 8.

53 Ray, *Ethnic Restaurateur*, 10.

54 Ray, *Ethnic Restaurateur*, 10.

55 Reese, *Black Food Geographies.* .

56 Reese, *Black Food Geographies*, 12.

57 Reese, *Black Food Geographies*, 9.

58 Paul Gilroy, *After Empire: Melancholia or Convivial Culture?* (New York: Routledge, 2004).

59 Gilroy, *After Empire*, xi.

60 Gilroy, *After Empire*, xi.

61 Michèle Lamont and Sada Aksartova, "Ordinary Cosmopolitanisms: Strategies for Bridging Racial Boundaries among Working-class Men," *Theory, Culture & Society* 19, no. 4 (2002): 1–25; and Greg Noble, "Everyday Cosmopolitanism and the Labour of Intercultural Community," in *Everyday Multiculturalism*, ed. Amanda Wise and Selvaraj Velayutham, 46–65 (London: Palgrave Macmillan, 2009).

62 Elijah Anderson, *The Cosmopolitan Canopy: Race and Civility in Everyday Life* (New York: Norton, 2011), 136.

63 Anderson, *Cosmopolitan Canopy*, xv.

64 Anderson, *Cosmopolitan Canopy*, 43.

65 Nir Avieli, "The Hummus Wars Revisited: Israeli-Arab Food Politics and Gastromediation," *Gastronomica* 16, no. 3 (2016): 19–30.

66 May, "'A Little Taste of Something More Exotic.'"

67 Meghan A. Burke, *Racial Ambivalence in Diverse Communities: Whiteness and the Power of Color-Blind Ideologies* (Lanham, MD: Lexington Books, 2012); and Gill Valentine, "Living with Difference: Reflections on Geographies of Encounter," *Progress in Human Geography* 32, no. 3 (2008): 323–37.

68 Valentine, "Living with Difference," 333.

69 Valentine, "Living with Difference," 329.

70 Caroline Knowles, "Nigerian London: Re-mapping Space and Ethnicity in Superdiverse Cities," *Ethnic and Racial Studies* 36, no. 4 (2013): 651–69.

71 John Berger and Jean Mohr, *A Fortunate Man* (New York: Pantheon, 1967), 13.

72 Don Mitchell, *The Lie of the Land: Migrant Workers and the California Landscape* (Minneapolis: University of Minnesota Press, 1996).

2 FOOD APARTHEID

1 Daniel Wheaton, "Mapping San Diego's 'Food Desert' Spots," *San Diego Union Tribune*, May 15, 2016; and Troy Johnson, "A National Treasure," *San Diego Magazine* (Winter 2016).

2 Barbarella Fokos, "Mountain View Backyard Bent to His Will," *San Diego Reader*, May 9, 2018.

3 San Diego Food System Alliance, "County of San Diego Supervisor Candidate Questionnaire: Nathan Fletcher's Response," San Diego Food System Alliance, San Diego, 2018.

4 USDA, "Food Access Research Atlas: Documentation," USDA Economic Research Service, 2017, www.ers.usda.gov/data-products/food-access-research-atlas/documentation/.

5 Elizabeth Eisenhauer, "In Poor Health: Supermarket Redlining and Urban Nutrition," *GeoJournal* 53, no. 2 (2001): 125–33; Naa Oyo A. Kwate, "Fried Chicken and Fresh Apples: Racial Segregation As a Fundamental Cause of Fast Food Density in Black Neighborhoods," *Health & Place* 14, no. 1 (2008): 32–44; Nathan McClintock, "From Industrial Garden to Food Desert: Demarcated Devaluation in the Flatlands of Oakland, California," in *Cultivating Food Justice: Race, Class and Sustainability*, ed. Alison Hope Alkon and Julian Agyeman, 89–120 (Cambridge, MA: MIT Press, 2011); and Reese, *Black Food Geographies*.

6 Brones, "Karen Washington"; Penniman, *Farming While Black*; Reese, *Black Food Geographies*; and Bradley and Galt, "Practicing Food Justice at Dig Deep Farms & Produce, East Bay Area, California."

7 Hélène Charreire, Romain Casey, Paul Salze, Chantal Simon, Basile Chaix, Arnaud Banos, Dominique Badariotti, Christiane Weber, and Jean-Michel Oppert, "Measuring the Food Environment Using Geographical Information Systems: A Methodological Review," *Public Health Nutrition* 13, no. 11 (2010): 1773–85.

8 Joassart-Marcelli, Rossiter, and Bosco, "Ethnic Markets and Community Food Security"; Samina Raja, Ma Changxing, and Pavan Yadav, "Beyond Food Deserts: Measuring and Mapping Racial Disparities in Neighborhood Food Environments," *Journal of Planning Education and Research* 27, no. 4 (2008): 469–82; and Anne Short, Julie Guthman, and Samuel Raskin, "Food Deserts, Oases, or Mirages?: Small Markets and Community Food Security in the San Francisco Bay Area," *Journal of Planning Education and Research* 26, no. 3 (2007): 352–64.

9 Cynthia Gordon, Marnie Purciel-Hill, Nirupa R. Ghai, Leslie Kaufman, Regina Graham, and Gretchen Van Wye, "Measuring Food Deserts in New York City's Low-Income Neighborhoods," *Health & Place* 17, no. 2 (2011): 696–700.

10 Caitlin E. Caspi, Glorian Sorensen, S. V. Subramanian, and Ichiro Kawachi, "The Local Food Environment and Diet: A Systematic Review," *Health & Place* 18, no. 5 (2012): 1172–87.

11 Eisenhauer, "In Poor Health"; Kwate, "Fried Chicken and Fresh Apples"; and Jerry Shannon, "Dollar Stores, Retailer Redlining, and the Metropolitan Geographies

of Precarious Consumption," *Annals of the American Association of Geographers* (2020): 1–19.

12 Frank Norris, "Logan Heights," *Journal of San Diego History* 29, no. 1 (1983), www.sandiegohistory.org/journal/1983/january/logan/.

13 City Clerk Archives, City Directories, San Diego Public Library, 2018.

14 Samuel Black, ed., *San Diego and Imperial Counties of California: A Record of Settlement, Organization, Progress and Achievement*, vol. 1 (Chicago: Clarke Publishing, 2013).

15 Adrian Florido, "How Segregation Defined San Diego's Neighborhoods," *Voice of San Diego*, March 21, 2011.

16 Norris, "Logan Heights."

17 LeRoy E. Harris, "The Other Side of the Freeway: A Study of Settlement Patterns of Negroes and Mexicans in San Diego, California," PhD dissertation, Carnegie Mellon University, 1974.

18 City Clerk Archives, City Directories.

19 Robert E. Park and Ernest W. Burgess, *The City* (Chicago: University of Chicago Press, 1925).

20 Richard Rothstein, *The Color of Law: A Forgotten History of How Our Government Segregated America* (New York: Norton, 2018).

21 Larry Ford and Ernst Griffin, "The Ghettoization of Paradise," *Geographical Review* 69, no. 2 (1979): 140–58.

22 Robert Fishman, "The American Metropolis at Century's End: Past and Future Influences," *Housing Policy Debates* 11, no. 1 (2000): 199–213.

23 FHA, *Underwriting Manual: Underwriting and Valuation Procedure under Title II of the National Housing Act* (Washington, DC: FHA, 1938), section 909.

24 FHA, *Underwriting Manual: Underwriting and Valuation Procedure under Title II of the National Housing Act with Revisions to April 1, 1936* (Washington, DC: FHA, 1936).

25 Rothstein, *Color of Law.*

26 Robert K. Nelson and Edward L. Ayers, "Mapping Inequality: Redlining in New Deal America," Digital Scholarship Lab, University of Richmond, 2018, https://dsl.richmond.edu/panorama/redlining/#loc=5/39.1/-94.58.

27 FHA, *Underwriting Manual: Underwriting and Valuation Procedure Under Title II of the National Housing Act with Revisions to April 1, 1936*, 284.

28 John Nolen, *A Comprehensive City Plan for San Diego, California* (San Diego, CA: The City Planning Commission, 1926).

29 Ford and Griffin, "Ghettoization of Paradise."

30 Jill Replogle and Tom Fudge, "San Diego Voters Reject Barrio Logan's Community Plan," KPBS, San Diego, 2014, www.kpbs.org/news/2014/jun/03/council-plan-barrio-logan-losing-early-returns/.

31 FHA, *Underwriting Manual: Underwriting and Valuation Procedure Under Title II of the National Housing Act with Revisions to April 1, 1936.*

32 Steven P. Erie, Vladimir Kogan, and Scott A. MacKenzie, "Redevelopment, San Diego Style: The Limits of Public-Private Partnerships," *Urban Affairs Review* 45, no. 5 (2010): 644–78.

33 Penniman, *Farming While Black*, 4, italics in original.

34 Eisenhauer, "In Poor Health," 27.

35 USDA, "USDA Food Plans: Cost of Food Report for December 2108," USDA Center for Nutrition Policy and Promotion, 2019, www.cnpp.usda.gov/sites/default/files/CostofFoodDec2018.pdf.

36 Eisenhauer, "In Poor Health."

37 Spencer M. Cowan, *Patterns of Disparity: Small Business Lending in the Chicago and Los Angeles–San Diego Regions* (Chicago: Woodstock Institute, 2017), www.documentcloud.org/documents/5028189-Chicago-and-LASD-Report-CC-License-Update.html.

38 Rebecca de Souza, *Feeding the Other: Whiteness, Privilege and Neoliberal Stigma in Food Pantries* (Cambridge, MA: MIT Press, 2019); and Guthman, "'If They Only Knew.'"

39 Smith, "Gentrification and Uneven Development," 147 and 149.

40 Smith, "Gentrification and Uneven Development," 149, italics in original.

41 Tom Slater, "Territorial Stigmatization: Symbolic Defamation and the Contemporary Metropolis," in *The Sage Handbook of New Urban Studies*, ed. Sean Hannigan and Greg Richards, 111–25 (London: Sage, 2017), 117.

42 Slater, "Territorial Stigmatization," 118.

3 WORK IN THE URBAN FOOD ECONOMY

1 Lori Weisberg, "San Diego Bakery Shuts Down after ICE Audit of Workers," *Los Angeles Times*, January 15, 2020.

2 Jeff McAdam, "Bakery Shuts Down after ICE Raid Finds Unauthorized Employees," *Fox5 San Diego*, January 16, 2020.

3 Winifed R. Poster, Marion Crain, and Miriam A. Cherry, eds., *Invisible Labor: Hidden Work in the Contemporary World* (Berkeley: University of California Press, 2016), 6.

4 Philip Martin, *Rural California Report* (Davis: California Institute for Rural Studies, 2019), www.cirsinc.org/rural-california-report/entry/federal-survey-shows-aging-and-settled-farmworker-population.

5 Eric Holt-Giménez, *Overcoming the Barrier of Racism in Our Capitalist Food System* (Oakland, CA: Food First, 2018).

6 Ghassan Hage, "At Home in the Entrails of the West: Multiculturalism, Ethnic Food and Migrant Home-building," in *Home/World: Space, Community and Marginality in Sydney's West*, ed. Helen Grace, 99–153 (Sydney: Pluto Press, 1997), 118.

7 Alkon and Guthman, *New Food Activism*.

8 Ruth Wilson Gilmore, *Golden Gulag: Prisons, Surplus, Crisis, and Opposition in Globalizing California* (Berkeley: University of California Press, 2007); Katherine McKittrick and Clyde Adrian Woods, *Black Geographies and the Politics of Place* (Cambridge, MA: South End Press, 2007); Pulido, "Geographies of Race and Ethnicity II"; Cedric J. Robinson, *Black Marxism: The Making of the Black Radical Tradition* (Chapel Hill: University of North Carolina Press, 2000); Andrew Herod,

Labor Geographies: Workers and the Landscapes of Capitalism (New York: Guilford Press, 2001); Linda McDowell, "Roepke Lecture in Economic Geography—The Lives of Others: Body Work, the Production of Difference, and Labor Geographies," *Economic Geography* 91, no. 1 (2015): 1–23; Don Mitchell, "Labor's Geography: Capital, Violence, Guest Workers and the Post–World War II landscape," *Antipode* 43, no. 2 (2011): 563–95; and Jamie Peck, "Pluralizing Labor Geography," in *The New Oxford Handbook of Economic Geography*, ed. Gordon L. Clark, Maryann P. Feldman, Meric S. Gertler, and Dariusz Wójcik, 465–84 (Oxford: Oxford University Press, 2018).

9 Anne Bonds and Joshua Inwood, "Beyond White Privilege: Geographies of White Supremacy and Settler Colonialism," *Progress in Human Geography* 40, no. 6 (2016): 715–33; Nancy Fraser, "Roepke Lecture in Economic Geography—From Exploitation to Expropriation: Historic Geographies of Racialized Capitalism," *Economic Geography* 94, no. 1 (2018): 1–17; Katherine McKittrick, "On Plantations, Prisons, and a Black Sense of Place," *Social & Cultural Geography* 12, no. 8 (2011): 947–63; and Pulido, "Geographies of Race and Ethnicity II."

10 Ray, *Ethnic Restaurateur*; Jill Esbenshade, *Shorted: Wage Theft, Time Theft, and Discrimination in San Diego County Restaurant Jobs* (San Diego: San Diego State University, 2015); Food Chain Workers Alliance, *The Hands That Feed Us: Opportunities and Challenges for Workers along the Food Chain* (Los Angeles: Food Chain Workers Alliance, 2012), https://foodchainworkers.org/wp-content/uploads/2012/06/Hands-That-Feed-Us-Report.pdf; Sarumathi Jayaraman, *Behind the Kitchen Door* (Ithaca, NY: Cornell University Press, 2013); and Heidi Shierholz, *Low Wages and Few Benefits Mean Many Restaurant Workers Can't Make Ends Meet* (Washington, DC: Economic Policy Institute, 2014), www.epi.org/files/2014/restaurant-workers-final.pdf.

11 Ray, *Ethnic Restaurateur*.

12 David D. Kallick, *Bringing Vitality to Main Street: How Immigrant Small Businesses Help Local Economies Grow* (New York: Fiscal Policy Institute and Council of the Americas, 2015), www.as-coa.org/sites/default/files/ImmigrantBusinessReport.pdf.

13 Krishnendu Ray, "Ethnic Succession and the New American Restaurant Cuisine," in *The Restaurants Book: Ethnographies of Where We Eat*, ed. David Beriss and David Sutton, 97–113 (New York: Berg, 2007).

14 Ivan Light, "The Ethnic Economy," in *Handbook of Economic Sociology*, ed. Neil Smelser, 650–77 (New York: Russel Sage Foundation, 2005).

15 Jan Rath, Robert Kloosterman, and Eran Razin, "Editorial: The Economic Context, Embeddedness and Immigrant Entrepreneurs," *International Journal of Entrepreneurial Behavior and Research* 8, no. 1 (2002): 6–10.

16 Saskia Sassen, *The Global City: New York, London, Tokyo*, second edition (Princeton, NY: Princeton University Press, 2013); and Saskia Sassen-Koob, "New York City: Economic Restructuring and Immigration," *Development and Change* 17, no. 1 (1986): 85–119.

17 Richard L. Florida, *The Rise of the Creative Class: And How It's Transforming Work, Leisure, Community and Everyday Life* (New York: Basic Books, 2002).

18 Sassen, *Global City*, 9.

19 David J. Karjanen, *The Servant Class City: Urban Revitalization versus the Working Poor in San Diego* (Minneapolis: University of Minnesota Press, 2016).

20 Jamie Peck, Nik Theodore, and Neil Brenner, "Neoliberal Urbanism: Models, Moments, Mutations," *SAIS Review of International Affairs* 29, no. 1 (2009): 49–66; and Erik Swyngedouw, Frank Moulaert, and Arantxa Rodriguez, "Neoliberal Urbanization in Europe: Large-Scale Urban Development Projects and the New Urban Policy," *Antipode* 34, no. 3 (2002): 542–77.

21 I identify individuals with food service jobs in the Public Use Microdata Sample (PUMS) of the American Community Survey using a combination of industry and occupation variables (see US Census, "American Community Survey Five-Year Estimates, 2013–2017. Public Use Microdata Sample," 2019). Sale jobs are those in industries 4470 (wholesale grocery), 4970 (retail grocery), 4980 (retail specialty food), and 4990 (liquor stores), according to the 2012 4-digit IND classification used by the US Census. I then use the four-digit occupational code to further distinguish between types of jobs (e.g., managers, cashiers, preparer). Restaurant jobs are those in occupational categories 4000 to 4150, based on 2010 four-digit occupational code used by the US Census. They include a wide range of occupations such as chef, cook, dishwasher, bartender, host, waiter, busser, and cafeteria worker.

22 Computed with data from Federal Reserve Bank of Saint Louis and US Bureau of Labor Statistics, "Employment in San Diego-Carlsbad, CA (MSA)," Federal Reserve Economic Data, 2019.

23 US Census, "American Community Survey Five-Year Estimates, 2013–2017. Public Use Microdata Sample."

24 Kallick, *Bringing Vitality to Main Street.*.

25 Amy Glasmeier, "Living Wage Calculator," Massachusetts Institute of Technology, 2019. http://livingwage.mit.edu/.

26 Esbenshade, *Shorted: Wage Theft, Time Theft, and Discrimination in San Diego County Restaurant Jobs.*

27 ILO, *Women and Men in the Informal Economy: A Statistical Picture* (Geneva: ILO, 2014).

28 Pascale Joassart-Marcelli, "Measuring Informal Work in Developed Nations," in *Informal Work in Developed Nations*, ed. Enrico Marcelli, Colin Williams, and Pascale Joassart, 24–44 (London: Routledge, 2010); and Pascale Joassart-Marcelli, "The New Normal: Freelancing, Hustling, and Informal Labor," in *City Rising* (Los Angeles: KCET, 2019), www.kcet.org/shows/city-rising/the-new-normal-freelancing-hustling-and-informal-labor.

29 Daniel Flaming, Brent Haydamack, and Pascale Joassart-Marcelli, *Hopeful Workers, Marginal Jobs: LA's Off-the-Book Labor Force* (Los Angeles: The Economic Roundtable, 2005).

30 Enrico Marcelli and Manuel Pastor, *Unauthorized and Uninsured* (San Diego: San Diego State University; Los Angeles: University of Southern California, 2015), https://dornsife.usc.edu/assets/sites/731/docs/Web_01_City_Heights_San_Diego_Final.pdf.

31 James Bliesner and Mirle Rabinowitz Bussell, *The Informal Economy in City Heights* (San Diego: University of California San Diego Center for Urban Economics and Design, 2013).

32 Esbenshade, *Shorted: Wage Theft, Time Theft, and Discrimination in San Diego County Restaurant Jobs.*

33 Annette Bernhardt, Ruth Milkman, Nik Theodore, Douglas D Heckathorn, Mirabai Auer, James DeFilippis, Ana Luz González, Victor Narro, and Jason Perelshteyn, *Broken Laws, Unprotected Workers: Violations of Employment and Labor Laws in America's Cities* (New York: National Employment Law Project, 2009).

34 Carolyn Sachs, Patricia Allen, A. Rachel Terman, Jennifer Hayden, and Christina Hatcher, "Front and Back of the House: Socio-Spatial Inequalities in Food Work," *Agriculture and Human Values* 31, no. 1 (2014): 3–17.

35 Greta Foff Paules, *Dishing It Out: Power and Resistance among Waitresses in a New Jersey Restaurant* (Philadelphia: Temple University Press, 1991).

36 Karla Erickson, "Bodies at Work: Performing Service in American Restaurants," *Space and Culture* 7, no. 1 (2004): 76–89.

37 Restaurant Opportunities Center United, *Ending Jim Crow in America's Restaurants: Racial and Gender Occupational Segregation in the Restaurant Industry* (New York: ROC United, 2015), 1

38 Valerie Preston and Sara McLafferty, "Spatial Mismatch Research in the 1990s: Progress and Potential," *Papers in Regional Science* 78, no. 4 (1999): 387–402.

39 Pascale Joassart-Marcelli, "The Spatial Determinants of Wage Inequality: Evidence from Recent Latina Immigrants in Southern California," *Feminist Economics* 15, no. 2 (2009): 33–72; and Virginia Parks, "The Uneven Geography of Racial and Ethnic Wage Inequality: Specifying Local Labor Market Effects," *Annals of the Association of American Geographers* 102, no. 3 (2012): 700–25.

40 Katherine Michelle Hill, "Sweet and Sour: Social Networks and Inequality in a Chinese Restaurant," *Sociology of Race and Ethnicity* 4, no. 1 (2018): 114–27.

41 H. G. Parsa, John T. Self, David Njite, and Tiffany King, "Why Restaurants Fail," *Cornell Hotel and Restaurant Administration Quarterly* 46, no. 3 (2005): 304–22.

42 Rupali Agarwal and Molly J. Dahm, "Success Factors in Independent Ethnic Restaurants," *Journal of Foodservice Business Research* 18, no. 1 (2015): 20–33.

43 Hill, "Sweet and Sour," 114.

44 Cowan, *Patterns of Disparity.*

45 Cowan, *Patterns of Disparity.*

46 Sarah D. Wald, "Visible Farmers/Invisible Workers: Locating Immigrant Labor in Food Studies," *Food, Culture & Society* 14, no. 4 (2011): 567–86.

47 Jayaraman, *Behind the Kitchen Door*, 350.

1 Lois Stanford, "Negotiating Food Security along the US-Mexico Border: Social Strategies, Practice and Networks among Mexican Immigrant Women," in *Women Redefining the Experience of Food Insecurity: Life off the Edge of the Table*, ed. Janet Page-Reeves, 105–26 (Lanham, MD: Lexington Books, 2014), 108.

2 Food Chain Workers Alliance Restaurant Opportunities Center of New York, Restaurant Opportunities Center of the Bay and Food First/Institute for Food and Development, *Food Insecurity of Restaurant Workers* (2014), www.scribd.com /document/234905417/Food-Insecurity-of-Restaurant-Workers.

3 FAO, *Food Security* (Rome: FAO, 2006).

4 Alisha Coleman-Jensen, Matthew P. Rabbitt, Christian A. Gregory, and Anita Singh, *Household Food Security in the United States in 2018* (Washington, DC: USDA, 2019).

5 US Census, "Current Population Survey Food Security Supplement, 2013 to 2017," US Census Bureau, 2019. Five years of data were combined to generate a large enough sample for comparisons.

6 Z-tests were used to test differences in the proportions of food-insecure people. Food workers were statistically significantly more food insecure than other workers ($p = 0.0003$). Among food workers, Latinos ($p = 0.04$), nonwhites ($p = 0.12$), and immigrants ($p = 0.10$) were also more food-insecure than their counterparts.

7 Coleman-Jensen et al., *Household Food Security in the United States in 2018*.

8 Craig Gundersen and James P. Ziliak, "Food Insecurity and Health Outcomes," *Health Affairs* 34, no. 11 (2015): 1830–39.

9 Mariana Chilton and Sue Booth, "Hunger of the Body and Hunger of the Mind: African American Women's Perceptions of Food Insecurity, Health and Violence," *Journal of Nutrition Education and Behavior* 39, no. 3 (2007): 116–25.

10 Chilton and Booth, "Hunger of the Body and Hunger of the Mind," 120.

11 Penny Van Esterik, "Right to Food; Right to Feed; Right to Be Fed: The Intersection of Women's Rights and the Right to Food," *Agriculture and Human Values* 16, no. 2 (1999): 225–32.

12 Megan A. Carney, "The Biopolitics of 'Food Insecurity': Towards a Critical Political Ecology of the Body in Studies of Women's Transnational Migration," *Journal of Political Ecology* 21, no. 1 (2014): 1–18; and Megan A. Carney, *The Unending Hunger: Tracing Women and Food Insecurity Across Borders* (Berkeley: University of California Press, 2015).

13 Michel Foucault, *The History of Sexuality*, in *History of Sexuality: An Introduction*, ed. Robert Hurley (New York: Vintage Books, 1988).

14 Carney, *Unending Hunger*; and de Souza, *Feeding the Other*.

15 Linda McDowell and Joanne Sharp, eds., *Space, Gender, Knowledge: A Reader for Feminist Geographers* (New York: John Wiley & Sons, 1997), 3.

16 Allison Hayes-Conroy and Jessica Hayes-Conroy, "Political Ecology of the Body: A Visceral Approach," in *The International Handbook of Political Ecology*, ed. Raymond Bryant, 659–72 (Northampton, MA: Edward Elgar Publishing, 2015).

17 Kirsten Simonsen, "In Quest of a New Humanism: Embodiment, Experience and Phenomenology As Critical Geography," *Progress in Human Geography* 37, no. 1 (2013): 10–26.

18 David Harvey, *Spaces of Hope* (Edinburgh: Edinburgh University Press, 2000), 130.

19 Rachel Colls, "Materialising Bodily Matter: Intra-Action and the Embodiment of 'Fat,'" *Geoforum* 38, no. 2 (2007): 353–65; Julie Guthman, "Opening Up the Black Box of the Body in Geographical Obesity Research: Toward a Critical Political Ecology of Fat," *Annals of the Association of American Geographers* 102, no. 5 (2012): 951–57; Hayes-Conroy and Hayes-Conroy, "Visceral Geographies"; Kate Boyer, "Affect, Corporeality and the Limits of Belonging: Breastfeeding in Public in the Contemporary UK," *Health & Place* 18, no. 3 (2012): 552–60; and Robyn Longhurst, Lynda Johnston, and Elsie Ho, "A Visceral Approach: Cooking 'at Home' with Migrant Women in Hamilton, New Zealand," *Transactions of the Institute of British Geographers* 34, no. 3 (2009): 333–45.

20 Nik Heynen, "Bringing the Body Back to Life through Radical Geography of Hunger: The Haymarket Affair and Its Aftermath," *ACME: An International E-Journal for Critical Geographies* 7, no. 1 (2008): 32–44, 34.

21 Ruth Wilson Gilmore, *Golden Gulag: Prisons, Surplus, Crisis, and Opposition in Globalizing California* (Berkeley: University of California Press, 2007), 247.

22 Carney, "Biopolitics of 'Food Insecurity'"; and Carney, *Unending Hunger*.

23 Teresa Marie Mares, "We Are Made of Our Food: Latino/a Immigration and the Practices and Politics of Eating" PhD dissertation, University of Washington, 2010; and Teresa Marie Mares, "Another Time of Hunger," in *Women Redefining the Experience of Food Insecurity: Life Off the Edge of the Table*, ed. Janet Page-Reeves, 45–64 (Lanham, MD: Lexington Books, 2014).

24 Nik Heynen, "Justice of Eating in the City: The Political Ecology of Urban Hunger," in *In the Nature of Cities*, ed. Nik Heynen, Maria Kaika, and Erik Swyngedouw, 129–42 (New York: Routledge, 2006), 129.

25 Reese, *Black Food Geographies*.

26 I interviewed 73 individuals between 2016 and 2018 in City Heights (n = 45), Barrio Logan (n = 15), and Southeastern San Diego (n = 13) about their everyday food practices and their experiences with food insecurity. Some of these individuals worked in restaurants (n = 18) and food stores (n = 22), and the remaining were consumers (n = 33). Among those who worked in food businesses, the majority were owners or managers (n = 34 out of 40). All were considered "ethnic" according the definition I outline in chapter 3 (i.e., people of color) and immigrants (n = 58). The majority of consumers were women (n = 30 out of 33), while most workers were men (n = 36 out of 40), for a total of 34 women and 39 men interviewed.

27 Lefebvre, "Right to the City."

28 Lucy Jarosz, "Defining World Hunger: Scale and Neoliberal Ideology in International Food Security Policy Discourse," *Food, Culture & Society* 14, no. 1 (2011): 117–39.

29 Jennifer R. Wolch, *The Shadow State: Government and the Voluntary Sector in Transition* (New York: The Foundation Center, 1990).

30 Daniel N. Warshawski, "Food Banks and the Devolution of Anti-Hunger Policy," in *Food and Place: A Critical Exploration*, ed. Pascale Joassart-Marcelli and Fernando J. Bosco, 166–84 (Lanham, MD: Rowman and Littlefield, 2018); and Janet Poppendieck, *Sweet Charity?: Emergency Food and the End of Entitlement* (New York: Viking, 1998).

31 Carney, "Biopolitics of 'Food Insecurity.'"

32 Hamutal Bernstein, Dulce Gonzalez, Michael Karpman, and Stephen Zuckerman, "One in Seven Adults in Immigrant Families Reported Avoiding Public Benefit Programs in 2018," Urban Institute, 2019, www.urban.org/research/publication /oneseven-adults-immigrant-families-reported-avoiding-public-benefitpro grams-2018.

33 Elizabeth Hewitt, "'They Go to Work, Come Back, and Starve': Why Immigrant Families Are Avoiding Food Assistance," *Civil Eats*, October 14, 2019.

34 Randy Capps, Michael Fix, and Everett Henderson, "Trends in Immigrants' Use of Public Assistance after Welfare Reform," in *Immigrants and Welfare: The Impact of Welfare Reform on America's Newcomers*, ed. Michael Fix, 123–52 (New York: Russel Sage Foundation, 2009).

35 US Census, "American Community Survey Five-Year Estimates, 2013–2017. Public Use Microdata Sample," US Census Bureau, 2019.

36 Emily Moon, "Why Is Participation in Food Assistance Program Like WIC Declining?" *Pacific Standard*, June 12, 2019.

37 Zaidee Stavely, "School Lunch Could Be Slashed for Thousands of California Children under New Proposal," *EdSource*, August 2, 2019.

38 Warshawski, "Food Banks and the Devolution of Anti-Hunger Policy."

39 de Souza, *Feeding the Other.*

40 Colleen Hammelman and Allison Hayes-Conroy, "Understanding Cultural Acceptability for Urban Food Policy," *Journal of Planning Literature* 30, no. 1 (2015): 37–48.

41 Allison Hayes-Conroy and Jessica Hayes-Conroy, *Doing Nutrition Differently: Critical Approaches to Diet and Dietary Intervention* (Burlington, VT: Ashgate, 2013).

42 Ilana Redstone Akresh, "Dietary Assimilation and Health among Hispanic Immigrants to the United States," *Journal of Health and Social Behavior* 48, no. 4 (2007): 404–17.

43 Bosco, Joassart-Marcelli, and O'Neal, "Food Journeys."

44 Susan J. Popkin, Molly M. Scott, and Marta Glavez, *Impossible Choices: Teens and Food Insecurity in America* (Washington, DC: Urban Institute, 2016), www.urban .org/sites/default/files/publication/83971/impossible-choices-teens-and-food -insecurity-in-america_0.pdf.

45 Samantha Punch, Ian McIntosh, and Ruth Emond, "Children's Food Practices in Families and Institutions," *Children's Geographies* 8, no. 3 (2010): 227–32.

46 Melissa L. Salazar, "Public Schools, Private Foods: Mexicano Memories of Culture and Conflict and American School Cafeterias," *Food and Foodways* 14, no. 3/4 (2007): 153–81.

47 Bosco, Joassart-Marcelli, and O'Neal, "Food Journeys."

48 Carney, "Biopolitics of 'Food Insecurity'"; and Pascale Joassart-Marcelli and Enrico Marcelli, "Cooking at Home: Gender, Class, Race, and Social Reproduction," in *Food and Place: A Critical Exploration*, ed. Pascale Joassart-Marcelli and Fernando J. Bosco, 270–89 (Lanham, MD: Rowman and Littlefield, 2018).

49 Joassart-Marcelli, Rossiter, and Bosco, "Ethnic Markets and Community Food Security"; and Arijit Sen, "Food, Place, and Memory: Bangladeshi Fish Stores on Devon Avenue, Chicago," *Food and Foodways* 24, no. 1–2 (2016): 67–88.

50 Our team audited 167 businesses in Southeastern San Diego (i.e., 108 restaurants and 59 stores) in 2014 and 221 businesses in City Heights (i.e., 120 restaurants and 101 food stores) in 2017. In 2018, I updated these audits and audited 63 businesses in Barrio Logan (i.e., 48 restaurants and 15 stores). The lists of businesses were updated again in January 2020. Although no new audits were conducted at that time, some businesses were added and others deleted, reflecting openings and closures in the past two years.

51 Joassart-Marcelli, Rossiter, and Bosco, "Ethnic Markets and Community Food Security."

52 Mary Willis and Janet Buck, "From Sudan to Nebraska: Dinka and Nuer Refugee Diet Dilemmas," *Journal of Nutrition and Education Behavior* 39, no. 5 (2007): 273–80.

53 Kyeyoung Park, "Confronting the Liquor Industry in Los Angeles," *International Journal of Sociology and Social Policy* 24, no. 7/8 (2004): 103–36.

54 Betty Dawson, "Negotiating Chaldean Resettlement in El Cajon, California," *Jadaliyya*, January 25, 2019.

55 Katie Meehan and Kendra Stauss, eds., *Precarious Worlds: Contested Geographies of Social Reproduction* (Athens: University of Georgia Press, 2015).

56 Bliesner and Bussell, *Informal Economy in City Heights.*

57 David Garrick, "San Diego Considering Crackdown on Flood of New Sidewalk Vendors," *Union Tribune* (San Diego), August 26, 2019.

58 Julian Agyeman, Caitlin Matthews, and Hannah Sobel, eds., *Food Trucks, Cultural Identity, and Social Justice: From Loncheras to Lobsta Love* (Cambridge, MA: MIT Press, 2017).

59 Alkon and Agyeman, *Cultivating Food Justice.*

60 Julie Guthman, "Bringing Good Food to Others: Investigating the Subjects of Alternative Food Practice," *Cultural Geographies* 15, no. 4 (2008): 431–47; Ramírez, "Elusive Inclusive"; and Slocum, "Whiteness, Space and Alternative Food Practice."

61 Alkon, Kato, and Sbicca, *Recipe for Gentrification*; Joassart-Marcelli and Bosco, "Food and Gentrification."

62 Joassart-Marcelli and Bosco, "Alternative Food Projects, Localization and Neo-liberal Urban Development"; and Nathan McClintock, "Radical, Reformist, and Garden-Variety Neoliberal: Coming to Terms with Urban Agriculture's Contra-dictions," *Local Environment: Subversive and Interstitial Food Spaces* 19, no. 2 (2014): 147–71.

63 Branden Born and Mark Purcell, "Avoiding the Local Trap: Scale and Food Systems in Planning Research," *Journal of Planning Education and Research* 26, no. 2 (2006): 195–207; and Joassart-Marcelli and Bosco, "Alternative Food Projects, Localization and Neoliberal Urban Development."

64 International Rescue Committee, "IRC in San Diego's Refugee Entrepreneurial Agriculture Program," grant proposal, National Institute of Food and Agricul-ture, US Department of Agriculture, 2011.

65 Mara Gittleman, Kelli Jordan, and Eric Brelsford, "Using Citizen Science to Quan-tify Community Garden Crop Yields," *Cities and the Environment* 5, no. 1 (2012): 1–14.

66 Reese, *Black Food Geographies*.

5 "BEST FOR FOODIES"

1 Elizabeth Salaam, "San Diego's City Heights on the Way Up. Not Quite Like North Park Yet," *San Diego Reader*, February 14, 2018.

2 Marie Tutko and Anne Wycoff, "San Diego Home Buyers' Guide 2019," *San Diego Magazine*, April 25, 2019.

3 Kinsee Morlan, "A Renaissance on Logan Avenue," *San Diego City Beat*, July 21, 2015; E'Louise Ondash, "Renaissance in Barrio Logan," *The Coast News*, July 10, 2013; Chelsea Pelayo, "Art Galleries Fuel a Barrio Logan Renaissance," *The Sun*, Sep-tember 12, 2017; and Josh Baxt, Erin Meanley Glenny, Jennifer Mcentee, Hoa Quach, and Marie Tutko, "San Diego's Next Hot Neighborhood: Where Every-one Will Be Living in 2016," *San Diego Magazine*, February 26, 2016.

4 Roger Showley, "Diversity, Progress Apparent in Area Rich with History," *San Diego Union Tribune*, June 30, 2019; and San Diego Real Estate Hunter, "Four Reasons Why Encanto Is a Great Place to Live," *San Diego Real Estate Hunter*, 2019, www.sandiegorealestatehunter.com/blog/4-reasons-why-encanto-san-diego-great -place-live/.

5 Pelayo, "Art Galleries Fuel a Barrio Logan Renaissance."

6 San Diego Tourism Authority, "City Heights: Fertile Ground for Creativity," 2019, www.sandiego.org/campaigns/district-arts/city-heights.aspx.

7 San Diego Tourism Authority, "Southeastern San Diego: An Unexpected Cultural Journey," 2019, www.sandiego.org/campaigns/district-arts/southeastern.aspx.

8 Paul Krueger, "The Most Dangerous Part of San Diego," *San Diego Reader*, May 2, 1991.

9 "City Heights Hell," *San Diego Reader*, October 4, 2007.

10 Loïc Wacquant, Tom Slater, and Virgílio Borges Pereira, "Territorial Stigmatization in Action," *Environment and Planning A* 46, no. 6 (2014): 1270–80, 1279.

11 Harvey Molotch, "The City as a Growth Machine: Toward a Political Economy of Place," *American Journal of Sociology* 82, no. 2 (1976): 309–32.

12 Molotch, "City as a Growth Machine," 309–10.

13 John R. Logan and Harvey Molotch, *Urban Fortunes: The Political Economy of Place*, 20th anniversary edition (Berkeley: University of California Press, 2007).

14 Andrew E. G. Jonas and David Wilson, *The Urban Growth Machine: Critical Perspectives Two Decades Later* (Albany: State University of New York Press, 1999).

15 David Harvey, "From Managerialism to Entrepreneurialism: The Transformation in Urban Governance in Late Capitalism," *Geografiska Annaler Series B, Human Geography* 71, no. 1 (2017): 3–17; Phil Hubbard and Tim Hall, "The Entrepreneurial City and the 'New Urban Politics,'" in *The Entrepreneurial City: Geographies of Politics, Regime and Representation*, ed. Tim Hall and Phil Hubbard, 199–202 (Chichester, UK: Wiley, 1998); Jonas and Wilson, *Urban Growth Machine*; and Peck, Theodore, and Brenner, "Neoliberal Urbanism."

16 Gordon MacLeod, "Urban Politics Reconsidered: Growth Machine to Postdemocratic City?," *Urban Studies* 48, no. 12 (2011): 2629–60; and Erik Swyngedouw, *Designing the Post-political City and the Insurgent Polis* (London: Bedford Press, 2011).

17 Richard L. Florida, *The Rise of the Creative Class: And How It's Transforming Work, Leisure, Community and Everyday Life* (New York: Basic Books, 2002).

18 Melanie Bedore, "The Convening Power of Food As Growth Machine Politics: A Study of Food Policymaking and Partnership Formation in Baltimore," *Urban Studies* 51, no. 14 (2014): 2979–95.

19 Peck, Theodore, and Brenner, "Neoliberal Urbanism."

20 Guthman, "Neoliberalism and the Making of Food Politics in California"; Joassart-Marcelli and Bosco, "Alternative Food Projects, Localization and Neoliberal Urban Development"; and Nathan McClintock, "Radical, Reformist, and Garden-Variety Neoliberal: Coming to Terms with Urban Agriculture's Contradictions," *Local Environment: Subversive and Interstitial Food Spaces* 19, no. 2 (2014): 147–71.

21 Harvey, "From Managerialism to Entrepreneurialism"; and Hubbard and Hall, "Entrepreneurial City and the 'New Urban Politics.'"

22 Erie, Kogan, and MacKenzie, "Redevelopment, San Diego Style; and Karjanen, *Servant Class City.*

23 Florida, *Rise of the Creative Class.*

24 City of San Diego, *Mid-City Communities Plan* (San Diego: City of San Diego, 1998), 102.

25 City of San Diego, *Barrio Logan Community Plan and Local Coastal Program* (San Diego: City of San Diego, 2013), LU-12.

26 City of San Diego, *Barrio Logan Community Plan and Local Coastal Program*, LU-13.

27 City of San Diego, *Southeastern San Diego Community Plan* (San Diego: City of San Diego, 2015), 8-15 to 8-16.

28 Lorlene Hoyt, "Collecting Private Funds for Safer Public Spaces: An Empirical Examination of the Business Improvement District Concept," *Environment and Planning B: Planning and Design* 31, no. 3 (2004): 367–80.

29 Kevin Ward, "'Creating a Personality for Downtown': Business Improvement Districts in Milwaukee," *Urban Geography* 28 (2007): 781–808.

30 North Park Main Street, "Home Page," 2020, https://northparkmainstreet.com /north-park-san-diego/.

31 City Heights Community Development Corporation, "City Heights Street Food Fest Invitation," Eventbrite, September 12, 2019, www.eventbrite.com/e/city -heights-street-food-fest-tickets-60420008873#.

32 San Diego Tourism Authority, "Barrio Logan: Arte y La Cultura Autentica," 2019, www.sandiego.org/campaigns/district-arts/barrio-logan.aspx.

33 Archana Ram, "Neighborhood Guide: City Heights," *San Diego Magazine*, April 24, 2015.

34 Tutko and Wycoff, "San Diego Home Buyers' Guide 2019."

35 The Infatuation, "Where to Eat and Drink in San Diego," 2019, www.theinfatu ation.com/san-diego/guides/san-diego-restaurants#guide.

36 The Infatuation, "Where to Eat and Drink in San Diego."

37 The Infatuation, "Where to Eat and Drink in San Diego."

38 Eater, "Essential San Diego Restaurants," *Eater San Diego*, Summer 2019, https:// sandiego.eater.com/maps/38-best-restaurants-in-san-diego; Eater, "The Hottest Restaurants in San Diego Right Now," *Eater San Diego*, December 2019, https:// sandiego.eater.com/maps/best-new-san-diego-restaurants-heatmap; The Infat- uation, "Where to Eat and Drink in San Diego"; Thrillist, "Fifty Things You Need to Eat in San Diego before You Die," October 2015, www.thrillist.com /eat/san-diego/50-best-things-to-eat-in-san-diego-bucket-list; Thrillist, "The Best Restaurants in San Diego Right Now," August 2019, www.thrillist.com /eat/san-diego/best-restaurants-san-diego; TimeOut, "The 18 Best Restaurants in San Diego," November 2019, www.timeout.com/san-diego/restaurants/best -restaurants-in-san-diego; Zagat, "Best Restaurants in San Diego," 2018, www .zagat.com/l/top-food-in-san-diego; and Zagat, "Hottest restaurants in San Diego," 2018, www.zagat.com/l/the-hottest-restaurants-in-san-diego. Every restaurant was geocoded based on their address in ArcMap using the ESRI's online geocoding tool. Kernel density analysis was performed using ArcTool with the default settings selected. Conceptually, a smoothly curved surface (kernel) is fitted over each point, with values equal to 1 at the point location and diminishing with distance until they reach zero at search radius automati- cally computed by ArcGIS based on the characteristics of the input data. The resulting density output is the sum of the kernel surface values at the center of each raster cell. Thus higher values indicate the presence of or proximity to multiple points (in this case, restaurants) in a given cell.

39 Neil Smith, *The New Urban Frontier: Gentrification and the Revanchist City* (New York: Routledge, 1996).

40 Zillow, "Homes for Sale," www.zillow.com/san-diego-ca/ (accessed May 2019).

6 THE TASTE OF GENTRIFICATION

1 Alex Zaragoza, "A Chicano Community in San Diego Is Outraged over a White Woman's Attempt to Open a 'Modern Fruteria,'" *Mitu*, October 27, 2017.

2 I recorded Twitter and Facebook postings for about a month following La Gracia's Kickstarter campaign launch on October 24, 2017. To protect the confidentiality of the individuals I followed, whose comments were public but who did not willingly choose to participate in my study, I keep their quotations anonymous.

3 Curti, Craine, and Aitken, *Fight to Stay Put.*

4 Gentrification status was computed using tract-level data from the Summary Files of the 1980, 1990, and 2000 Census of Population and Housing standardized in the Longitudinal Tract Database (LTDB 2019; see John R. Logan, Zengwang Xu, and Brian J. Stults, "Interpolating US Decennial Census Tract Data from as Early as 1970 to 2010: A Longitudinal Tract Database," *The Professional Geographer* 66, no. 3 [2014]: 412–20), and the 2008–12 and 2013–17 American Community Survey Five-Year Estimates of the US Census Bureau, 2014 and 2019—all of which use 2010 US Census tract boundaries. For each decade, building upon a method developed by Lance Freeman, "Displacement or Succession? Residential Mobility in Gentrifying Neighborhoods," *Urban Affairs Review* 40, no. 4 (2005): 463–91, I first identified two types of tracts: those affordable and poor enough to be eligible for gentrification at the beginning of the decade and those already too expensive and affluent to be eligible. Tracts where median property values and median household income were below the regional median at the start of the decade were part of the first group. All other tracts were included in the second group and further divided into high- and middle-income areas. Among tracts eligible to gentrify, those where increases in property values were in the top 25 percent for the county were considered to have gentrified. Rapid increases in property values reflect the type of socioeconomic change typically associated with gentrification—an influx of affluent, educated, and white residents that raises property values and displaces longtime low-income residents of color. I repeated the computations for each decade (1980–90, 1990–2000, 2000–2010, and 2010–18).

5 Zukin, *Naked City.*

6 Alkon, Kato, and Sbicca, *Recipe for Gentrification*; Anguelovski, "Healthy Food Stores, Greenlining and Food Gentrification"; Joassart-Marcelli and Bosco, "Alternative Food and Gentrification"; and Joassart-Marcelli and Bosco, "Food and Gentrification."

7 Lees, Slater, and Wyly, *Gentrification.*

8 Smith, "Gentrification and Uneven Development."

9 Rothstein, *Color of Law*; and Jason R. Hackworth, *The Neoliberal City: Governance, Ideology, and Development in American Urbanism* (Ithaca, NY: Cornell University Press, 2007).

10 Ley, "Artists, Aestheticization and the Field of Gentrification"; and Zukin, *Naked City*.

11 Tom Slater, "'A Literal Necessity to Be Re-Placed': A Rejoinder to the Gentrification Debate," *International Journal of Urban and Regional Research* 32, no. 1 (2008): 212–23, 216.

12 Lees, Annunziata, and Rivas-Alonso, "Resisting Planetary Gentrification."

13 McKittrick, "On Plantations, Prisons, and a Black Sense of Place."

14 Robinson, *Black Marxism*; Pulido, "Geographies of Race and Ethnicity II"; Erin McElroy and Alex Werth, "Deracinated Dispossessions: On the Foreclosures of 'Gentrification' in Oakland, CA," *Antipode* 51, no. 3 (2019): 878–98; and Margaret M Ramírez, "City as Borderland: Gentrification and the Policing of Black and Latinx Geographies in Oakland," *Environment and Planning D: Society and Space* 38, no. 1 (2020): 147–66.

15 Ananya Roy, "Racial Banishment," in *Keywords in Radical Geography: Antipode at 50*, ed. the Antipode Editorial Collective, 227–30 (Hoboken, NJ: Wiley, 2019).

16 Jaime Guzmán, "The Whiteness Project of Gentrification: The Battle over Los Angeles' Eastside," PhD dissertation, University of Denver, 2018.

17 Jean-Paul D. Addie and James C. Fraser, "After Gentrification: Social Mix, Settler Colonialism, and Cruel Optimism in the Transformation of Neighbourhood Space," *Antipode* 51, no. 5 (2019): 1369–94; Nathan McClintock, "Urban Agriculture, Racial Capitalism, and Resistance in the Settler-Colonial City," *Geography Compass* 12, no. 6 (2018): E12378; Jessica Ty Miller, "Temporal Analysis of Displacement: Racial Capitalism and Settler Colonial Urban Space," *Geoforum* 116 (2020): 180–92; and Jessica Parish, "Re-wilding Parkdale? Environmental Gentrification, Settler Colonialism, and the Reconfiguration of Nature in 21st Century Toronto," *Environment and Planning E, Nature and Space* 3, no. 1 (2020): 263–86.

18 Eve Tuck and K. Wayne Yang, "Decolonization Is Not a Metaphor," *Decolonization: Indigeneity, Education & Society* 1, no. 1 (2012): 1–40.

19 Sarah Launius and Geoffrey Alan Boyce, "More than Metaphor: Settler Colonialism, Frontier Logic, and the Continuities of Racialized Dispossession in a Southwest US City," *Annals of the American Association of Geographers* (2020): 1–18.

20 Ramírez, "City as Borderland."

21 Tone Huse, "Gentrification and Ethnicity," in *Handbook of Gentrification Studies*, ed. Loretta Lees and Martin Phillips, 186–204 (Northampton, MA: Edward Elgar Publishing, 2018).

22 Pascale Joassart-Marcelli and Fernando J. Bosco, "The Taste of Gentrification: Difference and Exclusion on San Diego's Urban Food Frontier," in *A Recipe for Gentrification: Food, Power, and Resistance*, edited by Alison Hope Alkon, Yuki Kato, and Joshua Sbicca, 31–53 (New York: New York University Press, 2020).

23 Pierre Bourdieu, *Distinction: A Social Critique of the Judgement of Taste* (Cambridge, MA: Harvard University Press, 1984).

24 Doreen Massey, "Places and Their Pasts," *History Workshop Journal* 39 (1995): 182–92, 182.

25 Arjun Appadurai, "How to Make a National Cuisine: Cookbooks in Contemporary India," *Comparative Studies in Society and History* 30, no. 1 (1988): 3–24.

26 Emily Deruy, "Mexican Food Enters the Fine-Dining Realm," *The Atlantic*, April 18, 2016; and Claudi McNeally, "How Filipino Food Is Becoming the Next Great American Cuisine," *Vogue*, June 1, 2017.

27 Edward F. McQuarrie, Jessica Miller, and Barbara J. Phillips, "The Megaphone Effect: Taste and Audience in Fashion Blogging," *Journal of Consumer Research* 40, no. 1 (2013): 136–58.

28 Dylan Gottlieb, "Dirty, Authentic . . . Delicious: Yelp, Mexican Restaurants, and the Appetites of Philadelphia's New Middle Class," *Gastronomica* 15, no. 2 (2015): 39–48, 39.

29 Gottlieb, "Dirty, Authentic . . . Delicious"; and Sharon Zukin, Scarlett Lindeman, and Laurie Hurson, "The Omnivore's Neighborhood? Online Restaurant Reviews, Race, and Gentrification," *Journal of Consumer Culture* 17, no. 3 (2015): 459–79.

30 Using the Data Miner extension on Google Chrome, I downloaded data on each "ethnic" restaurant, including street address, rating, number of reviews, and type, using the term *ethnic restaurant* in my search. Although it is unclear what algorithm Yelp uses to identify ethnic restaurants, the categorization appears to be based on how restaurants define themselves, with Thai, Indian, Ethiopian, Mexican, Vietnamese, and other cuisines of the Global South considered as "ethnic"—a common bias noted by many observers (Ray, *Ethnic Restaurateur*). The data had to be cleaned to eliminate sponsored listings, fill in occasional missing information that failed to download, and add city and zip code information that are not shown on the parent page and therefore could not be "scraped" in the simple version of the application. From the 752 restaurants originally identified as "ethnic," I also removed any "nonethnic" restaurants (e.g., traditional diners serving huevos rancheros and gastropubs with a taco plate on the menu) as well as large chains (e.g., P.F. Chang's, Chipotle, Papa John's, and El Pollo Loco), leaving a total of 451 ethnic restaurants to analyze. I geocoded each one based on their address in ArcMap using ESRI's online geocoding tool.

31 Wei Li, *Ethnoburb: The New Ethnic Community in Urban America* (Honolulu: University of Hawaii Press, 2008).

32 To analyze the perspective of Yelpers, I downloaded reviews for the ten most highly rated and ten lowest rated restaurants in the three study neighborhoods of City Heights, Barrio Logan, and Southeastern San Diego (as of March 1, 2020). For each of these restaurants I selected the twenty best and twenty lowest reviews, giving me a total of twenty-four hundred reviews to analyze. I focused on the "extremes" in an attempt to understand what people really liked or disliked about particular establishments. I uploaded the reviews into NVivo to

analyze their content by looking for repetition and coding for themes such as décor, safety, health, service, food, authenticity, ethnicity, cosmopolitanism, democracy, community, and price.

33 Barrio Dogg, https://barriodogg.com (accessed January 2021).

34 Storymakers, Facebook post, www.facebook.com/Storymakers-Coffee-Roasters-113184613812818/ (accessed January 2021).

35 Lees, Slater, and Wyly, *Gentrification*.

36 LTDB, "Longitudinal Tract Database," American Communities Project, Brown University, 2019.

37 US Census, "Census of Population and Housing. Public Use Microdata Sample," US Census Bureau, 2000; and US Census, "American Community Survey Five-Year Estimates, 2013–2017. Public Use Microdata Sample," US Census Bureau, 2019.

38 Caspi et al., "Local Food Environment and Diet."

39 Smith, *New Urban Frontier*.

40 Henri Lefebvre, *Rhythmanalysis: Space, Time and Everyday Life*, trans. Stuart Elden and Gerald Moore (New York: Continuum, 1992).

41 Kern, "Rhythms of Gentrification."

42 Kern, "Rhythms of Gentrification," 442.

43 Kevin Hetherington, "Rhythm and Noise: The City, Memory and the Archive," *Sociological Review* 61 (2013): 17–33.

44 Anderson, *Cosmopolitan Canopy*, 10.

45 Alkon and McCullen, "Whiteness and Farmers Markets"; Guthman, "If They Only Knew"; Brandon Hoover, "White Spaces in Black and Latino Places: Urban Agriculture and Food Sovereignty," *Journal of Agriculture, Food Systems, and Community Development* 3, no. 4 (2013): 109–15; and Slocum, "Whiteness, Space and Alternative Food Practice."

46 Sara Ahmed, *The Promise of Happiness* (Durham, NC: Duke University Press, 2010).

47 Arun Saldanha, *Psychedelic White: Goa Trance and the Viscosity of Race* (Minneapolis: University of Minnesota Press, 2007).

48 Slocum, "Whiteness, Space and Alternative Food Practice."

49 Tyler Cowen, "Six Rules for Dining Out: How a Frugal Economist Finds the Perfect Lunch," *The Atlantic*, May 2012.

7 RECLAIMING THE ETHNIC FOODSCAPE

1 Marvin Lemus and Linda Y. Chávez, *Gentefied*, Netflix, 2020.

2 Emanuel Delgado and Kate Swanson, "Gentefication in the Barrio: Displacement and Urban Change in Southern California," *Journal of Urban Affairs* (2019): 1–16, https://doi.org/10.1080/07352166.2019.1680245; and Ubaldo Escalante, "There Goes the Barrio: Measuring Gentefication in Boyle Heights, Los Angeles," PhD dissertation, Columbia University, 2017.

3 Julia Herbst, "Guillermo Uribe on the 'Gentefication' of East LA," *LA Magazine*, September 9, 2014.

4 Uribe as quoted in Jennifer Medina, "Los Angeles Neighborhood Tries to Change, but Avoid the Pitfalls," *New York Times*, August 17, 2013.

5 Amador as quoted in Medina, "Los Angeles Neighborhood Tries to Change, but Avoid the Pitfalls."

6 La Via Campesina, "Declaration of Nyéléni," Nyéléni Forum for Food Sovereignty, Mali, 2007, https://nyeleni.org/spip.php?article290.

7 Zoe W. Brent, Christina M. Schiavoni, and Alberto Alonso-Fradejas, "Contextualising Food Sovereignty: The Politics of Convergence among Movements in the USA," *Third World Quarterly* 36, no. 3 (2015): 618–35; and Amy Trauger, *Food Sovereignty in International Context: Discourse, Politics and Practice of Place* (New York: Routledge, 2015).

8 Kristin Reynolds and Nevin Cohen, *Beyond the Kale: Urban Agriculture and Social Justice Activism in New York City* (Athens: University of Georgia Press, 2016); and Monica M. White, *Freedom Farmers: Agricultural Resistance and the Black Freedom Movement* (Chapel Hill: University of North Carolina Press, 2018).

9 Alison Hope Alkon and Teresa Marie Mares, "Food Sovereignty in US Food Movements: Radical Visions and Neoliberal Constraints," *Agriculture and Human Values* 29, no. 3 (2012): 347–59; and Jessica Clendenning, Wolfram H. Dressler, and Carol Richards, "Food Justice or Food Sovereignty? Understanding the Rise of Urban Food Movements in the USA," *Agriculture and Human Values* 33, no. 1 (2015): 165–77.

10 Alkon and Agyeman, *Cultivating Food Justice*; and Gottlieb and Joshi, *Food Justice*.

11 Clendenning, Dressler, and Richards, "Food Justice or Food Sovereignty?"; and Lucy Jarosz, "Comparing Food Security and Food Sovereignty Discourses," *Dialogues in Human Geography* 4, no. 2 (2014): 168–81.

12 Kirsten Valentine Cadieux and Rachel Slocum, "What Does It Mean to Do Food Justice?," *Journal of Political Ecology* 22, no. 1 (2015): 1–26; and Eric Holt-Giménez and Annie Shattuck, "Food Crises, Food Regimes and Food Movements: Rumblings of Reform or Tides of Transformation?," *Journal of Peasant Studies* 38, no. 1 (2011): 109–44.

13 Rasheed Salaam Hislop, "Reaping Equity: A Survey of Food Justice Organizations in the U.S.A.,"MS thesis, University of California Davis, 2014.

14 Katharine Bradley and Hank Herrera, "Decolonizing Food Justice: Naming, Resisting, and Researching Colonizing Forces in the Movement: Decolonizing Food Justice," *Antipode* 48, no. 1 (2016): 97–114; Guthman, "Bringing Good Food to Others"; Hoover, "White Spaces in Black and Latino Places"; and Slocum, "Whiteness, Space and Alternative Food Practice."

15 Alison Hope Alkon, "Food Justice and the Challenge to Neoliberalism," *Gastronomica: The Journal of Food and Culture* 14, no. 2 (2014): 27–40; Guthman, "Neoliberalism and the Making of Food Politics in California"; Joassart-Marcelli and Bosco,

"Alternative Food Projects, Localization and Neoliberal Urban Development"; and McClintock, "Radical, Reformist, and Garden-Variety Neoliberal."

16 Steve Pile, "Introduction: Opposition, Political identities, and Spaces of Resistance," in *Geographies of Resistance*, ed. Steve Pile and Michael Keith, 1–12 (New York: Routledge, 1997), 3.

17 J. K. Gibson-Graham, *A Postcapitalist Politics* (Minneapolis: University of Minnesota Press, 2006).

18 Guthman, "Bringing Good Food to Others," 437.

19 Winnifred Curran and Trina Hamilton, *Just Green Enough: Urban Development and Environmental Gentrification* (New York: Routledge, 2017); and Jennifer R. Wolch, Jason Byrne, and Joshua P. Newell, "Urban Green Space, Public Health, and Environmental Justice: The Challenge of Making Cities 'Just Green Enough,'" *Landscape and Urban Planning* 125 (2014): 234–44.

20 John Joe Schlichtman, Jason Patch, and Marc Lamont Hill, *Gentrifier* (Toronto: University of Toronto Press, 2017).

21 Alkon, Kato, and Sbicca, *Recipe for Gentrification*, 330.

22 National Restaurant Association, *What Is Hot: 2018 Culinary Forecast* (Washington, DC: NRA, 2018).

23 Reese, *Black Food Geographies*.

24 Pascale Joassart-Marcelli, *The Good Food District: Historical Background and Current Needs* (San Diego: San Diego State University, Department of Geography, and Project New Village, 2018), https://fep.sdsu.edu/Docs/Report_V3.pdf; and Joassart-Marcelli, Bosco, and Delgado, *Southeastern San Diego's Food Landscape*.

25 Reese, *Black Food Geographies*, 104.

26 Environmental Health Coalition, "Barrio Logan's Community Garden," *Toxic Free Neighborhood Blog*, June 12, 2017, www.environmentalhealth.org/index.php/en /media-center/blog-for-environmental-justice/127-toxic-free-neighborhoods /623-barrio-logan-s-community-garden.

27 Emmanuelle Le Texier, "The Struggle against Gentrification," in *Chicano San Diego: Cultural Space and the Struggle for Justice*, ed. Richard Griswold del Castillo, 202–21 (Tucson: University of Arizona Press, 2007).

28 Mareike Ahrens, "'Gentrify? No! Gentefy? Sí!': Urban Redevelopment and Ethnic Gentrification in Boyle Heights, Los Angeles," *Aspeers* 8 (2015): 9–26; and Delgado and Swanson, "Gentefication in the Barrio."

29 Guzmán, "Whiteness Project of Gentrification."

30 Brenda Kayzar, "Interpreting Philanthropic Interventions: Media Representations of a Community Savior," in *The Fight to Stay Put: Social Lessons through Media Imaginings of Urban Transformation and Change*, ed. Giorgio Hadi Curti, Jim Craine, and Stuart Aitken, 209–28 (Stuttgart: Verlag, 2013).

31 David Goodman, E. Melanie DuPuis, and Michael K. Goodman, *Alternative Food Networks: Knowledge, Practice, and Politics* (New York: Routledge, 2012); Guthman, "Bringing Good Food to Others"; Guthman, "Neoliberalism and

the Making of Food Politics in California"; and Joassart-Marcelli and Bosco, "Alternative Food Projects, Localization and Neoliberal Urban Development."

32 Andrea Brower, "Agri-food Activism and the Imagination of the Possible," *New Zealand Sociology* 28, no. 4 (2013): 80–100; and Guthman, "Neoliberalism and the Making of Food Politics in California."

33 Erik Swyngedouw, "Apocalypse Forever?: Post-Political Populism and the Spectre of Climate Change," *Theory, Culture & Society* 27, no. 2 (2010): 213–32, 219.

34 Agyeman, Matthews, and Sobel, *Food Trucks, Cultural Identity, and Social Justice.*

35 Joshua Sbicca, "Food Labor, Economic Inequality, and the Imperfect Politics of Process in the Alternative Food Movement," *Agriculture and Human Values* 32, no. 4 (2015): 675–87.

36 David Card and Alan B. Krueger, *Myth and Measurement: The New Economics of the Minimum Wage* (Princeton, NJ: Princeton University Press, 2016).

37 Union of Concerned Scientists, *Purchasing Power: How Institutional "Good Food" Procurement Policies Can Shape a Food System That's Better for People and Our Planet* (Cambridge, MA: UCS, 2018), www.ucsusa.org/sites/default/files/attach/2017/11 /purchasing-power-report-ucs-2017.pdf.

38 Julian Agyeman and Sydney Giacalone, eds., *The Immigrant-Food Nexus: Borders, Labor, and Identity in North America* (Cambridge, MA: MIT Press, 2020).

39 White, *Freedom Farmers.*

40 Luz Calvo and Catrióna Rueda Esquibel, *Decolonize Your Diet: Plant-based Mexican-American Recipes for Health and Healing* (Vancouver, BC: Arsenal, 2015).

41 Charles Z. Levkoe, Josh Brem-Wilson, and Colin R. Anderson, "People, Power, Change: Three Pillars of a Food Sovereignty Research Praxis," *Journal of Peasant Studies* 46, no. 7 (2019): 1389–412.

BIBLIOGRAPHY

Addie, Jean-Paul D., and James C. Fraser. "After Gentrification: Social Mix, Settler Colonialism, and Cruel Optimism in the Transformation of Neighbourhood Space." *Antipode* 51, no. 5 (2019): 1369–94.

Agarwal, Rupali, and Molly J. Dahm. "Success Factors in Independent Ethnic Restaurants." *Journal of Foodservice Business Research* 18, no. 1 (2015): 20–33.

Agyeman, Julian, and Sydney Giacalone, eds. *The Immigrant-Food Nexus: Borders, Labor, and Identity in North America.* Cambridge, MA: MIT Press, 2020.

Agyeman, Julian, Caitlin Matthews, and Hannah Sobel, eds. *Food Trucks, Cultural Identity, and Social Justice: From Loncheras to Lobsta Love.* Cambridge, MA: MIT Press, 2017.

Ahmed, Sara. *The Promise of Happiness.* Durham, NC: Duke University Press, 2010.

Ahrens, Mareike. "'Gentrify? No! Gentefy? Sí!': Urban Redevelopment and Ethnic Gentrification in Boyle Heights, Los Angeles." *Aspeers* 8 (2015): 9–26.

Akresh, Ilana Redstone. "Dietary Assimilation and Health among Hispanic Immigrants to the United States." *Journal of Health and Social Behavior* 48, no. 4 (2007): 404–17.

Alkon, Alison, and Julie Guthman, eds. *The New Food Activism: Opposition, Cooperation, and Collective Action.* Berkeley: University of California Press, 2017.

Alkon, Alison Hope. "Food Justice and the Challenge to Neoliberalism." *Gastronomica: The Journal of Food and Culture* 14, no. 2 (2014): 27–40.

Alkon, Alison Hope, and Christie Grace McCullen. "Whiteness and Farmers Markets: Performances, Perpetuations . . . Contestations?" *Antipode* 43, no. 4 (2011): 937–59.

Alkon, Alison Hope, and Julian Agyeman, eds. *Cultivating Food Justice: Race, Class, and Sustainability.* Cambridge, MA: MIT Press, 2011.

Alkon, Alison Hope, and Teresa Marie Mares. "Food Sovereignty in US Food Movements: Radical Visions and Neoliberal Constraints." *Agriculture and Human Values* 29, no. 3 (2012): 347–59.

Alkon, Alison Hope, Yuki Kato, and Joshua Sbicca, eds. *A Recipe for Gentrification: Food, Power, and Resistance in the City.* New York: New York University Press, 2020.

Anderson, Elijah. *The Cosmopolitan Canopy: Race and Civility in Everyday Life.* New York: Norton, 2011.

Anguelovski, Isabelle. "Healthy Food Stores, Greenlining and Food Gentrification: Contesting New Forms of Privilege, Displacement and Locally Unwanted Land

Uses in Racially Mixed Neighborhoods." *International Journal of Urban and Regional Research* 39, no. 6 (2015): 1209–30.

Appadurai, Arjun. "How to Make a National Cuisine: Cookbooks in Contemporary India." *Comparative Studies in Society and History* 30, no. 1 (1988): 3–24.

———. *Modernity at Large: Cultural Dimensions of Globalization.* Minneapolis: University of Minnesota Press, 1996.

Avieli, Nir. "The Hummus Wars Revisited: Israeli-Arab Food Politics and Gastromediation." *Gastronomica* 16, no. 3 (2016): 19–30.

Baxt, Josh, Erin Meanley Glenny, Jennifer Mcentee, Hoa Quach, and Marie Tutko. "San Diego's Next Hot Neighborhood. Where Everyone Will Be Living in 2016." *San Diego Magazine,* February 26, 2016.

Bedore, Melanie. "The Convening Power of Food as Growth Machine Politics: A Study of Food Policymaking and Partnership Formation in Baltimore." *Urban Studies* 51, no. 14 (2014): 2979–95.

Bell, David, and Gill Valentine. *Consuming Geographies: We Are Where We Eat.* London: Routledge, 1997.

Berger, John, and Jean Mohr. *A Fortunate Man.* New York: Pantheon, 1967.

Bernhardt, Annette, Ruth Milkman, Nik Theodore, Douglas D Heckathorn, Mirabai Auer, James DeFilippis, Ana Luz González, Victor Narro, and Jason Perelshteyn. *Broken Laws, Unprotected Workers: Violations of Employment and Labor Laws in America's Cities.* New York: National Employment Law Project, 2009.

Bernstein, Hamutal, Dulce Gonzalez, Michael Karpman, and Stephen Zuckerman. "One in Seven Adults in Immigrant Families Reported Avoiding Public Benefit Programs in 2018." Urban Institute, 2019. www.urban.org/research/publication/oneseven -adults-immigrant-families-reported-avoiding-public-benefitprograms-2018.

Black, Samuel, ed. *San Diego and Imperial Counties of California: A Record of Settlement, Organization, Progress and Achievement.* Vol. 1. Chicago: Clarke Publishing, 2013.

Bliesner, James, and Mirle Rabinowitz Bussell. *The Informal Economy in City Heights.* San Diego: University of California San Diego Center for Urban Economics and Design, 2013.

Bonds, Anne, and Joshua Inwood. "Beyond White Privilege: Geographies of White Supremacy and Settler Colonialism." *Progress in Human Geography* 40, no. 6 (2016): 715–33.

Born, Branden, and Mark Purcell. "Avoiding the Local Trap: Scale and Food Systems in Planning Research." *Journal of Planning Education and Research* 26, no. 2 (2006): 195–207.

Bosco, Fernando J., and Pascale Joassart-Marcelli. "Spaces of Alternative Food: Urban Agriculture, Community Gardens and Farmers Markets." In *Food and Place: A Critical Exploration,* edited by Pascale Joassart-Marcelli and Fernando J. Bosco, 187–205. Lanham, MD: Rowman and Littlefield, 2018.

Bosco, Fernando J., Pascale Joassart-Marcelli, and Blaire O'Neal. "Food Journeys: Place, Mobility, and the Everyday Food Practices of Young People." *Annals of the American Association of Geographers* 107, no. 6 (2017): 1479–98.

Bourdieu, Pierre. *Distinction: A Social Critique of the Judgement of Taste*. Cambridge, MA: Harvard University Press, 1984.

Boyer, Kate. "Affect, Corporeality and the Limits of Belonging: Breastfeeding in Public in the Contemporary UK." *Health & Place* 18, no. 3 (2012): 552–60.

Bradley, Katharine, and Hank Herrera. "Decolonizing Food Justice: Naming, Resisting, and Researching Colonizing Forces in the Movement: Decolonizing Food Justice." *Antipode* 48, no. 1 (2016): 97–114.

Bradley, Katharine, and Ryan E. Galt. "Practicing Food Justice at Dig Deep Farms & Produce, East Bay Area, California: Self-Determination as a Guiding Value and Intersections with Foodie Logics." *Local Environment* 19, no. 2 (2014): 172–86.

Brenner, Neil, Peter Marcuse, and Margit Mayer. *Cities for People, Not for Profit: Critical Urban Theory and the Right to the City*. New York: Routledge, 2012.

Brent, Zoe W., Christina M. Schiavoni, and Alberto Alonso-Fradejas. "Contextualising Food Sovereignty: The Politics of Convergence among Movements in the USA." *Third World Quarterly* 36, no. 3 (2015): 618–35.

Brones, Anna. "Karen Washington: It's Not a Food Desert, It's Food Apartheid." *Guernica*, May 7, 2018.

Brower, Andrea. "Agri-Food Activism and the Imagination of the Possible." *New Zealand Sociology* 28, no. 4 (2013): 80–100.

Burgoine, Thomas. "Collecting Accurate Secondary Foodscape Data: A Reflection on the Trials and Tribulations." *Appetite* 55, no. 3 (2010): 522–27.

Burke, Meghan A. *Racial Ambivalence in Diverse Communities: Whiteness and the Power of Color-Blind Ideologies*. Lanham, MD: Lexington Books, 2012.

Cadieux, Kirsten Valentine, and Rachel Slocum. "What Does It Mean to Do Food Justice?" *Journal of Political Ecology* 22, no. 1 (2015): 1–26.

California Department of Public Health. "Communities of Excellence: Retail Food Environment." 2016.

Calvo, Luz, and Catrióna Rueda Esquibel. *Decolonize Your Diet: Plant-Based Mexican-American Recipes for Health and Healing*. Vancouver, BC: Arsenal, 2015.

Capps, Randy, Michael Fix, and Everett Henderson. "Trends in Immigrants' Use of Public Assistance after Welfare Reform." In *Immigrants and Welfare: The Impact of Welfare Reform on America's Newcomers*, edited by Michael Fix, 123–52. New York: Russel Sage Foundation, 2009.

Card, David, and Alan B. Krueger. *Myth and Measurement: The New Economics of the Minimum Wage*. Princeton, NJ: Princeton University Press, 2016.

Carney, Megan A. "The Biopolitics of 'Food Insecurity': Towards a Critical Political Ecology of the Body in Studies of Women's Transnational Migration." *Journal of Political Ecology* 21, no. 1 (2014): 1–18.

———. *The Unending Hunger: Tracing Women and Food Insecurity across Borders*. Berkeley: University of California Press, 2015.

Caspi, Caitlin E., Glorian Sorensen, S. V. Subramanian, and Ichiro Kawachi. "The Local Food Environment and Diet: A Systematic Review." *Health & Place* 18, no. 5 (2012): 1172–87.

Charreire, Hélène, Romain Casey, Paul Salze, Chantal Simon, Basile Chaix, Arnaud Banos, Dominique Badariotti, Christiane Weber, and Jean-Michel Oppert. "Measuring the Food Environment Using Geographical Information Systems: A Methodological Review." *Public Health Nutrition* 13, no. 11 (2010): 1773–85.

Chilton, Mariana, and Sue Booth. "Hunger of the Body and Hunger of the Mind: African American Women's Perceptions of Food Insecurity, Health and Violence." *Journal of Nutrition Education and Behavior* 39, no. 3 (2007): 116–25.

City Clerk Archives. City Directories. San Diego Public Library, San Diego, CA, 2018.

City Heights Community Development Corporation. "City Heights Street Food Fest Invitation." Eventbrite, September 12, 2019. www.eventbrite.com/e/city-heights -street-food-fest-tickets-60420008873#.

"City Heights Hell." *San Diego Reader* (October 4, 2007).

City of San Diego. *Barrio Logan Community Plan and Local Coastal Program*. San Diego: City of San Diego, 2013.

———. *Mid-City Communities Plan*. San Diego: City of San Diego, 1998.

———. *Southeastern San Diego Community Plan*. San Diego: City of San Diego, 2015.

Clendenning, Jessica, Wolfram H. Dressler, and Carol Richards. "Food Justice or Food Sovereignty? Understanding the Rise of Urban Food Movements in the USA." *Agriculture and Human Values* 33, no. 1 (2015): 165–77.

Coleman-Jensen, Alisha, Matthew P. Rabbitt, Christian A. Gregory, and Anita Singh. *Household Food Security in the United States in 2018*. Washington, DC: United States Department of Agriculture, 2019.

Colls, Rachel. "Materialising Bodily Matter: Intra-Action and the Embodiment of 'Fat.'" *Geoforum* 38, no. 2 (2007): 353–65.

Cook, Ian, and Philip Crang. "The World on a Plate: Culinary Culture, Displacement and Geographical Knowledge." *Journal of Material Culture* 1, no. 2 (1996): 131–53.

Cosgrove, Denis E. *Social Formation and Symbolic Landscape*. London: Croom Helm, 1984.

Cowan, Spencer M. *Patterns of Disparity: Small Business Lending in the Chicago and Los Angeles–San Diego Regions*. Chicago: Woodstock Institute, 2017. www.documen tcloud.org/documents/5028189-Chicago-and-LASD-Report-CC-License-Update .html.

Cowen, Tyler. "Six Rules for Dining Out: How a Frugal Economist Finds the Perfect Lunch." *The Atlantic*, May 2012.

Curran, Winifred, and Trina Hamilton. *Just Green Enough: Urban Development and Environmental Gentrification*. New York: Routledge, 2017.

Curti, Giorgio Hadi, Jim Craine, and Stuart C. Aitken, eds. *The Fight to Stay Put: Social Lessons through Media Imaginings of Urban Transformation and Change*. Stuttgart: Verlag, 2013.

Daniels, Stephen. "Marxism, Culture, and the Duplicity of Landscape." In *New Models in Geography*, edited by Richard Peet and Nigel Thrift, 212–36. New York: Routledge, 1989.

Dawson, Betty. "Negotiating Chaldean Resettlement in El Cajon, California." *Jadaliyya*, January 25, 2019.

Delgado, Emanuel, and Kate Swanson. "Gentefication in the Barrio: Displacement and Urban Change in Southern California." *Journal of Urban Affairs* (2019): 1–16. www.tandfonline.com/doi/full/10.1080/07352166.2019.1680245.

Deruy, Emily. "Mexican Food Enters the Fine-Dining Realm." *The Atlantic*, April 18, 2016.

de Souza, Rebecca. *Feeding the Other: Whiteness, Privilege and Neoliberal Stigma in Food Pantries*. Cambridge, MA: MIT Press, 2019.

Diner, Hasia R. *Hungering for America: Italian, Irish, and Jewish Foodways in the Age of Migration*. Cambridge, MA: Harvard University Press, 2001.

Duruz, Jean. "Adventuring and Belonging: An Appetite for Markets." *Space & Culture* 7, no. 4 (2004): 427–45.

Eater. "Essential San Diego Restaurants." *Eater San Diego*, Summer 2019. https://san diego.eater.com/maps/38-best-restaurants-in-san-diego.

———. "The Hottest Restaurants in San Diego Right Now." *Eater San Diego*, December 2019. https://sandiego.eater.com/maps/best-new-san-diego-restaurants -heatmap.

Eisenhauer, Elizabeth. "In Poor Health: Supermarket Redlining and Urban Nutrition." *GeoJournal* 53, no. 2 (2001): 125–33.

Environmental Health Coalition. "Barrio Logan's Community Garden." *Toxic Free Neighborhood Blog*, June 12, 2017. www.environmentalhealth.org/index.php/en /media-center/blog-for-environmental-justice/127-toxic-free-neighborhoods/623 -barrio-logan-s-community-garden.

Erickson, Karla. "Bodies at Work: Performing Service in American Restaurants." *Space and Culture* 7, no. 1 (2004): 76–89.

Erie, Steven P., Vladimir Kogan, and Scott A. MacKenzie. "Redevelopment, San Diego Style: The Limits of Public—Private Partnerships." *Urban Affairs Review* 45, no. 5 (2010): 644–78.

Esbenshade, Jill. *Shorted: Wage Theft, Time Theft, and Discrimination in San Diego County Restaurant Jobs*. San Diego: Center on Policy Initiatives and San Diego State University, Department of Sociology, 2015.

Escalante, Ubaldo. "There Goes the Barrio: Measuring Gentefication in Boyle Heights, Los Angeles." PhD dissertation, Columbia University, 2017.

ESRI (Environmental Systems Research Institute). "Business Data." ArcGIS Community Analyst. ESRI, 2018.

Federal Housing Administration (FHA). *Underwriting Manual: Underwriting and Valuation Procedure under Title II of the National Housing Act*. Washington, DC: FHA, 1938.

———. *Underwriting Manual: Underwriting and Valuation Procedure under Title II of the National Housing Act with Revisions to April 1, 1936*. Washington, DC: FHA, 1936.

Federal Reserve Bank of Saint Louis and US Bureau of Labor Statistics. "Employment in San Diego-Carlsbad, CA (MSA)." Federal Reserve Economic Data, 2019.

Ferrero, Sylvia. "Comida Sin Par. Consumption of Mexican Food in Los Angeles: Foodscapes in a Transnational Consumer Society." In *Food Nations: Selling Taste in*

Consumer Societies, edited by Warren Belasco and Philip Scranton, 194–219. New York: Routledge, 2002.

Fishman, Robert. "The American Metropolis at Century's End: Past and Future Influences." *Housing Policy Debates* 11, no. 1 (2000): 199–213.

Flaming, Daniel, Brent Haydamack, and Pascale Joassart-Marcelli. *Hopeful Workers, Marginal Jobs: LA's Off-the-Book Labor Force*. Los Angeles: The Economic Roundtable, 2005.

Florida, Richard L. *The Rise of the Creative Class: And How It's Transforming Work, Leisure, Community and Everyday Life*. New York: Basic Books, 2002.

Florido, Adrian. "How Segregation Defined San Diego's Neighborhoods." *Voice of San Diego*, March 21, 2011.

Fokos, Barbarella. "Mountain View Backyard Bent to His Will." *San Diego Reader*, May 9, 2018.

Food and Agriculture Organization of the United Nations (FAO). *Food Security*. Rome: FAO, 2006.

Food Chain Workers Alliance. *The Hands That Feed Us: Opportunities and Challenges for Workers along the Food Chain*. Los Angeles: Food Chain Workers Alliance, 2012. https://foodchainworkers.org/wp-content/uploads/2012/06/Hands-That-Feed-Us-Report.pdf.

Food Chain Workers Alliance, Restaurant Opportunities Center of New York, Restaurant Opportunities Center of the Bay, and Food First/Institute for Food and Development. "Food Insecurity of Restaurant Workers," 2014. www.scribd.com/document/234905417/Food-Insecurity-of-Restaurant-Workers.

Ford, Larry, and Ernst Griffin. "The Ghettoization of Paradise." *Geographical Review* 69, no. 2 (1979): 140–58.

Foucault, Michel. *The History of Sexuality*. Volume 1: *An Introduction*. Translated from French by Robert Hurley. New York: Vintage Books, 1988.

Fraser, Nancy. "Roepke Lecture in Economic Geography—from Exploitation to Expropriation: Historic Geographies of Racialized Capitalism." *Economic Geography* 94, no. 1 (2018): 1–17.

Freeman, Lance. "Displacement or Succession? Residential Mobility in Gentrifying Neighborhoods." *Urban Affairs Review* 40, no. 4 (2005): 463–91.

Gabaccia, Donna R. *We Are What We Eat: Ethnic Food and the Making of Americans*. Cambridge, MA: Harvard University Press, 1998.

Garrick, David. "San Diego Considering Crackdown on Flood of New Sidewalk Vendors." *Union Tribune* (San Diego), August 26, 2019.

Gibson–Graham, J. K. *A Postcapitalist Politics*. Minneapolis: University of Minnesota Press, 2006.

Gilmore, Ruth Wilson. "Fatal Couplings of Power and Difference: Notes on Racism and Geography." *The Professional Geographer* 54, no. 1 (2002): 15–24.

———. *Golden Gulag: Prisons, Surplus, Crisis, and Opposition in Globalizing California*. Berkeley: University of California Press, 2007.

Gilroy, Paul. *After Empire: Melancholia or Convivial Culture?* New York: Routledge, 2004.

Gittleman, Mara, Kelli Jordan, and Eric Brelsford. "Using Citizen Science to Quantify Community Garden Crop Yields." *Cities and the Environment* 5, no. 1 (2012): 1–14.

Glasmeier, Amy. "Living Wage Calculator." Massachusetts Institute of Technology, 2019. http://livingwage.mit.edu/.

Goodman, David, E. Melanie DuPuis, and Michael K. Goodman. *Alternative Food Networks: Knowledge, Practice, and Politics.* New York: Routledge, 2012.

Goodman, Michael K., Damian Maye, and Lewis Holloway. "Ethical Foodscapes?: Premises, Promises, and Possibilities." *Environment and Planning A* 42, no. 8 (2010): 1782–96.

Gordon, Cynthia, Marnie Purciel-Hill, Nirupa R. Ghai, Leslie Kaufman, Regina Graham, and Gretchen Van Wye. "Measuring Food Deserts in New York City's Low-Income Neighborhoods." *Health & Place* 17, no. 2 (2011): 696–700.

Gottlieb, Dylan. "Dirty, Authentic . . . Delicious: Yelp, Mexican Restaurants, and the Appetites of Philadelphia's New Middle Class." *Gastronomica* 15, no. 2 (2015): 39–48.

Gottlieb, Robert, and Anupama Joshi. *Food Justice.* Cambridge, MA: MIT Press, 2010.

Gundersen, Craig, and James P. Ziliak. "Food Insecurity and Health Outcomes." *Health Affairs* 34, no. 11 (2015): 1830–39.

Guthman, Julie. "Bringing Good Food to Others: Investigating the Subjects of Alternative Food Practice." *Cultural Geographies* 15, no. 4 (2008): 431–47.

———. "'If They Only Knew': Color Blindness and Universalism in California Alternative Food Institutions." *Professional Geographer* 60, no. 3 (2008): 387–97.

———. "Neoliberalism and the Making of Food Politics in California." *Geoforum* 39, no. 3 (2008): 1171–83.

———. "Opening up the Black Box of the Body in Geographical Obesity Research: Toward a Critical Political Ecology of Fat." *Annals of the Association of American Geographers* 102, no. 5 (2012): 951–57.

———. *Weighing In: Obesity, Food Justice, and the Limits of Capitalism.* Berkeley: University of California Press, 2011.

Guzmán, Jaime. "The Whiteness Project of Gentrification: The Battle over Los Angeles' Eastside." PhD dissertation, University of Denver, 2018.

Hackworth, Jason R. *The Neoliberal City: Governance, Ideology, and Development in American Urbanism.* Ithaca, NY: Cornell University Press, 2007.

Hackworth, Jason, and Neil Smith. "The Changing State of Gentrification." *Tijdschrift voor Economische en Sociale Geografie* 92, no. 4 (2002): 464–77.

Hage, Ghassan. "At Home in the Entrails of the West: Multiculturalism, Ethnic Food and Migrant Home-Building." In *Home/World: Space, Community and Marginality in Sydney's West*, edited by Helen Grace, 99–153. Sydney: Pluto Press, 1997.

Hall, Stuart. *The Fateful Triangle: Race, Ethnicity, Nation*, edited by Kobena Mercer. Cambridge, MA: Harvard University Press, 2007.

———. "New Ethnicities (1988)." In *Writing Black Britain 1948–1998: An Interdisciplinary Anthology*, edited by James Proctor, 265–74. New York: Manchester University Press, 2000.

Hammelman, Colleen, and Allison Hayes-Conroy. "Understanding Cultural Accept-ability for Urban Food Policy." *Journal of Planning Literature* 30, no. 1 (2015): 37–48.

Harris, LeRoy E. "The Other Side of the Freeway: A Study of Settlement Patterns of Negroes and Mexicans in San Diego, California." PhD dissertation, Carnegie Mellon University, 1974.

Harrison, Steve, and Paul Dourish. "Re-Place-Ing Space: The Roles of Place and Space in Collaborative Systems." In *Computer Supported Cooperative Work*, 67–76. Cambridge, MA: ACM, 1996.

Hartman, Chester. "The Right to Stay Put." In *The Gentrification Reader*, edited by Loretta Lees, Tom Slater, and Elvin K. Wyly, 531–41. Abingdon: Routledge, 1984.

Harvey, David. "From Managerialism to Entrepreneurialism: The Transformation in Urban Governance in Late Capitalism." *Geografiska Annaler Series B, Human Geography* 71, no. 1 (2017): 3–17.

———. *Spaces of Hope*. Edinburgh: Edinburgh University Press, 2000.

Hayes-Conroy, Allison, and Jessica Hayes-Conroy. *Doing Nutrition Differently: Critical Approaches to Diet and Dietary Intervention*. Burlington, VT: Ashgate, 2013.

———. "Political Ecology of the Body: A Visceral Approach." In *The International Handbook of Political Ecology*, edited by Raymond Bryant, 659–72. Northampton, MA: Elgar Publishing, 2015.

Hayes-Conroy, Jessica, and Allison Hayes-Conroy. "Visceral Geographies: Mattering, Relating, and Defying: Visceral Geographies." *Geography Compass* 4, no. 9 (2010): 1273–83.

Heldke, Lisa M. *Exotic Appetites: Ruminations of a Food Adventurer*. New York: Routledge, 2003.

Herbst, Julia. "Guillermo Uribe on the 'Gentefication' of East La." *LA Magazine*, September 9, 2014.

Herod, Andrew. *Labor Geographies: Workers and the Landscapes of Capitalism*. New York: Guilford Press, 2001.

Hetherington, Kevin. "Rhythm and Noise: The City, Memory and the Archive." *Sociological Review* 61 (2013): 17–33.

Hewitt, Elizabeth. "'They Go to Work, Come Back, and Starve': Why Immigrant Families Are Avoiding Food Assistance." *Civil Eats*, October 14, 2019.

Heynen, Nik. "Bringing the Body Back to Life through Radical Geography of Hunger: The Haymarket Affair and Its Aftermath." *ACME: An International E-Journal for Critical Geographies* 7, no. 1 (2008): 32–44.

———. "Justice of Eating in the City: The Political Ecology of Urban Hunger." In *In the Nature of Cities*, edited by Nik Heynen, Maria Kaika, and Erik Swyngedouw, 129–42. New York: Routledge, 2006.

Hill, Katherine Michelle. "Sweet and Sour: Social Networks and Inequality in a Chinese Restaurant." *Sociology of Race and Ethnicity* 4, no. 1 (2018): 114–27.

Hislop, Rasheed Salaam. "Reaping Equity: A Survey of Food Justice Organizations in the U.S.A." MS thesis, University of California–Davis, 2014.

Holloway, Lewis, and Moya Kneafsey. "Reading the Space of the Farmers' Market: A Preliminary Investigation from the UK." *Sociologia Ruralis* 40, no. 3 (2000): 285–99.

Holt-Giménez, Eric. *Overcoming the Barrier of Racism in Our Capitalist Food System.* Oakland, CA: Food First, 2018.

Holt-Giménez, Eric, and Annie Shattuck. "Food Crises, Food Regimes and Food Movements: Rumblings of Reform or Tides of Transformation?" *Journal of Peasant Studies* 38, no. 1 (2011): 109–44.

hooks, bell. "Eating the Other: Desire and Resistance." In *Black Looks: Race and Representation*, edited by bell hooks, 21–39. Boston: South End Press, 1992.

Hoover, Brandon. "White Spaces in Black and Latino Places: Urban Agriculture and Food Sovereignty." *Journal of Agriculture, Food Systems, and Community Development* 3, no. 4 (2013): 109–15.

HoSang, Daniel Martinez, Oneka LaBennett, and Laura Pulido. *Racial Formation in the Twenty-first Century.* Berkeley: University of California Press, 2012.

Hoyt, Lorlene. "Collecting Private Funds for Safer Public Spaces: An Empirical Examination of the Business Improvement District Concept." *Environment and Planning B: Planning and Design* 31, no. 3 (2004): 367–80.

Hubbard, Phil, and Tim Hall. "The Entrepreneurial City and the 'New Urban Politics.'" In *The Entrepreneurial City: Geographies of Politics, Regime and Representation*, edited by Tim Hall and Phil Hubbard, 199–202. Chichester: Wiley, 1998.

Huse, Tone. "Gentrification and Ethnicity." In *Handbook of Gentrification Studies*, edited by Loretta Lees and Martin Phillips, 186–204. Northampton, MA: Elgar Publishing, 2018.

Hyra, Derek S. *Race, Class, and Politics in Cappuccino City.* Chicago: University of Chicago Press, 2017.

International Labor Office (ILO). *Women and Men in the Informal Economy: A Statistical Picture.* Geneva: ILO, 2014.

International Rescue Committee. "IRC in San Diego's Refugee Entrepreneurial Agriculture Program." Grant proposal. National Institute of Food and Agriculture, US Department of Agriculture, 2011.

Janowski, Monica. "Introduction: Consuming Memories of Home in Constructing the Present and Imagining the Future." *Food and Foodways* 20, no. 3–4 (2012): 175–39.

Jarosz, Lucy. "Comparing Food Security and Food Sovereignty Discourses." *Dialogues in Human Geography* 4, no. 2 (2014): 168–81.

———. "Defining World Hunger: Scale and Neoliberal Ideology in International Food Security Policy Discourse." *Food, Culture & Society* 14, no. 1 (2011): 117–39.

Jayaraman, Sarumathi. *Behind the Kitchen Door.* Ithaca, NY: Cornell University Press, 2013.

Jazeel, Tariq. "Spatializing Difference beyond Cosmopolitanism: Rethinking Planetary Futures." *Theory, Culture & Society* 28, no. 5 (2011): 75–97.

Joassart-Marcelli, Pascale. *The Good Food District: Historical Background and Current Needs.* San Diego, CA: San Diego State University, Department of Geography, and Project New Village, 2018. https://fep.sdsu.edu/Docs/Report_V3.pdf.

———. "Measuring Informal Work in Developed Nations." In *Informal Work in Developed Nations*, edited by Enrico Marcelli, Colin Williams, and Pascale Joassart, 24–44. London: Routledge, 2010.

———. "The New Normal: Freelancing, Hustling, and Informal Labor." KCET's *City Rising* program, Los Angeles, 2019. www.kcet.org/shows/city-rising/the-new -normal-freelancing-hustling-and-informal-labor.

———. "The Spatial Determinants of Wage Inequality: Evidence from Recent Latina Immigrants in Southern California." *Feminist Economics* 15, no. 2 (2009): 33–72.

Joassart-Marcelli, Pascale, and Enrico Marcelli. "Cooking at Home: Gender, Class, Race, and Social Reproduction." In *Food and Place: A Critical Exploration*, edited by Pascale Joassart-Marcelli and Fernando J. Bosco, 270–89. Lanham, MD: Rowman and Littlefield, 2018.

Joassart-Marcelli, Pascale, and Fernando J. Bosco. "Alternative Food and Gentrification: How Farmers' Markets and Community Gardens Are Transforming Urban Neighborhoods." In *Just Green Enough*, edited by Winnifred W. Curran and Trina Hamilton, 92–106. New York: Routledge, 2017.

———. "Alternative Food Projects, Localization and Neoliberal Urban Development: Farmers' Markets in Southern California." *Métropoles*, no. 15 (2014). https://jour nals.openedition.org/metropoles/4970.

———. "Contested Ethnic Foodscapes: Survival, Appropriation, and Resistance in Gentrifying Immigrant Neighborhoods." In *The Immigrant-Food Nexus: Borders, Labor, and Identity in North America*, edited by Julian Agyeman and Sydney Giacalone, 59–80. Cambridge, MA: MIT Press, 2020.

———. "Food and Gentrification: How Foodies Are Transforming Urban Neighborhoods." In *Food and Place: A Critical Exploration*, edited by Pascale Joassart-Marcelli and Fernando J. Bosco, 129–46. Lanham, MD: Rowman and Littlefield, 2018.

———. *Food and Place: A Critical Exploration*. Lanham, MD: Rowman & Littlefield, 2018.

———. "The Taste of Gentrification: Difference and Exclusion on San Diego's Urban Food Frontier." In *A Recipe for Gentrification: Food, Power, and Resistance*, edited by Alison Hope Alkon, Yuki Kato, and Joshua Sbicca, 31–53. New York: New York University Press, 2020.

Joassart-Marcelli, Pascale, Fernando J. Bosco, and Emanuel Delgado. *Southeastern San Diego's Food Landscape: Challenges and Opportunities*. San Diego, CA: Department of Geography, San Diego State University and Project New Village, 2014.

Joassart-Marcelli, Pascale, Jaime S. Rossiter, and Fernando J. Bosco. "Ethnic Markets and Community Food Security in an Urban 'Food Desert.'" *Environment and Planning. A* 49, no. 7 (2017): 1642–63.

Johnson, Troy. "A National Treasure." *San Diego Magazine* (Winter 2016).

Johnston, Josée, and Shyon Baumann. *Foodies: Democracy and Distinction in the Gourmet Foodscape*. New York: Routledge, 2010.

Johnston, Josée, Andrew Biro, and Norah MacKendrick. "Lost in the Supermarket: The Corporate-Organic Foodscape and the Struggle for Food Democracy." *Antipode* 41, no. 3 (2009): 509–32.

Jonas, Andrew E. G., and David Wilson. *The Urban Growth Machine: Critical Perspectives Two Decades Later*. Albany: State University of New York Press, 1999.

Kallick, David D. *Bringing Vitality to Main Street: How Immigrant Small Businesses Help Local Economies Grow*. New York: Fiscal Policy Institute and Council of the Americas, 2015. www.as-coa.org/sites/default/files/ImmigrantBusinessReport.pdf.

Karjanen, David J. *The Servant Class City: Urban Revitalization Versus the Working Poor in San Diego*. Minneapolis: University of Minnesota Press, 2016.

Kayzar, Brenda. "Interpreting Philanthropic Interventions: Media Representations of a Community Savior." In *The Fight to Stay Put: Social Lessons through Media Imaginings of Urban Transformation and Change*, edited by Giorgio Hadi Curti, Jim Craine, and Stuart Aitken, 209–28 Stuttgart: Verlag, 2013.

Kern, Leslie. "Connecting Embodiment, Emotion and Gentrification: An Exploration through the Practice of Yoga in Toronto." *Emotion, Space and Society* 5, no. 1 (2012): 27–35.

———. "From Toxic Wreck to Crunchy Chic: Environmental Gentrification through the Body." *Environment and Planning D, Society & Space* 33, no. 1 (2015): 67–83.

———. "Rhythms of Gentrification: Eventfulness and Slow Violence in a Happening Neighbourhood." *Cultural Geographies* 23, no. 3 (2016): 441–57.

Knowles, Caroline. "Nigerian London: Re-Mapping Space and Ethnicity in Superdiverse Cities." *Ethnic and Racial Studies* 36, no. 4 (2013): 651–69.

Kobayashi, Audrey, and Linda Peake. "Racism out of Place: Thoughts on Whiteness and an Antiracist Geography in the New Millennium." *Annals of the Association of American Geographers* 90, no. 2 (2000): 392–403.

Krueger, Paul. "The Most Dangerous Part of San Diego." *San Diego Reader*, May 2, 1991.

Kwate, Naa Oyo A. "Fried Chicken and Fresh Apples: Racial Segregation as a Fundamental Cause of Fast Food Density in Black Neighborhoods." *Health & Place* 14, no. 1 (2008): 32–44.

Lamont, Michèle, and Sada Aksartova. "Ordinary Cosmopolitanisms: Strategies for Bridging Racial Boundaries among Working-Class Men." *Theory, Culture & Society* 19, no. 4 (2002): 1–25.

Launius, Sarah, and Geoffrey Alan Boyce. "More Than Metaphor: Settler Colonialism, Frontier Logic, and the Continuities of Racialized Dispossession in a Southwest US City." *Annals of the American Association of Geographers* (2020): 1–18.

La Via Campesina. "Declaration of Nyéléni." Nyéléni Forum for Food Sovereignty, Mali, 2007. https://nyeleni.org/spip.php?article290.

Lees, Loretta, Sandra Annunziata, and Clara Rivas-Alonso. "Resisting Planetary Gentrification: The Value of Survivability in the Fight to Stay Put." *Annals of the American Association of Geographers* 108, no. 2 (2017): 346–55.

Lees, Loretta, Tom Slater, and Elvin Wyly. *Gentrification*. New York: Routledge, 2008.

Lefebvre, Henri. *Rhythmanalysis: Space, Time and Everyday Life*. Translated by Stuart Elden and Gerald Moore. New York: Continuum, 1992.

———. "The Right to the City." In *Writings on Cities*, edited by Henri Lefebvre, 108–23. Oxford: Blackwell, 1996.

Lemus, Marvin, and Linda Y. Chávez. *Gentefied*. Netflix, 2020.

Le Texier, Emmanuelle. "The Struggle against Gentrification." In *Chicano San Diego: Cultural Space and the Struggle for Justice*, edited by Richard Griswold del Castillo, 202–21. Tucson: University of Arizona Press, 2007.

Levkoe, Charles Z., Josh Brem-Wilson, and Colin R Anderson. "People, Power, Change: Three Pillars of a Food Sovereignty Research Praxis." *Journal of Peasant Studies* 46, no. 7 (2019): 1389–412.

Ley, David. "Artists, Aestheticization and the Field of Gentrification." *Urban Studies* 40, no. 12 (2003): 2527–44.

Light, Ivan. "The Ethnic Economy." In *Handbook of Economic Sociology*, edited by Neil Smelser, 650–77. New York: Russel Sage Foundation, 2005.

Lipsitz, George. *How Racism Takes Place*. Philadelphia: Temple University Press, 2011.

Li, Wei. *Ethnoburb: The New Ethnic Community in Urban America*. Honolulu: University of Hawaii Press, 2008.

Logan, John R., and Harvey Molotch. *Urban Fortunes: The Political Economy of Place*. Twentieth anniversary edition. Berkeley: University of California Press, 2007.

Logan, John R., Zengwang Xu, and Brian J. Stults. "Interpolating US Decennial Census Tract Data from as Early as 1970 to 2010: A Longitudinal Tract Database." *The Professional Geographer* 66, no. 3 (2014): 412–20.

Longhurst, Robyn, Lynda Johnston, and Elsie Ho. "A Visceral Approach: Cooking 'at Home' with Migrant Women in Hamilton, New Zealand." *Transactions of the Institute of British Geographers* 34, no. 3 (2009): 333–45.

Lott-Schwartz, Hannah. "Barrio Logan: A Thriving Hub of Chicano Culture Emerges from the Shadows." *Hemisphere* (March 2018): 20.

LTDB. "Longitudinal Tract Database." American Communities Project. Brown University, 2019.

Luttrell, Wendy. "'Good Enough' Methods for Ethnographic Research." *Harvard Educational Review* 70, no. 4 (2000): 499–523.

MacLeod, Gordon. "Urban Politics Reconsidered: Growth Machine to Post-Democratic City?" *Urban Studies* 48, no. 12 (2011): 2629–60.

Mannur, Anita. *Culinary Fictions: Food in South Asian Diasporic Culture*. Philadelphia: Temple University Press, 2009.

———. "Culinary Nostalgia: Authenticity, Nationalism, and Diaspora." *Melus* 32, no. 4 (2007): 11–31.

Marcelli, Enrico, and Manuel Pastor. *Unauthorized and Uninsured*. San Diego, CA: San Diego State University; Los Angeles: University of Southern California, 2015. https://dornsife.usc.edu/assets/sites/731/docs/Web_01_City_Heights_San_Diego_Final.pdf.

Mares, Teresa Marie. "Another Time of Hunger." In *Women Redefining the Experience of Food Insecurity: Life off the Edge of the Table*, edited by Janet Page-Reeves, 45–64. Lanham, MD: Lexington Books, 2014.

———. "We Are Made of Our Food: Latino/a Immigration and the Practices and Politics of Eating." PhD dissertation, University of Washington, 2010.

Martin, Philip. *Rural California Report*. Davis: California Institute for Rural Studies, 2019. www.cirsinc.org/rural-california-report/entry/federal-survey-shows-aging-and-settled-farmworker-population.

Massey, Doreen. *For Space*. London: Sage, 2005.

———. "Landscape as a Provocation: Reflections on Moving Mountains." *Journal of Material Culture* 11, no. 1 (2006): 33–48.

———. "Places and Their Pasts." *History Workshop Journal* 39 (1995): 182–92.

May, Jon. "'A Little Taste of Something More Exotic': The Imaginative Geographies of Everyday Life." *Geography* 81, no. 1 (1996): 57–64.

McAdam, Jeff. "Bakery Shuts Down after ICE Raid Finds Unauthorized Employees." *Fox5 San Diego*, January 16, 2020.

McClintock, Nathan. "From Industrial Garden to Food Desert: Demarcated Devaluation in the Flatlands of Oakland, California." In *Cultivating Food Justice: Race, Class and Sustainability*, edited by Alison Hope Alkon and Julian Agyeman, 89–120. Cambridge, MA: MIT Press, 2011.

———. "Radical, Reformist, and Garden-Variety Neoliberal: Coming to Terms with Urban Agriculture's Contradictions." *Local Environment: Subversive and Interstitial Food Spaces* 19, no. 2 (2014): 147–71.

———. "Urban Agriculture, Racial Capitalism, and Resistance in the Settler-Colonial City." *Geography Compass* 12, no. 6 (2018): E12378.

McDowell, Linda. "Roepke Lecture in Economic Geography—The Lives of Others: Body Work, the Production of Difference, and Labor Geographies." *Economic Geography* 91, no. 1 (2015): 1–23.

McDowell, Linda, and Joanne Sharp, eds. *Space, Gender, Knowledge: A Reader for Feminist Geographers*. New York: John Wiley & Sons, 1997.

McElroy, Erin, and Alex Werth. "Deracinated Dispossessions: On the Foreclosures of 'Gentrification' in Oakland, Ca." *Antipode* 51, no. 3 (2019): 878–98.

McKittrick, Katherine. "On Plantations, Prisons, and a Black Sense of Place." *Social & Cultural Geography* 12, no. 8 (2011): 947–63.

McKittrick, Katherine, and Clyde Adrian Woods. *Black Geographies and the Politics of Place*. Cambridge, MA: South End Press, 2007.

McNeally, Claudi. "How Filipino Food Is Becoming the Next Great American Cuisine." *Vogue*, June 1, 2017.

McQuarrie, Edward F., Jessica Miller, and Barbara J. Phillips. "The Megaphone Effect: Taste and Audience in Fashion Blogging." *Journal of Consumer Research* 40, no. 1 (2013): 136–58.

Medina, Jennifer. "Los Angeles Neighborhood Tries to Change, but Avoid the Pitfalls." *New York Times*, August 17, 2013.

Meehan, Katie, and Kendra Stauss, eds. *Precarious Worlds: Contested Geographies of Social Reproduction*. Athens: University of Georgia Press, 2015.

Miller, Jessica Ty. "Temporal Analysis of Displacement: Racial Capitalism and Settler Colonial Urban Space." *Geoforum* 116 (2020): 180–92.

Mitchell, Don. "Imperial Landscape." In *Landscape and Power: Space, Place and Landscape*, edited by Don Mitchell, 5–35. Chicago: University of Chicago Press, 2002.

———. "Labor's Geography: Capital, Violence, Guest Workers and the Post–World War II Landscape." *Antipode* 43, no. 2 (2011): 563–95.

———. *The Lie of the Land: Migrant Workers and the California Landscape*. Minneapolis: University of Minnesota Press, 1996.

———. *The Right to the City: Social Justice and the Fight for Public Space*. New York: Guilford Press, 2003.

Molotch, Harvey. "The City as a Growth Machine: Toward a Political Economy of Place." *American Journal of Sociology* 82, no. 2 (1976): 309–32.

Molz, Jennie Germann. "Eating Difference: The Cosmopolitan Mobilities of Culinary Tourism." *Space and Culture* 10, no. 1 (2007): 77–93.

Moon, Emily. "Why Is Participation in Food Assistance Program Like WIC Declining?" *Pacific Standard*, June 12, 2019.

Morlan, Kinsee. "A Renaissance on Logan Avenue." *San Diego City Beat*, July 21, 2015.

National Restaurant Association. *What Is Hot: 2018 Culinary Forecast*. Washington, DC: NRA, 2018.

Nelson, Robert K., and Edward L. Ayers. "Mapping Inequality: Redlining in New Deal America." Digital Scholarship Lab, University of Richmond, 2018. https://dsl.richmond.edu/panorama/redlining/#loc=5/39.1/-94.58.

Noble, Greg. "Everyday Cosmopolitanism and the Labour of Intercultural Community." In *Everyday Multiculturalism*, edited by Amanda Wise and Selvaraj Velayutham, 46–65. London: Palgrave Macmillan, 2009.

Nolen, John. *A Comprehensive City Plan for San Diego, California*. San Diego: City Planning Commission, 1926.

Norris, Frank. "Logan Heights." *Journal of San Diego History* 29, no. 1 (1983). www.sandiegohistory.org/journal/1983/january/logan/.

North Park Main Street. "Home Page." 2020. https://northparkmainstreet.com/north-park-san-diego/.

Omi, Michael, and Howard Winant. *Racial Formation in the United States*. Third edition. New York: Routledge, 2014.

———. "Racial Formation Rules: Continuity, Instability, and Change." In *Racial Formation in the Twenty-first Century*, edited by Daniel Martinez HoSang, Oneka LaBennett, and Laura Pulido, 302–31. Berkeley: University of California Press, 2012.

Ondash, E'Louise. "Renaissance in Barrio Logan." *The Coast News*, July 10, 2013.

Parham, Susan. *Food and Urbanism: The Convivial City and a Sustainable Future*. Boston: Bloomsbury, 2015.

Parish, Jessica. "Re-Wilding Parkdale? Environmental Gentrification, Settler Colonialism, and the Reconfiguration of Nature in 21st Century Toronto." *Environment and Planning E: Nature and Space* 3, no. 1 (2020): 263–86.

Park, Kyeyoung. "Confronting the Liquor Industry in Los Angeles." *International Journal of Sociology and Social Policy* 24, no. 7/8 (2004): 103–36.

Park, Robert E., and Ernest W. Burgess. *The City.* Chicago: University of Chicago Press, 1925.

Parks, Virginia. "The Uneven Geography of Racial and Ethnic Wage Inequality: Specifying Local Labor Market Effects." *Annals of the Association of American Geographers* 102, no. 3 (2012): 700–25.

Parsa, H. G., John T. Self, David Njite, and Tiffany King. "Why Restaurants Fail." *Cornell Hotel and Restaurant Administration Quarterly* 46, no. 3 (2005): 304–22.

Paules, Greta Foff. *Dishing It Out: Power and Resistance among Waitresses in a New Jersey Restaurant.* Philadelphia: Temple University Press, 1991.

Peck, Jamie. "Pluralizing Labor Geography." In *The New Oxford Handbook of Economic Geography,* edited by Gordon L. Clark, Maryann P. Feldman, Meric S. Gertler, and Dariusz Wójcik, 465–84. Oxford: Oxford University Press, 2018.

Peck, Jamie, Nik Theodore, and Neil Brenner. "Neoliberal Urbanism: Models, Moments, Mutations." *SAIS Review of International Affairs* 29, no. 1 (2009): 49–66.

Pelayo, Chelsea. "Art Galleries Fuel a Barrio Logan Renaissance." *The Sun,* September 12, 2017.

Penniman, Leah. *Farming While Black: Soul Fire Farm's Practical Guide to Liberation on the Land.* White River Junction, VT: Chelsea Green Publishing, 2018.

Pile, Steve. "Introduction: Opposition, Political Identities, and Spaces of Resistance." In *Geographies of Resistance,* edited by Steve Pile and Michael Keith, 1–12. New York: Routledge, 1997.

Popkin, Susan J., Molly M. Scott, and Marta Glavez. *Impossible Choices: Teens and Food Insecurity in America.* Washington, DC: Urban Institute, 2016. www.urban.org/sites /default/files/publication/83971/impossible-choices-teens-and-food-insecurity -in-america_0.pdf.

Poppendieck, Janet. *Sweet Charity?: Emergency Food and the End of Entitlement.* New York: Viking, 1998.

Poster, Winifed R., Marion Crain, and Miriam A. Cherry, eds. *Invisible Labor: Hidden Work in the Contemporary World.* Berkeley: University of California Press, 2016.

Preston, Valerie, and Sara McLafferty. "Spatial Mismatch Research in the 1990s: Progress and Potential." *Papers in Regional Science* 78, no. 4 (1999): 387–402.

Price, Patricia L. "At the Crossroads: Critical Race Theory and Critical Geographies of Race." *Progress in Human Geography* 34, no. 2 (2010): 147–74.

Pulido, Laura. "Geographies of Race and Ethnicity II: Environmental Racism, Racial Capitalism and State-Sanctioned Violence." *Progress in Human Geography* 41, no. 4 (2017): 524–33.

———. "Rethinking Environmental Racism: White Privilege and Urban Development in Southern California." *Annals of the Association of American Geographers* 90, no. 1 (2000): 12–40.

Punch, Samantha, Ian McIntosh, and Ruth Emond. "Children's Food Practices in Families and Institutions." *Children's Geographies* 8, no. 3 (2010): 227–32.

Raja, Samina, Ma Changxing, and Pavan Yadav. "Beyond Food Deserts: Measuring and Mapping Racial Disparities in Neighborhood Food Environments." *Journal of Planning Education and Research* 27, no. 4 (2008): 469–82.

Ram, Archana. "Neighborhood Guide: City Heights." *San Diego Magazine*, April 24, 2015.

Ramírez, Margaret M. "City as Borderland: Gentrification and the Policing of Black and Latinx Geographies in Oakland." *Environment and Planning D: Society and Space* 38, no. 1 (2020): 147–66.

Ramírez, Margaret Marietta. "The Elusive Inclusive: Black Food Geographies and Racialized Food Spaces." *Antipode* 47, no. 3 (2015): 748–69.

Rath, Jan, Robert Kloosterman, and Eran Razin. "Editorial: The Economic Context, Embeddedness and Immigrant Entrepreneurs." *International Journal of Entrepreneurial Behavior and Research* 8, no. 1 (2002): 6–10.

Ray, Krishnendu. *The Ethnic Restaurateur.* Boston: Bloomsbury, 2016.

———. "Ethnic Succession and the New American Restaurant Cuisine." In *The Restaurants Book: Ethnographies of Where We Eat*, edited by David Beriss and David Sutton, 97–113. New York: Berg, 2007.

———. *The Migrant's Table: Meals and Memories in Bengali-American Households.* Philadelphia: Temple University Press, 2004.

Reese, Ashanté M. *Black Food Geographies: Race, Self-Reliance, and Food Access in Washington, D.C.* Chapel Hill: University of North Carolina Press, 2019.

Relph, E. *Place and Placeness.* London: Pion, 1976.

Replogle, Jill, and Tom Fudge. "San Diego Voters Reject Barrio Logan's Community Plan." San Diego: KPBS, 2014. www.kpbs.org/news/2014/jun/03/council-plan-barrio-logan-losing-early-returns/.

Restaurant Opportunities Center United. *Ending Jim Crow in America's Restaurants: Racial and Gender Occupational Segregation in the Restaurant Industry.* New York: ROC United, 2015.

Reynolds, Kristin, and Nevin Cohen. *Beyond the Kale: Urban Agriculture and Social Justice Activism in New York City.* Athens: University of Georgia Press, 2016.

Robinson, Cedric J. *Black Marxism: The Making of the Black Radical Tradition.* Chapel Hill: University of North Carolina Press, 2000.

Rose, Mitch. "Landscape and Labyrinths." *Geoforum* 33, no. 4 (2002): 455–67.

Rothstein, Richard. *The Color of Law: A Forgotten History of How Our Government Segregated America.* New York: Norton, 2018.

Roy, Ananya. "Racial Banishment." In *Keywords in Radical Geography: Antipode at 50*, edited by The Antipode Editorial Collective, 227–30. Hoboken: Wiley, 2019.

Sachs, Carolyn, Patricia Allen, A. Rachel Terman, Jennifer Hayden, and Christina Hatcher. "Front and Back of the House: Socio-Spatial Inequalities in Food Work." *Agriculture and Human Values* 31, no. 1 (2014): 3–17.

Sáenz, Rogelio, and Karen Manges Douglas. "A Call for the Racialization of Immigration Studies: On the Transition of Ethnic Immigrants to Racialized Immigrants." *Sociology of Race and Ethnicity* 1, no. 1 (2015): 166–80.

Salaam, Elizabeth. "San Diego's City Heights on the Way Up. Not Quite Like North Park Yet." *San Diego Reader*, February 14, 2018.

Salazar, Melissa L. "Public Schools, Private Foods: Mexicano Memories of Culture and Conflict and American School Cafeterias." *Food and Foodways* 14, no. 3/4 (2007): 153–81.

Saldanha, Arun. *Psychedelic White: Goa Trance and the Viscosity of Race.* Minneapolis: University of Minnesota Press, 2007.

———. "Reontologising Race: The Machinic Geography of Phenotype." *Environment and Planning D: Society & Space* 24, no. 1 (2016): 9–24.

San Diego Food System Alliance. "County of San Diego Supervisor Candidate Questionnaire: Nathan Fletcher's Response." San Diego Food System Alliance, San Diego, 2018.

San Diego Real Estate Hunter. "Four Reasons Why Encanto Is a Great Place to Live." 2019. www.sandiegorealestatehunter.com/ blog/4-reasons-why-encanto-san-diego-great-place-live/.

San Diego Tourism Authority. "Barrio Logan: Arte y La Cultura Autentica." 2019. www.sandiego.org/campaigns/district-arts/barrio-logan.aspx.

———. "City Heights: Fertile Ground for Creativity." 2019. www.sandiego.org/cam paigns/district-arts/city-heights.aspx.

———. "Southeastern San Diego: An Unexpected Cultural Journey." 2019. www .sandiego.org/campaigns/district-arts/southeastern.aspx.

Sassen, Saskia. *The Global City: New York, London, Tokyo.* Second edition. Princeton, NJ: Princeton University Press, 2013.

Sassen-Koob, Saskia. "New York City: Economic Restructuring and Immigration." *Development and Change* 17, no. 1 (1986): 85–119.

Sauer, Carl. "The Morphology of Landscape." *University of California Publications in Geography* 2 (1925): 19–54.

Sbicca, Joshua. *Food Justice Now.* Minneapolis: University of Minnesota Press, 2018.

———. "Food Labor, Economic Inequality, and the Imperfect Politics of Process in the Alternative Food Movement." *Agriculture and Human Values* 32, no. 4 (2015): 675–87.

———. "Growing Food Justice by Planting an Anti-Oppression Foundation: Opportunities and Obstacles for a Budding Social Movement." *Agriculture and Human Values* 29, no. 4 (2012): 455–66.

Schlichtman, John Joe, Jason Patch, and Marc Lamont Hill. *Gentrifier.* Toronto: University of Toronto Press, 2017.

Sen, Arijit. "Food, Place, and Memory: Bangladeshi Fish Stores on Devon Avenue, Chicago." *Food and Foodways* 24, no. 1–2 (2016): 67–88.

Shannon, Jerry. "Dollar Stores, Retailer Redlining, and the Metropolitan Geographies of Precarious Consumption." *Annals of the American Association of Geographers* (2020): 1–19.

Shierholz, Heidi. *Low Wages and Few Benefits Mean Many Restaurant Workers Can't Make Ends Meet.* Washington, DC: Economic Policy Institute, 2014. www.epi.org/files /2014/restaurant-workers-final.pdf.

Short, Anne, Julie Guthman, and Samuel Raskin. "Food Deserts, Oases, or Mirages?: Small Markets and Community Food Security in the San Francisco Bay Area." *Journal of Planning Education and Research* 26, no. 3 (2007): 352–64.

Showley, Roger. "Diversity, Progress Apparent in Area Rich with History." *San Diego Union Tribune*, June 30, 2019.

Simonsen, Kirsten. "In Quest of a New Humanism: Embodiment, Experience and Phenomenology as Critical Geography." *Progress in Human Geography* 37, no. 1 (2013): 10–26.

Slater, Tom. "'A Literal Necessity to Be Re-Placed': A Rejoinder to the Gentrification Debate." *International Journal of Urban and Regional Research* 32, no. 1 (2008): 212–23.

———. "Territorial Stigmatization: Symbolic Defamation and the Contemporary Metropolis." In *The Sage Handbook of New Urban Studies*, edited by Sean Hannigan and Greg Richards, 111–25. London: Sage Publications, 2017.

Slocum, Rachel. "Race in the Study of Food." *Progress in Human Geography* 35, no. 3 (2011): 303–27.

———. "Whiteness, Space and Alternative Food Practice." *Geoforum* 38, no. 3 (2007): 520–33.

Smith, Neil. "Gentrification and Uneven Development." *Economic Geography* 58, no. 2 (1982): 139–55.

———. *The New Urban Frontier: Gentrification and the Revanchist City.* New York: Routledge, 1996.

Stanford, Lois. "Negotiating Food Security along the US-Mexico Border: Social Strategies, Practice and Networks among Mexican Immigrant Women." In *Women Redefining the Experience of Food Insecurity: Life off the Edge of the Table*, edited by Janet Page-Reeves, 105–26. Lanham, MD: Lexington Books, 2014.

Stavely, Zaidee. "School Lunch Could Be Slashed for Thousands of California Children under New Proposal." *EdSource*, August 2, 2019.

Swyngedouw, Erik. "Apocalypse Forever?: Post-Political Populism and the Spectre of Climate Change." *Theory, Culture & Society* 27, no. 2 (2010): 213–32.

———. *Designing the Post-Political City and the Insurgent Polis.* London: Bedford Press, 2011.

Swyngedouw, Erik, Frank Moulaert, and Arantxa Rodriguez. "Neoliberal Urbanization in Europe: Large-Scale Urban Development Projects and the New Urban Policy." *Antipode* 34, no. 3 (2002): 542–77.

The Infatuation. "Where to Eat and Drink in San Diego." 2019. www.theinfatuation.com/san-diego/guides/san-diego-restaurants#guide.

Thrillist. "The Best Restaurants in San Diego Right Now." August 2019. www.thrillist.com/eat/san-diego/best-restaurants-san-diego.

———. "Fifty Things You Need to Eat in San Diego before You Die." October 2015. www.thrillist.com/eat/san-diego/50-best-things-to-eat-in-san-diego-bucket-list.

TimeOut. "The 18 Best Restaurants in San Diego." November 2019. www.timeout.com/san-diego/restaurants/best-restaurants-in-san-diego.

Tonkiss, Fran. *Space, the City and Social Theory: Social Relations and Urban Forms.* Malden, MA: Polity, 2005.

Trauger, Amy. *Food Sovereignty in International Context: Discourse, Politics and Practice of Place*. New York: Routledge, 2015.

Tuan, Yi-Fu. "Space and Place: Humanistic Perspective." *Progress in Human Geography* 6 (1974): 211–52.

Tuck, Eve, and K. Wayne Yang. "Decolonization Is Not a Metaphor." *Decolonization: Indigeneity, Education & Society* 1, no. 1 (2012): 1–40.

Tutko, Marie, and Anne Wycoff. "San Diego Home Buyers' Guide 2019." *San Diego Magazine*, April 25, 2019.

Union of Concerned Scientists (UCS). *Purchasing Power: How Institutional "Good Food" Procurement Policies Can Shape a Food System That's Better for People and Our Planet*. Cambridge: UCS, 2018. www.ucsusa.org/sites/default/files/attach/2017/11/pur chasing-power-report-ucs-2017.pdf.

US Census. "American Community Survey Five-Year Estimates, 2013–2017. Public Use Microdata Sample." US Census Bureau, Washington, DC, 2019.

———. "American Community Survey Five-Year Estimates, 2013–2017. Summary File Data." US Census Bureau, Washington, DC, 2019.

———. "American Community Survey Five-Year Estimates, 2008–2012. Public Use Microdata Sample." US Census Bureau, Washington, DC, 2014.

———. "American Community Survey Five-Year Estimates, 2008–2012. Summary File Data." US Census Bureau, Washington, DC, 2014.

———. "Census of Population and Housing. Public Use Microdata Sample." US Census Bureau, Washington, DC, 2000.

———. "Current Population Survey Food Security Supplement, 2013 to 2017." US Census Bureau, Washington, DC, 2019.

US Department of Agriculture (USDA). "Food Access Research Atlas: Documentation." USDA Economic Research Service, 2017. www.ers.usda.gov/data-products /food-access-research-atlas/documentation/.

———. "USDA Food Plans: Cost of Food Report for December 2108." USDA Center for Nutrition Policy and Promotion, 2019. www.cnpp.usda.gov/sites/default/files /CostofFoodDec2018.pdf.

Valentine, Gill. "Living with Difference: Reflections on Geographies of Encounter." *Progress in Human Geography* 32, no. 3 (2008): 323–37.

van den Berghe, Pierre L. "Ethnic Cuisine: Culture in Nature." *Ethnic and Racial Studies* 7, no. 3 (1984): 387–97.

Van Esterik, Penny. "Right to Food; Right to Feed; Right to Be Fed: The Intersection of Women's Rights and the Right to Food." *Agriculture and Human Values* 16, no. 2 (1999): 225–32.

Wacquant, Loïc, Tom Slater, and Virgílio Borges Pereira. "Territorial Stigmatization in Action." *Environment and Planning A* 46, no. 6 (2014): 1270–80.

Wald, Sarah D. "Visible Farmers/Invisible Workers: Locating Immigrant Labor in Food Studies." *Food, Culture & Society* 14, no. 4 (2011): 567–86.

Ward, Kevin. "'Creating a Personality for Downtown': Business Improvement Districts in Milwaukee." *Urban Geography* 28 (2007): 781–808.

Warshawski, Daniel N. "Food Banks and the Devolution of Anti-Hunger Policy." In *Food and Place: A Critical Exploration*, edited by Pascale Joassart-Marcelli and Fernando J. Bosco, 166–84. Lanham, MD: Rowman and Littlefield, 2018.

Weisberg, Lori. "San Diego Bakery Shuts Down after ICE Audit of Workers." *Los Angeles Times*, January 15, 2020.

Wheaton, Daniel. "Mapping San Diego's 'Food Desert' Spots." *San Diego Union Tribune*, May 15, 2016.

White, Monica M. *Freedom Farmers: Agricultural Resistance and the Black Freedom Movement*. Chapel Hill: University of North Carolina Press, 2018.

Willis, Mary, and Janet Buck. "From Sudan to Nebraska: Dinka and Nuer Refugee Diet Dilemmas." *Journal of Nutrition and Education Behavior* 39, no. 5 (2007): 273–80.

Wolch, Jennifer R. *The Shadow State: Government and the Voluntary Sector in Transition*. New York: The Foundation Center, 1990.

Wolch, Jennifer R., Jason Byrne, and Joshua P. Newell. "Urban Green Space, Public Health, and Environmental Justice: The Challenge of Making Cities 'Just Green Enough.'" *Landscape and Urban Planning* 125 (2014): 234–44.

Yasmeen, Gisèle. "Bangkok's Foodscape: Public Eating, Gender Relations and Urban Change." PhD dissertation, University of British Columbia, 1997.

Zagat. "Best Restaurants in San Diego." 2018. www.zagat.com/l/top-food-in-san-diego.

———. "Hottest Restaurants in San Diego." 2018. www.zagat.com/l/the-hottest-restaurants-in-san-diego.

Zaragoza, Alex. "A Chicano Community in San Diego Is Outraged over a White Woman's Attempt to Open a 'Modern Fruteria.'" *Mitu*, October 27, 2017.

Zillow. "Homes for Sale." 2019. www.zillow.com/san-diego-ca/ (accessed May 2019).

Zukin, Sharon. *The Cultures of Cities*. Cambridge, UK: Blackwell, 1995.

———. *Naked City: The Death and Life of Authentic Urban Places*. New York: Oxford University Press, 2009.

Zukin, Sharon, Scarlett Lindeman, and Laurie Hurson. "The Omnivore's Neighborhood? Online Restaurant Reviews, Race, and Gentrification." *Journal of Consumer Culture* 17, no. 3 (2015): 459–79.

Zukin, Sharon, Valerie Trujillo, Peter Frase, Danielle Jackson, Tim Recuber, and Abraham Walker. "New Retail Capital and Neighborhood Change: Boutiques and Gentrification in New York City." *City & Community* 8, no. 1 (2009): 47–64.

INDEX

fig denotes figure; *map* denotes map; *table* denotes table

A

Accion, 93

aesthetics: cosmopolitan aesthetics, 12, 144, 178, 189; restaurants as embracing new aesthetics, 174

African-Caribbean Market (City Heights), 206

Agyeman, Julian, 209

Alkon, Alison Hope, 9, 68, 195

alternative food practices/projects/ movement, 12, 23, 44, 64, 127–30, 136, 149, 191, 192, 195, 199, 207, 209

alternative foodscapes, 24, 158, 185

Amador, Marco, 189

"amazing finds," 166

American Community Survey (2013–17), 55*map*, 73, 77*fig*, 107, 153*map*

AmeriCorps, 198

Anderson, Elijah, 36, 185

antigentrification, 6, 187, 189, 201, 202

antiracism, 9, 12, 126, 198. *See also* racism

Appadurai, Arjun, 20

art crawls, 141, 183

authenticity: as business strategy, 33, 73, 86, 173–74, 189; as cosmopolitan aesthetic, 143, 144, 149, 159, 165, 171, 174, 178, 185, 189; and ethnicity, 29, 86, 165, 169, 170, 173–74, 197; praise for, 133, 159; shifting meaning of, 165; urbanites/foodies as searching for, 4, 5, 134, 186, 195

B

"bad food," 111

Barefoot Bohemian, 5, 18, 150

Barrio Dogg (Barrio Logan), 177, 177*fig*, 178

Barrio Logan (San Diego): acts of resistance in, 6, 56, 202; antigentrification stance in, 202; Barrio Art Crawl, 141; Barrio Dogg, 177, 177*fig*, 178; Barrio Logan Association, 141; as best destination for tacos, 161; Chicano Park Herb Garden, 201; Chicano Park Steering Committee, 202; community garden in, 129; Community Plan, 56; Community Village Area, 138; demographic change in, 52, 56; devaluation of, 52, 53–54; Environmental Health Coalition, 202; food apartheid in, 63, 154; food as providing significant source of employment in, 67; as food desert, 43, 46, 51, 59, 193; as foodie destination, 142, 145; food oases in, 50, 58; food stores and restaurants in, 60–61*map*, 62, 64, 118–19*table*, 120, 175; gentrification in, 154,

261

cosmopolitan food: popularity of, 4; socioeconomic obstacles underlying life of those producing it, 39–40

cosmopolitan foodscapes: as compared to ethnic foodscapes, 19, 40; creation/production of, 5, 134, 137–48; described, 36–40; invisibility of immigrants and ethnic others in, 39; reinvention of ethnic foodscapes into, 152, 163–65, 175, 179–86; use of term, 37

cosmopolitanism: defined, 4, 6; as lifestyle, 37; elitism of, 38–39; and gastrodevelopment projects, 148–49; writings about, 36–37

cosmopolitan restaurants: absence of ethnoracial people from, 184; as replacing ethnic ones, 180; in study neighborhoods, 175; unique style of, 171

cottage food operations, 126–28, 199

counternarratives, as strategy in reclaiming ethnic foodscapes, 209–10

Cowen, Tyler, 185–86

Crang, Philip, 24

creative cities, 24–25, 126, 137

creative class, 39, 71, 135, 136, 137

credit. See loans

culinary frontier, 145, 165

culinary "hot spots," 145, 146map, 165

culinary tourism, 32

cultural economy (urban), 24, 66, 135

cultural landscapes, described, 19–20

Current Population Survey Food Security Supplement, 98, 99

D

Daniels, Stephen, 20

Deanwood (Washington, DC), 35, 197, 199

democracy, as cosmopolitan aesthetic, 144, 162, 174, 189

Department of Health and Human Services, 205–6

de Souza, Rebecca, 110

devaluation: of neighborhood, 8, 43, 52–57; and race, 51, 58; symbolic devaluation and stigmatization, 63–64, 168

displacements: and gentrification, 9–10, 15, 81, 154, 155; involving state in prevention of, 203–8; and race, 157–58; resisting of through community-based organizing, 197–203; through urban development, 56, 57; in transformation from ethnic to cosmopolitan foodscape, 7, 8, 15, 26, 131, 179–86

Distinction (Bourdieu), 160

diversity: as cosmopolitan aesthetic, 31, 143, 144, 185, 186, 189, 195; food projects as emphasizing, 149; openness to cultural diversity, 4, 5, 8, 36, 37, 38; racialized understanding of, 39

Dourish, Paul, 23

Duarte Restaurant (Barrio Logan), 48

"dump," 168

Dur Dur Market (City Heights), 206

Duruz, Jean, 34, 35

E

East Village (San Diego), 109, 145, 148, 153

Eater, 143, 144

eating, empathic and careful: as strategy in reclaiming ethnic foodscapes, 195–97

"Eating the Other" (hooks), 31

economic informality, and the food service industry, 81–83

Edible San Diego, 143

Eisenhauer, Elizabeth, 58, 59

El Cajon, CA: ethnic restaurants reviewed on Yelp, 164map; food deserts in, 43; gentrification in, 153

Electronic Benefit Transfer (EBT), 121, 123–24, 199

El Golosito (Barrio Logan), 175–76, 176fig

Enterprise Zones, 57

Environmental Health Coalition (Barrio Logan), 202

Esbenshade, Jill, 83

Escondido, CA: food deserts in, 43; highly rated Mexican restaurants in, 164

ethnic, use of term, 8, 29, 74

ethnic entrepreneurs: earnings of, 89–90, 172–73; impact of gentrification on, 94, 175, 180; and New Roots Community Farm, 128; role of in everyday life of residents, 123, 124, 173; statistic on, in San Diego, 74, 76–77*table*, 78, 89; struggles to adapt, 94, 124, 172, 175; support for, 92, 200–201, 208

ethnic food: adaptation and appropriation of, 172–79; "cheap" as appeal of, 95; economy, 74, 78; empowerment potential of, 34; entrepreneurship in, 69–70; finance as challenge in most ethnic food businesses, 91; openness to as problematic, 31–32; people as rarely calling their own food ethnic, 31; popularity of, 6, 196; retelling story of, 209–10; use of term, 197. *See also* ethnic entrepreneurs

ethnic foodscapes: as compared to cosmopolitan foodscapes, 19, 40; consequences of historical devaluation of, 43; and critical food studies, 30–35; as fashioned by racially biased policies, 158; gentrification as producing curated version of, 159; as no longer serving needs of residents, 149; reclaiming of, 187–211; reinvention of into cosmopolitan foodscapes, 152, 163–65, 175, 179–86; as relational and dynamic, 33; sudden interest in, 134; systemic erasure of, 152; use of term, 29–30

ethnicity: boundaries of as being redrawn, 158; conceptualization of, 11; defined, 28; and race and immigration, 28–29;

as theme appealing to cosmopolitan eaters, 185

ethnic markets, 121–22, 124

ethnic restaurateurs: according to Krishnendu Ray, 34–35, 69; as being replaced by cosmopolitan ones, 180

ethnic workers, in food industry, ancestry of in San Diego, 74–75, 76–77*table*

"ethnoburbs," 163–64

ethnoracial, use of term, 11, 28–29, 74

Exotic Appetites (Heldke), 31–32

F

farmers' markets, 12, 14, 15, 23, 25, 37, 44, 127, 128, 137, 138, 139, 140, 147, 148, 149, 155, 183, 192, 197, 198–99, 201–2, 206

fast food restaurants: concentration in low-income neighborhoods, 44, 62; immigrants patronizing, 98, 111, 112, 113; independent, 117; negative health influence of, 44, 182; pricing at, 121; as replacing family-run businesses, 58; in study neighborhoods, 117, 118*table*, 181

Federal Housing Administration (FHA), 52–53, 54, 56, 59

Feeding America, 108

Ferrero, Sylvia, 33–34, 35

flea markets, 143, 183

Fletcher, Nathan, 41–42

Florida, Richard, 135

food: "bad food," 111; "cheap" food, 42, 95, 160, 161, 173, 196; "classic" dishes, 144, 173, 188; comfort food, 4, 114, 121, 122, 178; as commodity, 135, 147; cosmopolitan food, 4, 39–40; and gentrification, 25, 155, 156; home practices regarding, 112–15; as part of urban agendas, 138; and place, 5, 24, 161; and social inclusion, 6, 37, 136; as source of pleasure and tension, 101;

food (*continued*)

teenagers' perception of, 111–12; as tool for boosterism, 136–37; transformative role of, 4. *See also* good food; local food

Food, Conservation, and Energy Act (2008), 45

food access: economic resources that might constrain, 99; Healthy Food Access for All Americans Act, 45; limitations on, 130; navigating and resisting unequal food access, 35; projects to address, 205–6

Food and Place (Joassart-Marcelli and Bosco), 14–15

food apartheid: as context for food provisioning and social reproduction, 96, 97, 103, 125, 130, 154, 180, 190; communities of color as challenging, 131, 192, 194, 197; defined, 58; labor market segmentation as component of, 68, 72; illustrations of, 46; lending practices as contributing to, 92; and racism, 10, 12, 25, 33, 45, 58, 63, 68, 102, 157, 158; social production of, 41–65, 136, 157, 158, 165, 180; use of term, 42

food banks, 104–5, 108, 109

food-body-space nexus, 102

Food Chain Workers Alliance, 207

Food Desert Act, 45

food deserts, 41, 42, 43, 46, 58, 63

food districts, 129, 137, 198

food drives, 105, 147

food entrepreneurs: number of in San Diego, 89; support for home-based ones, 200; treatment by City of San Diego, 205. *See also* ethnic entrepreneurs

food environments: contributions of exciting food environments, 147; creation of more inclusive one, 206; literature on, 45; painting more nuanced picture of, 46; transformation of, 127

food fairs, 149, 201

food festivals, 25, 37, 126, 136, 137, 141, 155, 156, 206

food habits, 12, 21, 28, 37, 62, 111

food halls, 25, 136, 155

foodies, 22, 25, 29, 38, 68, 99, 128, 131, 133, 140, 142, 143, 157, 162, 163, 165, 166, 173, 174, 185, 188, 192, 195, 210

food industry: as built by ethnic workers, 72; earnings in, 79–80, 89; labor in, 66–95; as one of fastest growing sectors of San Diego economy, 66–67, 73; self-employment in, 73, 75, 78

food insecurity: among food workers, 67, 80, 97–99; biopolitics of, 103; consequences of, 100–103; coping with, 96–131; defined, 97, 100; as disproportionately affecting communities of color, 25, 42, 44, 99; effect of gentrification on, 180–81; as embodiment, 101; resources for, 104–30; rethinking of through the body, 99–104; role of ethnic markets in coping with/fighting against, 121–22, 124; social production of, 10, 25, 101–104, 130, 192; and urban political ecology of the body, 130–31

food justice: defined, 192; local efforts for, 198–99, 200, 203, 209; use of term, 191–92

food machine: in San Diego, 196; urban food machine, 134, 136, 149, 157, 206

food microentrepreneurs, 201

food movement: disconnect in, 95; food practices of immigrants as erased from, 209; labor as marginal to contemporary one, 94; limitations of contemporary one, 12; and responsibility of the state, 204. *See also* alternative food practices/projects/movement

food oases, 50, 58

food pantries, 108, 110, 111, 131, 182

food provision: as source of stress for immigrants, 122; dismantling of mechanisms for, 68, 159, 182; history of, 58. *See also* alternative food practices/projects/movement

food retailers: absence of, 45; acceptance of EBT by, 123; geographic distribution of in Central San Diego, 116–17*map*; lack of large food retailers, 42; self-employed workers as, 73. *See also* food stores; supermarkets

food sales, median individual earnings in, 79–80

foodscapes: conceptualization of, 20–22; as contested in gentrifying neighborhoods, 158; defined, 6, 20–21; places, spaces, and scales of, 22–27; production of, 32–33, 42; racialization and race in, 12, 26–27, 46, 63; studying of, 14; use of term, 18. *See also* alternative foodscapes; cosmopolitan foodscapes; ethnic foodscapes; urban foodscapes

food security: biopolitical project of, 97, 103, 105; "culturally appropriate" as aspect of, 110, 122; and forms of inequality, 191; impact of supermarket density on, 62; obstacles to, 127; role of informal economy in, 83; undermining of among people of color, 68

food service workers: median individual earnings of, 79, 80; residential neighborhoods of in San Diego, 87. *See also* labor

food sovereignty: defined, 190–91, 210; and food justice, 192; history of, 190–91; as opportunity to address food apartheid, 193; use of term, 192

food stamps (CalFresh), 80, 99, 105, 106, 107, 108, 121, 206

food stores: in Barrio Logan (San Diego), 118–19*table*, 120; in City Heights (San Diego), 118–19*table*, 120–21; cooperative food store, 129;

disappearance of, 51, 63; ethnic food stores, 117*map*; lack of, 57; in Southeastern San Diego, 118–19*table*, 120; specialty food stores, 50, 69; by type and ethnicity in study neighborhoods, 118–19*table*. *See also* food entrepreneurs; food retailers; supermarkets

food trucks/food truck gatherings, 4, 5, 25, 26, 44, 69, 126, 138, 141, 144, 147, 205

food waste, 109

Ford, Larry, 52

Foucault, Michel, 101

G

gardens: rooftop gardens, 136. *See also* community gardens

Gaslamp (San Diego), 145

gastrodevelopment: actors in, 137–48; components of, 156–57; defined, 135–36; urban food machine as key driver of, 134

gentefication: as alternative and more benevolent form of gentrification, 202–3; sites of, 189; use of term, 188–89

Gentefied (TV series), 187–88

gentrification: complexity of, 187–88; consequences of, 94, 159, 183; and colonization, 145; cultural aspects of, 156; defined, 152; devaluation as precondition for, 63; displacement in, 9–10, 15, 81, 154, 155; food, race, and ethnicity in theory of, 155–59; as form of settler colonialism, 157–58; geography of in San Diego, 152–54, 153*map*; as living on "borderlands," 158; low-wage jobs as required by, 71; making space for, 63–65; role of alternative food practices in, 128; self-gentrification, 189; "slow violence" of, 10; as supporting local ethnic businesses,

54–55, 203; as structuring foodscapes, 26, 45, 51, 101; in theory of gentrification, 155–59

racial capitalism, 68, 85, 157, 158

racial differentiation, as prerequisite for gentrification, 157

racialization: of food, 160, 161, 196, 209; of people/bodies, 11, 26, 28, 29, 31, 39, 58, 101, 158, 160, 168; of place/foodscape, 12, 36, 51, 58, 63, 87, 133, 157, 161, 167, 182; of work, 66, 168–69

racial segregation: race as spatially produced by, 28; in San Diego, 54–55

racism: according to Ruth Gilmore, 102; as constraining the agency of many immigrants and ethnic minorities, 33; defined, 87, 102; as embodied experience, 26, 31, 101–103, 158; environmental racism, 18, 202; experience of in foodscape, 26, 122, 192; and food apartheid, 25, 33, 158; and food security, 101, 191; and gentrification, 6, 157–58; and hunger, 102, 105; resistance against, 9, 12, 17, 36, 126, 191–93, 198; in restaurant industry, 72, 86; structural, 29, 30, 32, 59, 157–58

Ray, Krishnendu, 34–35, 69

Ray at Night, 140

real estate industry/market: and gastro-development, 147–48; and gentrification, 180, 182. *See also* housing; redlining

Recipe for Gentrification (Alkon, Kato, and Sbicca), 195–96

redlining, 46, 53, 55*map*, 58, 59, 92, 155, 203

Reese, Ashanté, 12, 35, 103–4, 131, 197, 199

Relph, Edward, 23

rent gap, 63, 155, 659

resistance: acts of in Barrio Logan, 6, 56, 202; geographic nature of, 193–94; lack of in City Heights and Southeastern San Diego, 203; to mainstream nutrition, 111; at

neighborhood level, 197; in reclaiming ethnic foodscapes, 194; by young people about food options, 112, 113

Restaurant Opportunities Center (ROC) United, 86, 87, 207

restaurant reviews, 14, 33, 143–44, 145, 156, 162, 163–72, 164*map*, 173, 176

restaurants: authentic, 165–172; "best" restaurants and culinary hot spots, 146*map*; as embracing new aesthetics, 173–179; ethnic restaurants reviewed on Yelp, 163–165, 164*map*; impact of in urban neighborhoods, 25, 139–142; labor, 66–95, 97–99; staff meals in, 98; in study neighborhoods, 47–49, 118–19*table*, 120, 139–142, 146*map*, 163–164, 175; volatility of, 90. *See also* cosmopolitan restaurants; fast food restaurants; restaurant reviews

retail redlining, 46

Robinson, Cedric, 157

ROC (Restaurant Opportunities Center) United, 86, 87, 207

Rolando's (Barrio Logan), 175–76, 176*fig*

rooftop gardens, 136

Rueda Esquibel, Catrióna, 209

Ruiz Bakery (Barrio Logan), 48

S

Safe Sidewalk Vending Act (SB946) (2018), 126, 205

Safeway (supermarket), 51

Saldanha, Arun, 185

San Diego, CA: as America's finest creative city, 137; Centre City Development Corporation (CCDC), 57; City Council actions, 205; culinary "hot spots," 146*map*; downtown area development, 47, 57, 71; ethnic restaurants reviewed on Yelp, 164*map*; food deserts in, 41, 42, 43, 44; food retailers in Central San Diego, 116–17*map*;

Special Supplemental Nutrition Program for Women, Infants, and Children (WIC), 108, 121, 206

Stanford, Lois, 97

Storymakers Coffee Roasters (Barrio Logan), 177, 177*fig*, 178

street fairs, 139, 206

street markets, 149

street vendors, 5, 69, 71, 82, 83, 97, 125–26, 131, 199, 200–201, 205, 208, 210

Sunset, 143

The Sun, 132

Super Cocina (City Heights), 144

supermarkets: decline of small ones, rise of large ones, 58; impact of high-end supermarkets in urban neighborhoods, 25; location and density of in Central San Diego, 60–61*map*; perceptions of customer base in low-income areas, 62; redlining of, 59. *See also specific supermarkets*

Supplemental Nutrition Assistance Program (SNAP), 105, 106, 107

T

Tamale Factory (Barrio Logan), 47

taste: according to Pierre Bourdieu, 160; defined, 159; of gentrification, 159–62, 174; "good taste" as more elusive, 161; place as contributor to, 160–61

telling different stories, as strategy in reclaiming ethnic foodscapes, 209–10

Thrillist, 143, 144

TimeOut, 143, 144

Tonkiss, Fran, 9

tourism: culinary tourism, 32; San Diego's promotion of, 71, 142–43

Trump, Donald, 106, 196

U

Ujaama Food Co-op (Detroit), 200

Underwriting Manual (FHA), 53, 56

Union Tribune, 132

United Food and Commercial Workers International Union, 207

United States Department of Agriculture (USDA): food assistance programs, 108, 124; thrifty food plan, 59; on urban food deserts, 42, 43

United Women of East Africa, 206

Urban Agriculture Incentive Zone Act (AB551) (2013), 205

urban agriculture projects, 127, 128, 129, 130, 131, 148, 149, 191, 198, 199, 200, 205, 206

urban coalitions, role of, 135

Urban Corps, 198

urban food machine: as driver of gastrodevelopment, 134; exclusion of immigrants and low-income residents in, 149; goal/intention of, 136, 157; power of, 136; state as actor of, 206

urban foodscapes: cultural economy of, 24; and spatial segregation, 27, 42. *See also* cosmopolitan foodscapes; ethnic foodscapes

urban growth machine, 134, 175, 183

urban neighborhoods: changing character of, 156; cosmopolitan character of, 38–39; devaluing and pathologizing of, 157; "eclectic" ones, 145; hollowing out of, 54; marginalization of, 42; marketing of, 158; policy interventions in, 45; revitalization of through foodscape, 25; stigmatization and symbolic defamation of, 63

urban pioneers, 4, 186